D0953774

What They Do With Your Money

What They Do With Your Money

*How the Financial System Fails Us
and How to Fix It*

STEPHEN DAVIS

JON LUKOMNIK

DAVID PITT-WATSON

Yale UNIVERSITY PRESS
New Haven and London

Published with assistance from the Louis Stern Memorial Fund.

Copyright © 2016 by Stephen Davis, Jon Lukomnik, and David Pitt-Watson.
All rights reserved.
This book may not be reproduced, in whole or in part, including illustrations, in any form (beyond that copying permitted by Sections 107 and 108 of the U.S. Copyright Law and except by reviewers for the public press), without written permission from the publishers.

Yale University Press books may be purchased in quantity for educational, business, or promotional use. For information, please e-mail sales.press@yale.edu (U.S. office) or sales@yaleup.co.uk (U.K. office).

Set in Minion type by Westchester Publishing Services
Printed in the United States of America

Library of Congress Control Number: 2015955527
ISBN 978-0-300-19441-8 (cloth : alk. paper)

A catalogue record for this book is available from the British Library.

This paper meets the requirements of ANSI/NISO Z39.48-1992
(Permanence of Paper).

10 9 8 7 6 5 4 3 2 1

Contents

Acknowledgments

No book is the product solely of the authors. We are indebted to the many thousands of people who work in the finance industry and try to do the right thing for their customers and society while buffeted by conflicting interests. They have been our inspiration.

In particular there are a number of people whose thinking and practice have contributed to the ideas in this book. Any new insights we provide are built on their accumulated wisdom. We cannot name them all, but here are some whose efforts have helped all of us to understand and reform the finance industry for the better.

Thanks go to Keith Ambachtsheer, Alissa Amico, David Anderson, Donna Anderson, Mats Andersson, Melsa Ararat, Phil Armstrong, Phillip Augur, the late Andre Baladi, Sir John Banham, David Beatty, Lucian Bebchuk, Marco Becht, Aaron Bernstein, Laura Berry, Kenneth Bertsch, Lary Bloom, Jack Bogle, Glenn Booraem, Peter J. C. Borgdorff, Amy Borrus, Erik Breen, Sally Bridgeland, Steve Brown, Maureen Bujno, Tim Bush, Peter Butler, Ann Byrne, the late Sir Adrian Cadbury, Anne Chapman, the late Jonathan Charkham, Douglas Chia, Peter Clapman, Paul Clements-Hunt, Andrew Cohen, Francis

Coleman, Tony Coles, Paul Coombes, Martijn Cremers, William Crist, Ken Daly, David Davis, Matthew de Ferrars, Sandy Easterbrook, Bob Eccles, Michelle Edkins, Ambassador Norm Eisen, Robin Ellison, Charles Elson, Luca Enriques, Fay Feeney, Rich Ferlauto, Peggy Foran, Tamar Frankel, Julian Franks, Mike Garland, Kayla Gillan, Harrison Goldin, Jeffrey Goldstein, the late Alastair Ross Goobey, Jeffrey Gordon, Gavin Grant, Sandra Guerra, Andrew Haldane, Paul Harrison, James Hawley, Scott Hirst, Hans Hirt, Catherine Howarth, Mostafa Hunter, Robert Jackson, Bess Joffe, Keith Johnson, Michael Johnson, Guy Jubb, Fianna Jurdant, Adam Kanzer, Erika Karp, John Kay, Con Keating, Matthew Kiernan, Jeff Kindler, Dan Konigsburg, Richard Koppes, Mike Krzus, Robert Kueppers, Paul Lee, Pierre-Henri Leroy, Suzanne Levine, Emily Lewis, Karina Litvack, Mindy Lubber, Mike Lubrano, Donald Mac-Donald, Hari Mann, Bob Massie, Michael McCauley, Greg McClymont, Bill McCracken, Alan McDougall, John McFall, Jane McQuillen, Jim McRitchie, Colin Melvin, Bob Meyers, Natasha Landell Mills, Ira Millstein, Nell Minow, Bob Monks, Peter Montagnon, Sir Mark Moody-Stuart, Susan Morgan, Roderick Munsters, Marcy Murningham, Lord Paul Myners, Bridget Neil, Stilpon Nestor, Saker Nusseibeh, Amy O'Brien, Matt Orsagh, Norman Ornstein, Barry Parr, William Patterson, Dan Pedrotty, John Plender, Julian Poulter, Mark Preisinger, Tracey Rembert, Iain Richards, Louise Rouse, Allie Rutherford, Sacha Sadan, Nichole Sandford, Kurt Schacht, Andrew Scott, Linda Scott, Joanne Segars, Uli Seibert, Ann Sheehan, Howard Sherman, Jim Shinn, Chris Sier, Anne Simpson, Anita Skipper, Tim Smith, Jeffrey Sonnenfeld, Nigel Stanley, Anne Stausboll, Christian Strenger, John Sullivan, David Swensen, Kenneth Sylvester, Henry Tapper, Jennifer Taub, Paul Taskier, Matthew Taylor, Sarah Teslik, Raj Thamotheram, Dario Trevisan, Mark van Clieaf, Jan van Eck, Alex van der Velden, Ed Waitzer, Kerrie Waring, Steve Waygood, Steve Webb, Andrew Weisman, Heidi Welsh, Kevin Wesbroom, Darrell West, Ralph Whitworth, John Wilcox, Eric Wollman, Simon Wong, Ann Yerger, and Beth Young.

We would also like to thank our spouses and children, our longtime agent, Gail Ross, and our patient and supportive editor, Bill Frucht, and his expert team at Yale University Press.

Finally, this book is dedicated to our parents.

Introduction
We the Capitalists

If you believe the advertisements, saving money over the long term weaves a reliable safety net, allowing us to retire comfortably, afford a house, or pay for extra care in the event of ill health. Behind the hype, though, our financial system can subject that hard-earned capital to a perfect crime. Undetected, a skein of routine practices can siphon savings from citizen nest eggs. This book is about what "they"—the investment firms, banks, and pension plans—do with your money once it enters their world. What happens can vary a lot from institution to institution and from country to country, and that in turn makes an enormous difference to our wealth and our welfare.

Consider a story of triplets. At the age of twenty-five, ready to join the workforce full time, Beth moves to Atlanta, Georgia; Cathy heads to London; and Sarah makes a new home in Amsterdam, where financial institutions are different from those prevailing on Wall Street or in the City of London. Each sister earns $60,000 per year, trying to balance the needs of today, such as how to feed the family, with those of tomorrow, such as how to afford retirement. They intend to give up work at the same age, and they want the same income in retirement. You would think that they would each have to set aside the same amount of savings every year. Wrong. Beth, who chose Atlanta, and Cathy, in London, will most likely pay 50 percent or more beyond what Amsterdam-based Sarah will have to spend to secure exactly the same retirement benefits at exactly the same age. Either Beth and Cathy will have to scrimp for years to afford the retirement income they want, or they face a postwork income much less than Sarah's.[1]

These huge variances in outcomes occur because small differences in annual charges compound over the years. Here is how it would work. From the age of twenty-five, Beth in Atlanta socks $6,000 annually into a commercial retirement savings plan selected by her employer. Beth can get a 5 percent return and so she could, in theory, have a savings pot of $725,000 when she retires at sixty-five. What she doesn't factor in is fees. The 1.5 percent that she is charged every year reduces her ultimate savings by more than $200,000, to $507,000.[2]

At sixty-five, when she retires, she has a difficult decision. She needs to know she won't run out of money if she lives for a long time. On average, Beth might expect to live another twenty years, until she is eighty-five. But Beth wants to be sure that she will still have an income even if she lives to ninety-five. Assuming she will have to pay the same annual charge of 1.5 percent, Beth will be able to spend just $27,600 each year.[3]

Over in London, Cathy has discovered she has an ultimate pension pot of the same size: $507,000. In Britain, many people buy an annuity that will keep paying no matter how

long they live. But annuities are expensive and give low returns. So Cathy might expect an annual payout of $31,000.[4]

In Amsterdam, though, Sarah has been enrolled into a
giant, low-cost, nonprofit fund that will cover her for the rest
of her life. Annual charges are just 0.5 percent, so at age sixty-
five she has a pension pot equivalent to $642,000. That gives
her an annual payout of $49,400—far higher than either of her
sisters'.[5]

Why the vast disparity? Rather than establish simple,
commonsense, low-cost vehicles for collective savings and retirement, such as the Dutch have, financial institutions and
policymakers in the United States and United Kingdom have
engineered a system that has transformed worker savings into
a virtual ATM for the financial industry. Complexity rules;
one study tracked no fewer than sixteen different intermediaries escorting the citizen-shareowner's money to an investment.[6] Each can justify, on the basis of the complex system
within which they operate, why their service is needed. And
each takes his or her slice of fees. Agents pay other agents to
advise us about investing in securities or mutual funds on
which there is little evidence that anyone has better knowledge than anyone else. Usually we aren't told that the agent
has been hired or how much they have cost us. We think we're
hiring expertise, but what we are really buying—expensively—
mostly is luck. The most rigorous studies suggest that over
more than a century, the financial system has plowed back
any productivity gains to serve itself rather than us.[7]

But it's worse than that. The investment industrial complex not only charges us disproportionate fees. It also fails
to provide adequate ownership when it invests our money in
public companies, leaving the entire business world vulnerable

to periodic systemic shock. The cash we hand to institutional investors such as pension, investment, and insurance companies has been used to purchase some 73 percent of shares in the world's largest companies.[8] That gives such collective investing bodies vast sway over corporate behavior around the globe. But they each tuck bits of our retirement savings into stocks of thousands of companies to which the investment managers cannot possibly provide the kind of oversight we expect from owners, and whose names they may not even know.

We, the providers of capital, may have an interest in growing our savings for the long haul. But the agents hunt rapid profits because that is what they are paid to do. Data are mixed about just how brief shareholding periods have really become. Some alarmists point to high-frequency trading to suggest that investor "ownership" of a company is sometimes measured in milliseconds. That approach converts stock exchanges into casinos rather than rational allocators of capital. Other researchers argue that underlying time frames may still be measured in years.[9] In any case, there is little dispute that many money managers trade in and out of stocks with scant attention to whether the companies they invest in are well managed, whether they contribute to climate change or corruption, or indeed whether they are poised to trigger a market meltdown.

Make no mistake: our financial system is one of the great achievements of modern times. It is the means by which the money we save is placed at the disposal of companies and individuals who wish to use it to create new things in the economy: businesses, factories, homes, and other goods. This process drives economic growth and prosperity. The financial system helps create social mobility, rewarding talent and hard work. Those of talent raise money to form their own companies, benefiting their customers, suppliers, and workers and enriching themselves. Even the way we save for the long term is an extraordinary achievement. We give our money to a retirement fund, which, in turn, gives it to a fund manager who invests in a company. Despite temptations to do so, the company normally does not defraud its investors, workers, and suppliers. The laws and institutions, behaviors, and ethics that allow this and many other financial transactions to take place constitute one of the great social innovations of our era.

This book's purpose is to show, though, that too often the financial system as it now exists in the United States, Britain, and elsewhere is built to fail, at least if success is defined as efficiently promoting our interests. This makes little sense if you think about where today's capital comes from. Since the end of the Cold War, almost all of the countries of the world have come to accept and protect the merits of private over state ownership. More of our private economy than ever has been handed over to "capitalists." Who are these people? We might once have thought of the stereotype of rapacious, cigar-chomping tycoons—the robber barons of America's Gilded Age. Today, however, in most developed countries and increasingly in the emerging economies, the capitalists are us. Citizens putting aside even small amounts in the bank or pension fund or for buying a home meet the dictionary's definition: "one who has accumulated capital." And the collective savings of hundreds of millions of citizens currently amount to a pool of some $85 trillion.[10] We may not feel like capitalist moguls, but, collectively, we are. The system should work for us.

But there is a catch to this new capitalism. We are typically not the ones who manage our money. We depend on "experts" such as financial advisors, brokers, mutual funds, and banks to invest our nest eggs with care so that they will deliver a reasonable return over time. Evidence, however, points to a hard truth: the money we save is often not managed solely in our best interests. Systemic conflicts benefit our financial agents. That chronic fault produces a cascade of distortions that can cut deeply into our own returns while subtracting from the real economy. Moreover, the siphoning is a perfect crime. Think back to Beth, who after forty years winds up with a $218,000 hole in her savings. Like most savers, she would typically never know of the pilfering. She would instead see a "gain" of $267,000 (the $507,000 she has in her account minus the $240,000 she had invested). As one authoritative probe concluded, the fund industry is "purpose built for ambiguity and lack of accountability; a condition that favors the interests of everyone but the [saver]."[11]

Influential studies map other chronic effects on savings when we cede control of our capital. Research has found that some mutual funds, apparently unchecked by their boards, often place "important business interests . . . in asset gathering ahead of their fiduciary duties" to savers.[12] Some fund companies make investment decisions designed to help gain and retain corporate clients, even at a substantial financial penalty to the savers whose interests they are there to serve.[13] Vanguard founder John C. Bogle has calculated the titanic costs to investors when investment funds with permissive boards tolerate excessive buying and selling of securities with attendant fees and sales loads.[14] Over twenty-five years ending in 2005, he suggests, fund companies reaped $500 billion in fees from overly complex products, while delivering returns to clients less than one third of the figure investors would have made had they put savings into a simple low-cost alternative. A 2009 Aspen Institute report came to similar conclusions, finding that "funds engage in behavior that is inconsistent with their investors' goals."[15] New York City revealed that "high fees and failures to hit performance benchmarks have cost the pension system some $2.5 billion in lost value" over the decade ended 2014.[16] Even fund managers admit that the rapid trading behavior that characterizes today's investment markets is counterproductive and subtracts value.[17] In short, thanks to experts operating with different interests, citizen savers have seen a bonfire of their nest eggs.

This book contends the capitalist system needs accountability in order to render it safe to use over the long term. We probe for symptoms of what has gone wrong and offer a diagnosis of causes and a prescription for treatment. Fixing markets requires marrying twenty-first-century ways of empowering individuals to neglected principles such as common sense, ownership, and real-economy economics. It also requires confronting a fact of life: financial institutions today have powerful motivations, as rational as they are perverse, to oppose reforms that could restore trust to the system. But capitalism, like political systems, must regularly be challenged by the citizens who live with it if it is to fulfill its purpose.

The cost of failing to challenge the financial system can be catastrophic on a grand scale. Think of the short-termism rife at banks implicated in the global financial crisis that unfolded in 2008. Mortgage brokers who bought and sold subprime loans for these institutions paid little attention to whether people taking out the loans could pay them back. By the time lenders ran into difficulty, the bankers hoped to have sold the loans on to others. As we will show, banks lost sight of real risk in a tangle of flawed models and calculations. That same reliance on inappropriate expertise and "mad mathematics" that helped bring us to crisis in 2008 still guides our financial institutions today.

One might have thought that the banks' "owners," meaning the institutional investors who use our money to hold the banks' stock, would have discouraged such behavior for fear of being burnt. In fact, their virtual fingerprints were all over the banks that undertook excessive risks. According to a forensic report by economist John Kay, Wall Street–style investors encouraged "companies to engage in financial engineering, to run their businesses 'to make the numbers,' or otherwise to emphasize short term financial goals at the expense of the development of the business capabilities."[18] "Short-termism is a disease that infects American business and distorts management and boardroom judgment," asserted Martin Lipton, Theodore Mirvis, and Jay Lorsch in a 2009 paper. "But it does not originate in the boardroom. [It] is bred in the trading rooms of the hedge funds and professional institutional investment managers."[19]

In thrall to these money machines, many corporations cut research and development and shrink jobs, in an effort to keep quarter-fixated investor analysts happy and stock prices buoyant.[20] Corporate boards even penalize chief executives if they opt for long-term growth.[21] One key study concluded: "The obsession with short-term results by investors, asset management firms, and corporate managers collectively leads to the unintended consequences of destroying long-term value, decreasing market efficiency, reducing investment returns, and impeding efforts to strengthen corporate governance."[22] As market guru Ira Millstein put it years ago, that's a recipe for "recurrent crisis."[23]

Let's be clear: it is not surprising that the financial system can be dysfunctional, any more than it is surprising that our political system can go wrong. As in politics, so in finance: there are many who labor tirelessly and honestly on behalf of the people who trust them.[24] Democracy, despite its flaws, is sometimes described as the best political model invented by humankind. So, too, some form of capitalism looks like the best economic system available. But the financial system that sits at the heart of the capitalist economy needs fundamental repair. There are ample reasons to question whether the structure of the financial sector, featuring the innumerable intermediary agents to whom we hand our money, is fit for purpose, either to channel our savings towards productive investment or to serve as long-term owner of companies.[25] In this book we will take an insider's look at some of the "tricks of the trade," ways in which we are led to believe that value is being delivered when it is not.

Many of the solutions framed by policymakers may even have made things worse. Over the last twenty years, lawmakers around the world have gambled that if corporate boards could be made more responsive to investors, then these shareowners would act to police failing, rogue, or rapacious corporations. Keeping markets clean would not only be government's responsibility. "If [investors] are unhappy, we don't want them just to sell up and move on," declared UK deputy prime minister Nick Clegg in a 2012 speech. "We want them to throw their weight around so that the company improves."[26] Measures such as the US Dodd-Frank Act, the European Commission's Action Plan on corporate governance, and legislation in Britain, Australia, South Africa, and other markets were meant to empower shareowners to intervene in executive pay, board composition, and corporate citizenship. But driven as they often are by short-term strategies, institutional investors may contribute to, rather than suppress, excessive focus on the short term by corporate boards.

To be sure, reforms have gone some distance to making corporations more open, but they are only partial. In the United States, regulations stemming from the Sarbanes-Oxley and Dodd-Frank Acts installed fresh protections against fraud and cavalier approaches to risk. For instance, board audit committees must now be fully independent and feature financial experts. Board elections, once all but meaningless exercises, are now conducted using majority-vote-style rules that carry the risk that directors will be ousted if they lose investor confidence.[27] Shareholders in 2011 were empowered with an annual vote on executive pay, but excessive compensation with too little accountability is still common. There are fewer imperial chief executives serving as their own bosses—in 2014 an unheard-of 47 percent of big US public companies featured a separate chair of the board—but that still leaves a majority of companies where the chair and the CEO are the same person.[28] Takeover defenses that protected even the worst CEOs are disappearing; companies with "poison pills," which can entrench management against action by shareholders, now number fewer than 900, compared to 2,200 a decade ago.[29] Some poor-performing CEOs are getting exit papers when trouble starts instead of when it is too late—but arguably too few.[30]

Moreover, while policymakers have devoted much effort to modernizing corporate boards, they have given comparatively little attention to the investors who are supposed to oversee the market. This brand of piecemeal rulemaking has enabled regulated entities to try to game the regulator with shrewd technical dodges.

If most institutional investors do not act as prudent stewards of public corporations, then it follows that the market adjustments adopted in the wake of scandal and crisis are fatally flawed for having empowered not the ultimate shareholders (that is, you and me), but our agents, who may have much less interest in stewardship. Some observers conclude, therefore, that remediation must begin with a rollback of shareowner powers. Independent, skilled corporate boards, they contend, unfettered by investor activism, are the best champions of invigorated business.[31] The 2012 JOBS Act even made a start at this by waiving some investor protections—for instance, permitting skimpier financial data—for certain classes of US companies.

This book offers a different path to making capitalism safe. We present an agenda that mirrors past efforts to overhaul corporate boards—but instead of focusing just on corporate boards and on economic incentives, we address how to get the system as a whole to fulfill its purpose. The epic transition in which financial institutions replaced tycoons as chief providers of capital wound up giving the powers of ownership to intermediaries. We don't think it is foreordained that the agents we hire to watch our money will work against our interests. To make sure they don't, we suggest practical public policy measures to strengthen institutional shareholders' capacity to act in the interests of citizens who give them capital, so that they behave as long-term owners and value creators. For instance, law should spell out that institutional investors have a fiduciary duty to act in the best interests of ultimate providers of capital instead of their own commercial aims. The key is to unlock the self-correcting abilities of the financial markets as a whole by encouraging market vigilance and accountability among and between market participants.

To be clear, shareowners should never be in the business of running public corporations, any more than patients should tell their surgeons how to perform an operation. That job is for managers to execute and boards to supervise.[32] The question is, how do we make sure companies are run in their citizen-owners' interests?

Absent systemic reform, capital markets around the world will continue to harbor an unsafe, underpowered governance system that may be hijacked by agents with misaligned incentives. But if we use tested means to modernize the institutions that manage our savings, research suggests we could wind up with a double benefit: more prudent oversight of public companies, and larger pools of citizen savings.

It is time to reboot capitalism with a return to common sense, ownership, and accountability.

This is no small task. Narrow concepts of how markets behave continue to dominate economic thought, which is the background operating system for financial markets. In recent decades, economics has morphed from an essential discipline describing the behavior of humans in the real world to one in which conditions necessary for capitalism to function are too often wrongly understood and real-world complications just assumed away, resulting in very precise models and formulas that are precisely wrong when needed most. Models were developed that simply "assumed" that the characteristics that make capitalism stable are indeed in place. Those who study risk learn that it can be accurately measured, and that complex systems, properly designed, are safe. It is with that core training that students are recruited to banks, treasuries, and regulators.

Some economists have tried to reinsert some of the nuance that punctuates daily life, cautioning that real-world uncertainty is very different from the calculable volatility and probability that financial economic engineers equate with risk.[33] Other great classical economists also saw that economic models were better suited to the classroom than the real world.[34] But the allure of predictable models and their pseudo-precision gradually took possession of modern finance and shaped prescriptions of behavior throughout the market.

Does that matter? You bet it does. We offer examples of how that thinking has sidetracked us to value destruction, a diversion that Adam Smith, as a practical economist, would fully have predicted.

We suggest that today's market requires that we start, as Adam Smith did, with thinking about economics as a pragmatic subject. It is not just about theory, but about institutions, about checks and balances, behaviors and values. To do that, economics—or the way economics is used in the real world—needs to match equations with insights into the behavior of political and social institutions such as companies, banks, private family businesses, global corporations, and governments. Organized well, these institutions can deliver the growth and prosperity that are capitalism's best promise. Organized poorly, they can help turn that same capitalist system into a generator of weapons of mass financial destruction.

Rebooting the financial system also involves an answer to a bedrock question at the core of capital market failure. How can we make sure that our financial system is fit for purpose? In particular how can we redirect long-term savings from leaky, inefficient, poorly accountable, and short-term-focused financial agents into a commonsense savings system that serves citizens ahead of Wall Street? Elements of a "people's pension plan" are buried in history. In the mid-eighteenth century, two remarkable ministers of the Church of Scotland,

Alexander Webster and Robert Wallace, devised the world's first retirement plan for the widows of their fellow clergy, a plan based on a clear sense of purpose, and a management approach that was both technically and morally trustworthy. In this book we show how you might get the best of both worlds by combining modern technology with the trust and risk-sharing approaches that allow much higher returns based on the same tested, commonsense principles pioneered by the Scottish duo. Similar commonsense considerations could help create a more effective banking system.

The irony is that the importance of ownership, accountability, and common sense would have been familiar ideas to economists in the past. We need to return to those ideas if the financial system is to offer a fair return to those whose money it invests. The prospective advantages of doing so are too big—a more robust economy, more jobs, higher returns from savings, less dependency in old age—for us to accept the status quo.

1

What's the Financial System For?

What is the purpose of the finance industry? That sounds like a simple question, but unless you have an answer, it is difficult to judge what a "good" finance industry would look like. If we want to understand why the finance industry goes wrong and why our current systems for managing it are imperfect, we first need to decide the purpose of the industry.

The purpose of most industries is clear. The pharmaceutical industry manufactures drugs to help cure or prevent illness; the drugs fulfill their mission if our condition is ameliorated. Agriculture exists to grow food and other products. The auto industry builds products that help us travel in safety, speed, and comfort.

So imagine we are showing someone around Wall Street or the City of London who knows little about finance. Say it's someone time-traveling from the medieval era, around the time of the Magna Carta, eight hundred years ago. He would marvel at the buildings and cars, at the well-fed and well-dressed people, at the screens on the trading floor, and at the opulence of the boardrooms. Then imagine we tried to explain to him the purpose of the finance industry.

Financial services make up about 7 percent[1] of the British economy—more than five times the value added by agriculture.[2] It's not much different around the developed world. Twenty percent of the value of all the companies listed on the New York Stock Exchange is accounted for by banks, insurance companies, and other financial service companies.[3]

But never having seen a modern bank or an insurance company, our companion might ask the deceptively simple question, "What is all this activity for? What is its use?" He would understand what food and shelter, clothing, and entertainment were for. But what does the financial services industry do to generate such displays of wealth?

Finance provides for four vital services.

Safe custody. It provides a safe spot to store wealth. Rather than stuffing our money and valuables under the mattress, where they might be stolen, we can place them on deposit at a bank, or in a safe deposit box, or in encrypted electronic bits on secure storage devices.[4]

A payments system. Once our money is stored in a financial institution, we can safely and easily give it to others. If my money is at the same bank as yours and I need to pay you for some service or good, I don't need to go into the bank, get the money, and give it to you as cash. We can ask the bank to make a bookkeeping entry that takes the money from my account and credits yours. If several banks agree that they will undertake the same transaction, no bills or coins need to change hands for any payment among holders of accounts at any of the banks. Instead, the banks just make a simple accounting entry. Most major banks around the world have signed on to just a few network agreements, permitting you to pay people around the world. This is an essential service in support of global commerce.

Intermediation between lenders and borrowers. The financial system can, as the third Lord Rothschild succinctly observed, "take money from point A where it is, to point B, where it is needed."[5] Money that has been deposited at a bank can be lent out to those who wish to invest. If this is done well, the saver's money can still be safe, even while it can be used to fund investment—hence boosting the economy—and give the saver a return. Of course, there are risks in lending: the bank needs to be sure that borrowers will pay back their loans. So it requires underwriting standards and expertise, and in the event a loan does default, the bank needs to have adequate reserves to pay its depositors. Banks need to be sure they have adequate cash (known as liquidity) in the event that lots of depositors want their money back at the same time.

Reducing risk. The finance industry allows us as a society and economy to take risks and harvest the rewards. It reduces risk for any one individual by sharing the risk among many people. For example, the bank where I deposit money may lend to some risky ventures, but as long as those ventures don't all get into trouble at the same time, this lending may be quite profitable. Some of the risky borrowers will pay back their loans, and the interest charged can more than compensate for any losses due to defaults. Similarly, an insurance company can offer life insurance to many people, allowing the premiums from all and the returns from investing those premiums to cover the claims when individuals die.

These four services are central to a modern economy and are one of the reasons we enjoy our high living standards. Before this system developed, it was very difficult to save wealth or for wealth to be deployed to create new wealth. Ambitious people often fought over land and other physical possessions because they were the only stores of wealth available. Land was passed from parent to child; those who had less wealth could find few places to raise money or begin an enterprise for their own self-betterment. There was little protection against old age, infirmity, or catastrophic life events, save to trust that your family would look after you.

The financial system allows people to create and store wealth, move money efficiently, and protect themselves from risks. It is thus a central feature of economic development and indispensable to a modern economy. It is impossible to find an advanced economy that does not have an advanced financial system.

Less obviously, the finance industry has outsized sway over corporate governance—the process by which the managers of companies are held accountable to the owners. Companies that borrow money agree to certain conditions in return for the cash. Those "indentures" often include such fundamental issues as how much more debt the company may issue and how its accounts will be audited. Sometimes the creditors set conditions that make it almost impossible for that company to be acquired. If the company defaults on its loans, creditors gain even more control. Companies that raise money by issuing stock give certain rights to their shareowners. For example, in most countries, shareowners have the right to appoint the board of directors. The reason we call our system "capitalist" is that those who control the capital decide who will run the companies in which they invest. The financial institutions that hold our money often play this role. So, for example, big fund managers such as Blackrock or Axa or Nippon

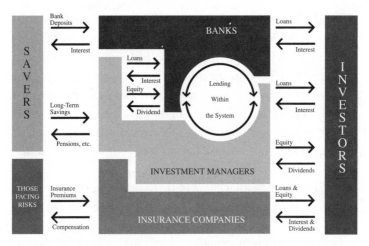

Figure 1. The Financial System: An Overview of Key Actors
and Flows of Money

Life will vote for board members of the companies in which
they own shares.

After we have explained all this (probably several times,
since so much of it is foreign to him), our medieval companion asks us to describe some of the roles played by different
institutions in the financial system. We sketch out a diagram
that looks a bit like the Figure 1. On the left-hand side are
people who deposit money they earn, while on the right-hand
side are people or companies that use the money. Between them
are three main intermediaries: banks, investment managers,
and insurance companies.

This diagram shows three sets of people. On the left are
people with money. They need a place to store it, they want to
receive some return on it, or they want to be shielded from
some kind of risk and are willing to pay for that service. On

the right are people who need money (whom we have described as investors), and who will use it to build wealth or to
consume today things that they will pay for later. They may
want to start new businesses or expand existing ones, buy
homes, or borrow money to buy goods that perhaps they then
hope to resell at a profit. In the middle are the people who me-
diate between those who have money and want to avoid risk,
and those who want to use that money in order to build new
wealth.

These middlemen come in three principal varieties. First
and most familiar are the banks. People make deposits and
loans to banks (a bank account is a loan to a bank) on which
they expect to receive interest. Fund managers also provide
banks with money, either in the form of partial ownership,
which we call shares or equity, or in loans, which we call debt
or fixed income investing. So, too, do central banks, though
those loans are very short term. In turn, banks lend that money
to individuals or companies that have need of it. They charge
the borrowers interest and fees on those loans, which in turn
pay for the bank's operations.[6]

Banks also provide safekeeping for money and offer a
payment system. Our traveler's jaw drops when you hand your
bank card to a shop assistant, who keeps it for a moment and
then returns it, and lets you take goods away from the shop.
You didn't pay anything for what you bought! You explain
that the bank will take money from your account and credit
it to the shop's account. No one (we hope) can steal your money,
or the shopkeeper's, because it never leaves the bank.

"This all looks great for the good times," our thoughtful
companion tells us once he recovers, "but it depends on almost
all the loans being repaid on schedule; otherwise, your bank
might lend out the money and never get it back." He comes

from a world in which farmers' crops often fail, and trading ships and fishing vessels regularly sail over the horizon and are never heard from again. "Surely many investments are much riskier than that. How do banks finance the risky ventures?"

Despite all our technology, we respond, some things haven't changed. Many businesses fail, and only a few make it to the big time. Lending lots of money to them is not likely to be a good prospect, since only a few will be successful. So the financial system has invented the "limited liability company,"[7] which issues "shares," or "equity," which entitle their owners to a proportion of the company's profit but don't make them liable for the company's debt. Since having the shares of only one company can also be risky, our savings are invested in portfolios of such shares, overseen by investment managers. Those managers invest in lots of companies, buying not only shares which give ownership but also loans and other securities that companies issue directly. The shares may pay a dividend—a portion of the profits, if any—and the loans pay interest.

Assuming our visitor is not completely overwhelmed, we go on to explain that investment funds are particularly appropriate for long-term investment. For example, they are designed to help people who might be saving to set aside money for income in old age. By buying the shares of many companies in many industries, they buy into the success of those companies rather than simply receiving the interest on a bank deposit, which may not offer a high return.

Furthermore, by investing in lots of companies, investment funds reduce the risk by ensuring we don't put all our eggs in one basket. "But how can you be sure," our friend asks, "that the managers of the companies in which you are invested won't steal all the profits?" This, we explain, is where governance comes in. With a share of ownership comes the right to help appoint the board of a company and hence control its management. That system is supposed to provide assurance that the managers of those companies, by and large, run operations in the interests of shareholders.

Finally, we point out the third of the intermediary institutions: insurance companies. These companies allow everyone to share risks. For example, you, and most other people in the country, pay a small amount known as a premium each year on the promise that, should something bad happen such as your house burning down, you will receive compensation. This disaster happens only to a few people, but for those unlucky few, the premiums paid by others are used to compensate for the loss. Many people, for example, take out life insurance so that when they die, their dependents will be provided for. In the meantime, insurance companies invest the premiums in loans and shares. These investments help pay for their operations and keep the cost of premiums low.

So there are the three main financial institutions: banks, which provide safe custody, a payments system, and intermediation between depositor and borrower; fund managers, who provide longer-term risk capital; and insurers, who help us to defray risk.

"And that building there, with 'PwC' emblazoned on it, must be a big bank or something. Is it?" Not exactly, we respond. That is one of the homes of those who provide assurance that the commercial institutions are measuring and reporting their success accurately—in particular, how much profit they have made. There are other advisors who service the financial community as well, like lawyers and actuaries, we explain.

"But how," our visitor asks, "do you know these people won't cheat you, that the bank or the insurance company won't just walk away with the money you have deposited?" We describe how the system is regulated, that it would be illegal to steal the money, that there are armies of people and volumes of laws to make sure the system works.

Our medieval companion doesn't buy it. "What happens if the banker or the insurer or the fund manager makes a mistake? Doesn't that mean you lose all your money? And how do they charge their fees? You tell me they are paid lots more than tailors or farmers or fishermen. Are you sure this is all honest? You've told me it is important that the finance industry works, but how can you know it works well? Are you comfortable that all these giant buildings are the result of the success of the industry, and not perhaps the result of someone taking some of your money for their own advantage? Are you sure that this very complicated industry is the best way to create those services you say are so important? What about that banking crisis you mentioned, where it looked as though the whole system would collapse? How did that come about?"

He's not done. Walking past one of the many churches in the City of London, our friend reminds us that in his day, churches were deeply respected. But they brought themselves into great disrepute by selling "indulgences," which allowed those who were wealthy enough to be forgiven their sins.[8] The indulgences, he reminds us, paid for a lot of beautiful religious architecture and a comfortable life for those members of the clergy willing to abuse the system. But it hardly helped with the spiritual well-being of the people, which was the proper purpose of the church. He turns to us. "Are you sure that the finance industry is not making a similar bargain?"

Takeaways

- Whatever you may think of its performance, the finance industry is vital to the success of our economy.
- We need the financial system to help us keep our money safe. We need it to trade with one another. It takes our savings and gives them to those who can invest the money well, pays us a return, and makes the economy grow. And it helps us insure against risks, particularly catastrophic ones.
- It also provides huge social benefits; it backs talent and hard work; it helps social mobility.
- Indeed, in our system of enterprise, it is the finance industry that is charged with the governance of much of the private sector economy. Directors of the world's largest companies are appointed with the votes of our savings and investing institutions.
- But there's a big question: "Does the finance industry do its job well?"

2
Incentives Gone Wild

I t is said that if you drop a frog into very hot water, it will try to jump out. But if you heat the water very slowly, it won't notice and will boil quite contentedly.

Financial disasters are a bit like being dropped into hot water. We notice them. The global financial crisis that began in 2007–2008 ravaged both the small and the mighty. Ordinary people watched the value of their houses, their retirement savings, and their living standards come crashing down while Lehman Brothers went bankrupt, the United Kingdom nationalized some of its leading banks, and Greece tottered on the edge of default. Everyone from Reykjavik to London to Washington to Madrid to Tokyo knew that catastrophic events were taking place.

Today, though the glare of the press is beginning to pass from the crisis, billions of dollars of wealth continue to be destroyed day after day. Yet barely anyone notices. Few seem concerned. We are like the frog being slowly boiled; we allow the finance industry to undertake activities that are not useful, and to charge us for the privilege. The result reduces not only our wealth but our children's wealth.

Today's wealth transfer is stealthy. There are no dramatic corporate decapitations. Instead of sudden cataclysm, there is a slow bleed—less dramatic, but no less harmful. It is not that the chains of agents handling our savings are bad people or that there is some calculated plan to swindle us. It is that the finance industry is not designed efficiently to create wealth for others—even as it has become positively awesome at creating wealth for itself.

Let's start with a landmark study by Thomas Philippon, professor of finance at New York University who has rigorously examined the efficiency of US finance. His studies track how much money has been lent to and borrowed from the finance industry since the 1880s, and how much this activity has cost. Hence he can calculate the productivity of the finance industry over time.

His central finding is as remarkable as it is simple. In a world where modern science, technology, and smart management have relentlessly driven down costs (consider how much a computer cost twenty years ago and how little computing power it had compared with your smartphone today), there has been no reduction of costs in the finance sector. Philippon estimates that the finance industry charges about 2 percent for each "intermediated" dollar, that is, each dollar "used to pool funds, share risks, transfer resources, produce information and provide incentives."[1]

That 2 percent has been pretty consistent over time; indeed, in the past thirty years, the cost of finance has actually risen. No matter how you cut the data (and Philippon adjusted for all sorts of variables), there has been no trend toward cheaper or better service. Compare that with other industries, and the results are staggeringly poor.[2]

Philippon's work has been subject to full academic scrutiny, and his conclusions hold good, which may surprise many in the finance industry. Today there is vastly more activity taking place in finance: lending, securities trading, and so on. But Philippon looked at the borrowing and lending that the financial services sector undertakes with the outside world, because that is where it ultimately adds value. His work suggests that though there may have been increases in productivity at a micro level, the benefits of that gain have been distributed within the industry itself, rather than to the outside world.

One possible explanation for his conclusion is that as an economy grows, it requires a disproportionately larger finance industry to support it. But the facts don't support that hypothesis either. In the 1920s, finance had a higher share of GDP than it had in the 1960s, when America was much richer. But since the 1960s, the amount of US income that has gone to the finance industry has exploded. The income of the financial sector accounted for just 4 percent of the gross domestic product in 1950. By 2010, that had doubled to 8 percent. And during that same period, the industry actually became less efficient in its ability to "intermediate," that is, to aggregate your and my savings and get it invested by companies seeking to grow, when almost every other industry in the United States was chalking up efficiency gains. As Philippon observes, "The finance industry that sustained the expansion of railroads, steel and chemical industries, and later the electricity and automobile revolutions, seems to have been more efficient than the current finance industry. Surprisingly, the tremendous improvements in information technologies of the past 30 years have not led to a decrease in the average cost of intermediation, or at least not yet."[3]

The effects Philippon identifies have an everyday impact on nearly every citizen with a bank account or savings plan. The fees really add up. For example, if you are paying someone 1.5 percent a year as a percentage of your assets to manage your pension savings,[4] you will end up paying nearly 38 percent of potential lifetime savings in fees.[5] That's huge. If you have spent a forty-year career contributing to a defined contribution retirement plan (typically a 401[k] in the United States), and you could have accumulated $1 million by age sixty-five, 1.5 percent a year in fees will reduce that to $700,000, and continuing fees during retirement will further reduce your savings' purchasing power to $620,000.[6]

Many people close to the situation understand this issue. Arthur Levitt, who founded one of Wall Street's seminal brokerage houses and was later the longest-serving chair of the Securities and Exchange Commission, is unequivocal on the subject: "Fees are the greatest drag on [investment] performance you can have. And they are not adequately appreciated."[7]

Tyranny of the Experts

Why have market forces not encouraged suppliers to serve customers better and drive costs down? The finance industry is very competitive, and competitive forces usually push down expenses and prices as suppliers compete for business. Why has the market for financial services itself not only remained inefficient but become worse over the past two generations?

It can't be for lack of skills or resources. The industry employs some of the best-educated people, spends billions on technology, and has developed standards for everything from how to transfer money across the world instantaneously to how to report investment performance. All that might have been expected to translate into ever-greater efficiency. Sometimes it does, but most often the primary benefits are realized by those in the industry itself, rather than by the savers and investors who are the ultimate customers. So, for example, the existence of stock exchanges where shares can be bought and sold is of enormous potential benefit. It allows companies to raise money, and it allows investors to support those companies, knowing that if they need to get their money back, they can sell their shares. It allows companies to invest for the long term, even as its shareholders might change. But today, activity on exchanges is becoming dominated by "high-frequency trading," where securities may be held for only milliseconds. That may have some positive benefit, but it also creates perverse incentives.[8] So, for instance, various stock exchanges and trading venues pay high-frequency traders to buy and sell, resulting in a multibillion-dollar payday to them. TD Ameritrade, the largest online broker in the United States, sells its trading volume to Citadel, a Chicago-based hedge fund. Citadel walls off those buy and sell orders from others. Why? So that it can run an internal high-frequency trading program. It paid TD Ameritrade some $236 million in 2013.[9] Nor is that an anomaly. Payments for order flow that year included about $100 million to Charles Schwab and $75 million to E*Trade. Ultimately, all these costs are a cost to other investors. As the *Wall Street Journal* notes, critics of the practices think "the arrangements can skew the priorities of brokers and sometimes result in a less than ideal outcome for investors."[10]

High-frequency trading, payment for order flow, and internal pools at hedge funds are all very efficient if looked at

from the point of view of the immediate participants, but they
provide little for the companies seeking money to invest, and
the savers seeking a return who are the ultimate customers.

Perversely, the very developments we normally associate
with well-functioning markets have added costs without returning much value. Specialization has been accepted as a positive influence since Adam Smith, in 1776, famously explained
how a pin factory, using specialized labor, could manufacture
vastly more pins per employee than if each were working alone.[11]
As a result, in a competitive market, the price of pins will
decrease.

It hasn't worked that way in finance. Financial markets
certainly embrace specialization. In investing, for instance,
few of us have the skill set or the time necessary to select a
stock, create a marketplace in which to trade it, and execute the
trade at the right price. The finance sector has created specialists for each of those functions. Similarly, to get a loan today, a
business may have to deal with multiple banks, relationship officers, credit officers, credit rating agencies, lawyers, appraisers,
risk managers, syndication managers, and others.

But specialization works to the customer's advantage
only if the customer can judge whether the product or service
she is buying is a good one. The chain of financial intermediaries has grown so lengthy that there is no longer a line of sight
between us, the providers of capital, and all of the agents. That
opacity allows those with expertise to use their knowledge to
serve themselves without passing on a commensurate benefit
to the customer. Specialization without transparency can create a financial system that is "institutionally corrupt": where
the power that is entrusted to it is improperly used. That
doesn't mean the people within the system are bad people;
rather, the incentives of the system encourage them to enrich

themselves while placing a cost on those they are supposed to serve.

The chain of specialists has reached a "reductio ad absurdum point" where the people and institutions that we entrust to act on our behalf have become so numerous that much, if not most, of their compensation comes from other agents, rather than from us directly. As a result, their business models are geared toward serving one another. Provided that we, the economic principals who have put our savings at risk or who are signing for that loan, will go along with it, then the system will continue, and the agents will profit. So, for example, if you invest your pension in a mutual fund, here is the chain of effect you unknowingly start. A record-keeper will make sure the correct amount of your paycheck deduction will go to the fund you select. Your money is then invested in the mutual fund. The mutual fund will decide what to buy partially through its own research and through third-party research. The mutual fund pays the third-party research. It may well also pay your record keeper or mutual fund platform (such as Schwab) for being listed, a practice known as revenue sharing that drives up the fees you pay the mutual fund. The fund sends a buy order to a broker. The broker sends the trade to an exchange. Then the trade must be settled, money sent or received, and the results reconciled by a custodian. There are variants on the specific agents involved. For instance, there may be a transfer agent to keep track of your mutual fund shares, custodians to hold the securities, and third-party pricing services to value those securities.

You can imagine a similar chain of agents for other financial transactions. When you take out a mortgage, there is a mortgage lending company which may sell your loan to a bank; a loan officer at the bank; a real estate agent; a loan

processor; a mortgage underwriter; a real estate appraiser; a
home inspector; and lawyers. Behind the scenes, after the mortgage closes, there may well be a guarantor (for example, Fannie
Mae or Freddie Mac in the United States) and a mortgage ser-
vicer. Your bank likely will sell your mortgage to an underwriter, who will combine your mortgage with others into a
pool of mortgages that can then be traded, which then adds a
plethora of other agents such as traders, mortgage desks at
investment banks, risk management professionals, derivative
salespeople, and financial engineers.

Every agent along the way gets paid and, to be sure, de-
serves to get paid, just as they do in any other industry that has
a complex supply chain. Each step along the way makes perfect
sense, but there are a lot of steps. Seemingly simple transactions become very complicated when you actually look at the
mechanics of finance, and at each step there are numerous
opportunities for agents to extract fees, often without our being aware of it.

The agency system has grown so large that it dwarfs what
we think of as conventional finance. John Kay, the economist
who chaired a UK investigation into the financial sector,
concluded that British banks engage in about $7 trillion of
lending each year. But only about $2 trillion of that is to the
nonfinancial service sector or, in Kay's words, to "businesses
that do things." The remaining $5 trillion effectively represents
trading with itself. "What that reveals is how small bank lending to business really is."[12] Yet, as Kay notes, virtually everyone in the sector is paid based on activity levels, so the other
$5 trillion of activity creates income for the intermediaries—
and costs for the rest of us. Think of it this way: if you are paying a 1 percent fee, you should be paying 1 percent on $2

trillion, or $20 billion. But because of all the intra-finance-sector trading, British savers are really paying $70 billion (1 percent on $7 trillion). That means the effective rate on the $2 trillion of nonfinancial intermediation is 3.5 times what it should be. If we are looking for proof of inefficiency, we need look no further.

Kay's study focused on banking, but "agency capitalism" also prevails in another piece of the financial world: investment management. A 2013 report by the United Kingdom's Law Commission noted that funds "rely on long lines of intermediaries, including consultants, investment managers, platforms and custodians to invest their assets. Furthermore, the chains appear to be growing, with some new participants finding a niche, including 'fiduciary managers' and proxy agents. These many intermediaries introduce costs into the system."[13] This is a worldwide phenomenon. Jeremy Cooper, chair of an Australian government panel that reviewed that country's retirement savings system, described the system as "purpose built for ambiguity and lack of accountability; a condition that favors the interests of everyone but the members."[14] Australia's pension system is generally considered one of the better ones.[15]

How did this develop? Adam Smith would have had a ready answer. If you give your money to other people to manage, "negligence and profusion" will prevail. People respond to incentives. If the incentives encourage it, the finance system will move resources away from the needs of the outside economy and toward the needs of the financial firms that manage those innovations. The focus of the financial sector turns inward, away from growing the real economy and toward growing the financial sector itself.

Tricks of the Trade

To understand how billions can continue to disappear from our savings, it helps to understand where it goes. Let us look at a few examples of how incentives have created an industry that is not designed to serve its customers.

In the fund management world—the sector of finance that manages our retirement accounts and other savings—people are paid either for their activity, such as the volume of trades or the number of loans underwritten, or on some other metric generally unrelated to how successfully they have fulfilled individual transactions. Asset managers, for instance, are generally compensated based on the amount of money they manage, not on how well they do it. Most asset managers, whether they manage mutual funds, exchange-traded products, hedge funds, or separate accounts, charge an asset-based fee: for every dollar in your account, you pay something, no matter the return.[16] In 2012, the explicit charge (the costs you are told about) for the average US stock fund was 77 cents per year for every $100 invested.[17] If you had $10,000 in a mutual fund, the asset manager would get $77 a year, and if the fund grew to $50,000, she would get $385. The more assets the manager has under management, the more money she gets paid, regardless of the performance of those funds. A billion-dollar fund, for example, would earn her about $7.7 million each year.

Customers tend to pay for good performance, and there is clearly a linkage between the amount of assets under management and performance. Assets gravitate to funds with better returns. Morningstar, a leading provider of research about investment products, rates funds with aggregate assets of nearly $14 trillion. Not surprisingly, funds that have been awarded four or five stars—the highest rankings, and largely based on performance—received new asset inflows of $462 billion in 2012, for example. By contrast, poorly performing funds (those with three, two, and one stars) had net outflows of $385 billion.[18] The fact that fund flows correlate to performance should be good for us. So what's the problem?

Playing the Averages

The hitch is that it is very, very difficult to outperform the market over the long term. Why do we have so many fund managers, all of whom assure us that they are doing well? The answer is that probabilities can create illusions of great performance, and investors are hard-pressed to determine who has real skill and who has been lucky. So we hire consultant experts to help us choose high-performing asset management experts, but these advisors are no better at picking experts than the experts are at picking stocks.[19]

While a well-designed investment system would offer some choice to savers, it would likely end up with a few large providers who used scale to keep costs low, plus some specialists to invest in niche areas. The reality, however, is that the fund-tracking firm Morningstar reports on no fewer than 53,000 different funds,[20] a number that is very costly to maintain and makes no sense from the point of view of the consumer. But it does allow suppliers to exploit the laws of probability.

Here are two simple illustrations of why the plethora of funds benefits the industry.

Plant a thousand flowers: Some will thrive and look pretty. A reasonable proliferation of funds does have benefits for savers. We can choose to be exposed to specific risks, such as the bond market rather than the equity market; to specific geographies such as Europe or Asia; to specific industries such as technology or utilities; to smaller companies or larger companies; or to safer but lower-yielding bonds versus riskier but higher-yielding ones. You can divide your savings among different fund families to diversify manager risk. But you quickly reach the limit of logical ways to divide up the investible universe. Most people think that number is orders of magnitude below 53,000. For example, the average defined contribution pension plan in the United States gives participants fewer than twenty-five investment options.[21]

To understand why tens of thousands of funds exist, remember that high-performing funds attract assets. How can a fund management company make sure it has a fund that outperforms the market? Create a whole lot of funds. If, for example, you establish thirty-two funds, after the first year, luck would suggest that sixteen will beat the average. After the second year, half of those sixteen, or eight, will again beat the average, and of those, four will beat the average for a third year. By year five, you will have one superstar fund that has outperformed the market for the past five years. That fund is very saleable. After all, such a performance record couldn't possibly have happened just by chance, could it?

Asset management firms understand this phenomenon very well, and they understand the flip side of the argument even better: a fund that has done poorly usually has difficulty raising money. While there are fund families with integrity that will stand behind those funds, working diligently to improve them and creating better products in the process, others just start anew. Creating a new fund, even if it is largely identical to one that was just closed, in effect wipes out the old fund's track record. As Morningstar wrote, "A . . . cynical take is that distributors prefer to sell unrated funds; after all, why sell a product with a track record that includes 2008 when you can sell one that is designed to cure everything that went wrong in that terrible year?"[22]

Most fund managers truly believe that it is their skill, not blind chance, that makes their funds perform well. But the incentive for the industry as a whole is to play the odds. Thus we have many more funds, at much greater cost, than we need for effective investment, misleading us into thinking that there are more fund managers who have the skill to outperform the market than there really are.

Picking up pennies off the railway track, hoping the train is far away. We all know not to buy an insurance policy from an insurer whose business strategy depends on never paying a claim. Yet some money managers run their portfolios, and some bankers lend money, as if following that strategy. Much like an insurance company collecting premiums, they construct portfolios that pay a small amount frequently in return for taking the risk that a low-probability event won't happen.

Suppose, for instance, a portfolio manager can receive a premium for giving someone else the right to sell her a stock for less than the current price, a strategy known as "writing a put option," because she has given someone else the right to "put" the stock to her. As long as the stock stays above that price, she collects a small premium. After all, no one is going to take advantage of the option to sell you a stock at less than what it's worth. But if the stock drops, the portfolio manager is obligated to buy it at the agreed-upon price, which may now be higher than the market price. As veteran investor Andrew Weisman pointed out in a seminal paper more than a decade ago, a number of hedge fund strategies are based on the same idea, although the method is more complex. Often it involves buying one security and selling another, and betting that the relationship between the two remains steady, so as to "permit a trader to collect a premium for assuming the risks associated [with] low-probability events."[23]

The problem, of course, is that "low probability" is not "no probability." Just as hurricanes do sometimes happen and insurance companies have to pay up, so, too, those otherwise stable relationships sometimes evaporate. When they do, they can take your life savings with them. It was just that sort of low-probability set of events that caused hedge fund Long-Term Capital Management to blow up in 1998, forcing the Federal Reserve to organize a $3.6 billion bailout of the fund, which at its height had controlled derivatives with a notional value of $1.25 trillion.[24]

Long-Term Capital Management used far more complex mathematical calculations than a manager who just writes put options. But fundamentally, it was exposed to the same risk.[25] Weisman calls these strategies "informationless" because you don't have to know much to create a great performance record—until disaster strikes. We call them "picking up pennies off the railway track." It seems like easy money, just lying there, waiting for you to pick it up. The train is usually far away, but every once in a while it is a lot closer than it looks— and the damage is extreme. This was precisely the strategy used by banks that invested in subprime mortgages, the ones that triggered the financial crisis. For many years, they looked like they were doing well, until the train arrived. They—and we—were caught up in the subsequent crash.

These two problems arise from the use, or rather the abuse, of probability. By creating lots of funds, investment managers can make it look like they have some way of outperforming the market. By betting against low-probability events, they can make their funds outperform, until they don't.

Mad Mathematics of Perfect Prediction

In financial markets, mathematical models are everywhere. They predict price movements and measure expected and realized risk.

Models are necessary and useful, but they are not infallible. The inconvenient truth is that the models, though often touted as risk management tools, work best for everyday situations, when they are least needed. They are often wrong in a crisis, precisely when you need them most, but their wrongness is dressed up in mathematical pseudo-precision. The financial crisis, it was said, was a "ten-standard-deviation event." The sudden drop in the market average was a "hundred-year storm." When we hear about another hundred-year storm just a few years after the last one, or about two ten-standard-deviation events occurring back to back (a virtual statistical impossibility), we can only conclude that the models are wrong. They are designed to work in perfectly calibrated, artificial conditions, not in reality.

We have worked as portfolio managers, risk managers, and academics, and we know that quantitative models can be great tools. But rational people make models their servants, not their masters. Unfortunately, something about a projection provided by technology seems to dazzle otherwise sophisticated people, occasionally even when their expertise and common sense should be crying out for caution. We have all read, for example, about car crashes caused by drivers following obviously flawed directions coming from their navigation systems. Somehow, our natural skepticism is dampened by sophisticated technology.

Perhaps the most widespread mathematical modeling system used by the finance sector is "value at risk," or "VaR," as it is known in trading rooms and risk management offices. Don't let the jargon intimidate you; value at risk is exactly what it sounds. It tries to predict, given how you are investing your money, how much value you lose, and with what probability, over any specified time period. VaR analysis might tell you, for instance, that over the next year you can be 95 percent sure that your portfolio will not lose more than 10 percent. Using clever statistics, you can see the probability of the property market going up when shares go down, or the other way around, or of stock A moving in lockstep with stock B. The applications can get really complicated.

In retrospect, for example, the global financial crisis looks like an accident waiting to happen. Subprime loans were made to people who were unlikely to be able to repay. So why, with all this sophisticated mathematical modeling, did we have a financial crisis? It's because the models predicted that no global financial crisis would happen, or, more precisely, that it was amazingly unlikely. Then, in October 2008, the Dow Jones Industrial Average experienced two daily changes of more than 10 percent. Risk models told us that such a movement occurs only "once every 73 to 603 trillion billion years. Yet it happened twice in the same month."[26] Sadly, the models were wrong, or else we have been very unfortunate to be alive at the one time in the history of the universe when disaster struck.

Why are models wrong when we need them the most, when a warning might have enabled us to avoid, or at least mitigate, the severity of the damage? Buried in the math are two colossal assumptions: that we can explain, or "model," both history and the future; and that in the future, things will behave largely as they did in the past.

Risk models, like other models used in the industry, are supposed to be windows into the future. To be that, they call for inputs about what the future looks like: what returns are likely to be, how volatile those returns will be, and so on. Many models deal with these inputs according to a simple but dangerous assumption: that the future will act like some combination of events in the past.[27]

Much of the time, that is true. Think about your life. Most days resemble the day before and the day before that. You get up, wash, dress, work, eat, sleep, talk to family and friends, prepare for bed, and then do it all over again. You might hit the snooze button one day and not the next, eat at a different restaurant, take a vacation, or make some other change, but the parameters around your routines are relatively limited. If we were to break down all of your daily actions over the last ten years into their component parts and apply some fancy computer programming, we could probably come up with a pretty good estimate of the things you are likely to do on a routine day in the near future.

But if during those ten years there were no crises, our model would predict that in the future there will be no crises. Equally, if you had no spectacular strokes of good fortune, it will predict none in your future.

Even if they change your life profoundly, such days are not likely to resemble the ones before and after. That is why the day you get married is so memorable. In fact, the elements of that day are not likely to be present in the sample of any of the previous 3,652 days.[28] So how could the computer possibly calculate the likelihood of their recurring tomorrow, or next week?

Similarly, in the financial world, if you feed a statistical model data that have come from a period where there has been no banking crisis, the model will predict that it is very unlikely you will have a banking crisis. When statisticians worked out that a financial crisis of the sort we witnessed in 2008 would occur once in billions of years, their judgment was based on years of data when there had not been such a crisis.[29]

It compounds the problem that people tend to simplify the outcome of risk models. For example, many people take comfort in the idea of a 95 percent probability that their maximum loss is predicted to be less than 10 percent in any particular year. But look at it the other way: one in twenty times, your portfolio will lose more than 10 percent, and *you don't know how big that loss can be*. Would you play Russian roulette if there were twenty chambers in a gun, and you knew that only one was loaded? Even worse, you don't know if it's loaded with a blank or live ammunition or a nuclear bomb. That is what an advisor is not saying when he tells you only that he's 95 percent confident you can only lose 10 percent.

In 2001, some 50,000 investors in the United Kingdom lost a total of $10 billion by investing in something called "split capital trusts." Split capital trusts were complex investments sold as "virtually risk free."[30] The risk calculations behind them were impeccable. There was only one problem: the assumptions on which those calculations were based never considered a serious fall in the value of UK stocks.[31] Given that unrealistically rosy view, the split capital trusts went out and borrowed money to lever up their returns. The resultant scandal, taken up in Parliament, became Britain's largest ever financial inquiry up to that time.[32]

The power of that lesson faded over the years. As Bob Herz of the Financial Accounting Standards Board (the entity entrusted with setting accounting standards in the United States) noted in a 2008 speech, "To me, the simple truth seems to be that the models work until they don't work. In a changing world, the past is not necessarily a reliable guide to the future, especially when the basics change."[33]

But the basics are always changing. Wall Street is an innovation machine; new financial products emerge every day. That can be a good thing; few of us want to return to an era without automated teller machines, electronic fund transfers, or the ability of farmers and airlines to hedge the cost of crops or fuel. But the inevitability of change does suggest that, however comforting it may be, assuming that the future will look like the past is not the best way to maintain the health of the financial sector.

What about requiring financial institutions to use more detailed or more robust models? Our regulators seem to be doing precisely that. But this just means that we end up with ever more detailed plans for fighting the last war. Here is how banking expert Stilpon Nestor put it. He was speaking to the United Kingdom's Parliamentary Commission on Banking Standards about the regulatory regime known as "Basel III," which is today's new, improved response to the crisis, but his description could apply to any doctrinaire modeling system. Before the crisis, he noted, "boards were following detailed Basel II capital adequacy metrics but ended up missing more than one elephant in the risk room, such as rapidly increasing gross leverage and decreasing liquidity. While Basel III now 'catches' these particular elephants, history teaches us that there are others roaming free and undetected— and that sooner or later they will strike. Sovereign risk exposures . . . are a good reminder of the dangers that lie ahead. If all banks are made to think inside the current regulatory box, it is unlikely that they will catch any of these new elephants."[34]

Mathematical models were designed to help us understand risk better, but they have been used in ways that make us believe we can predict it. To put it another way, the elephants about to trample you rarely show up in the rearview mirror. Not that these risk models are worthless. Because they are loaded with routine assumptions, they are fairly good at predicting the range of everyday, normal price movements. The problem is that the experts try to apply them to situations for which the models are ill suited.

Promiscuous Diversification

Unfortunately, the world of finance has other examples of taking a good idea and extending it or misapplying it until it becomes a bad one.

Diversification is truly one of the great concepts of investing, because it helps reduce risk. The concept is simple: don't put all your eggs in one basket. Why? Because the basket could fall, the eggs could break, and you would be left with no breakfast. Similarly, putting all your investment savings into a single stock, or even just a few, is risky. Even picking a great, well-known company is no defense. In the last few years, we have seen the fall of such titans as Merrill Lynch, Kodak, Bear Stearns, WorldCom, Enron, and Adelphia. Some were frauds, some were buffeted by change, some were mismanaged. But investors in all lost money, sometimes everything.

The investors were subject to "idiosyncratic risk," meaning factors that were specific to those companies rather than to the market as a whole. Diversification minimizes idiosyncratic risk, because if you invest in fifty companies, most of your money will still be safe even if one or two go bankrupt.

That's why academics call diversification the "only free lunch" for investors.[35]

All the free food at the diversification buffet may lead us to ignore a key fact: diversification is no defense against systemic risk, meaning risks to broad swaths of the market. That seems obvious; if the entire market declines, a diversified portfolio will decline, too. What is less obvious is that widespread diversification may actually increase systematic risk. It may even have helped cause the global financial crisis. To understand how, we first need to understand how the financial markets employ diversification.

Most people might think that a good investor is someone like Warren Buffett, who identifies good investment opportunities, doesn't place all his eggs in one basket, and watches those investments closely. Yet many more people, probably including you and definitely including the authors of this book, don't invest like Buffett. Instead, they invest through index funds—pools of money that buy shares of many companies listed in an index. The S&P 500 or the FTSE 100 are two such indices, comprising, respectively, the 500 largest companies listed in the United States and the 100 largest in the United Kingdom. Because the investments match an index, this is sometimes called "passive" investing, since it involves no "active" stock picking.

But few people stop to think how the indices themselves are determined: how much of stock A is included and how much of stock B. The most common method is to use the market capitalization of the stocks being considered, that is, how much the market values each stock. The amount of each stock within that index will vary with its market capitalization. As of this writing, for example, the largest company, Apple

Computer, comprises about 3 percent of the S&P 500 index, while the tenth largest, AT&T, comprises about 1.5 percent. The companies that rank 499th and 500th in the index account for only a few hundredths of a percent. To track accurately, an index fund comprises its portfolio by owning stocks in the same percentages as the index.

Index funds are constituted that way because modern portfolio theory says that the market overall is the result of thousands or millions of Warren Buffetts making active, considered decisions. The result, according to the theory, is a market that efficiently prices risk and reward. The market weights of the various stocks are therefore rational and can form the basis of a relatively efficient index.

That means that for indexation to work well there needs to be a robust market of active investors. These active traders need to be working relatively independently so that they don't suffer groupthink, have good information so that their decisions are well considered, and meet a host of other conditions.[36] It is those stock pickers who reduce systemic risk for the overall market by steering capital away from riskier situations and by engaging as owners with management of the portfolio companies.[37] (Some index fund managers implicitly recognize the limitations of their stock selection passivity in reducing systemic risk. They attempt to reduce systemic risk through discussions with public companies over issues such as governance structures and capital deployment, among others.)

But the same logic, when applied to banking, made diversification not a reducer of risk but a magnifier of it. We would all agree that it is crazy to lend money to someone with no assets, no job, and no prospects for paying it back. Yet the financial crisis was largely caused by experts thinking they had discovered the magic formula of financial alchemy, making it perfectly okay to lend to people who indeed had no assets, no job, and no way to pay back the loan. The secret formula that turned obviously poor loans into "safe" investments—in such numbers that when the poor quality finally manifested itself, those investments crashed economies around the world—was diversification. Instead of carefully underwriting each mortgage, bankers became "diversified" underwriters, thinking that if they could just make hundreds of thousands of loans, risk was mitigated.

Banks understand the risk of lending only to one sector or in one city. If you are a bank that only lends to farmers and the agricultural industry gets in trouble, so will you. Diversifying your loans to different types of borrowers mitigates that risk. But the alchemy took basic insight to extremes. Thousands of mortgages were packaged together in securities, which were sold to banks all around the world. The belief was that since no single bad loan amounted to a high percentage of the overall loan pool, you couldn't drown.

But there were too few active bankers making independent decisions on loan quality. The incentives in the industry encouraged lenders to manufacture mortgages as quickly as possible, according to identical flawed criteria. Many loan originators, moreover, were paid based on the number of loans they made, not the quality of those loans. They began writing no- or low-documentation loans in which so little corroboration of information was required of borrowers that the mortgages were commonly known as "liar loans."[38] None of it mattered to the bankers doing the underwriting. They thought they were protected by the magic of diversification; since they sold most of the loans and kept only small tranches of thousands of them, or hundreds of thousands, what could go wrong? If one egg broke, there were others. No one was watching the *baskets* of eggs. By overrelying on diversification, the bankers actually increased the risk: every basket and every egg were affected.

Diversification turned from a prudent strategy to a justification for sloppy lending. Mindless diversification was no substitute for lending standards. Nearly a decade after the collapse of the housing market, we are still feeling its effects. The health of the system depends on someone, somewhere, "minding the store."

Performance for Whom?

Investing for most people is about building long-term wealth.[39] We typically invest to buy a home, fund retirement, pay for our children's education, or just cushion against the unknown.[40] Endowments and foundations invest so as to continue their programs forever. Traditional pension plans invest to provide retirement income for their members. Insurance companies invest to offset claims that may or may not occur, and to stay solvent. In other words, the vast majority of investors, whether citizens or institutions, need adequate returns (a) over a long time, and (b) to offset liabilities, whether the cost of retirement, education, programmatic costs or insurance claims, or even just the financial needs of living day to day. So performance, to the owners of the assets, means how much we have and make and get to keep. It is the absolute value we accumulate, relative to our needs.

But since few of us have the skills to invest our own money, we hire asset managers: mutual fund companies, hedge funds, private equity funds, advisors, real estate funds, and so on. These actors measure performance very differently from the way we do. They look at performance relative to a broad market benchmark such as the S&P 500, and relative to their competitors. In other words, they measure themselves against the rest of the agent universe of which they are a part. And they generally measure performance over a short period—a calendar quarter, perhaps, or a year or three years. While this way of judging performance may show how they are doing against their competitors, it says little about how good a job they are doing for you and me.

Most investment managers are like sprinters, trained to perform over the short term, and not concerned about how fast they run the race provided they beat other runners. But the performance we need is more akin to a marathon, and our concern is not how fund managers perform relative to one another but their absolute performance; that is what determines how much we will have to live on.

Here is an example of the disconnect: If the S&P 500 is down 10 percent for the year, but manager X is down only 9 percent, he has outperformed. That fund will attract money and will likely get a high star rating. But we savers have still lost 9 percent. Our bills are no less, and our retirement is a year closer. Our fund manager outperformed, but we lost ground. Clearly, there is a mismatch between the performance we need to build wealth toward long-term goals, and the performance a fund manager needs to attract assets and get paid.

In the jargon of the business, portfolio managers are focused on "alpha" instead of "beta." Alpha is the return due to a manager's relative performance,[41] while beta means the return (and risk) from an entire asset class, such as government bonds or the American stock market, in which the manager is invested. Despite all the attention paid to superstar portfolio managers, relative performance has much less impact on wealth creation than the general direction of the market. According to widely accepted research, alpha is about one-tenth as important as beta. Beta drives some 91 percent of the average portfolio's return.[42]

That manager who outperformed by losing "only" 9 percent when the S&P was down 10 percent added 1 percent of alpha, but his clients probably didn't feel much better. Now let's take the opposite situation. If the S&P is up 10 percent but your manager returns "only" 9 percent, that manager will have underperformed. But your savings are up 9 percent. You might feel disappointed that you missed the last 1 percent, but which situation would you prefer?

Some fund managers counter that they can't do much, as individuals, to affect the performance of the market. But as we saw in the discussion of diversification, the entire class of fund managers has a strong effect on the market. If companies are to be managed well, they need active and engaged owners, but investment managers who focus on relative performance have little incentive to provide such ownership. As soon as they realize a company is in trouble, rather than try to improve things, they simply sell the shares. They have little patience with company directors who work to strengthen long-term performance, if that does not increase the stock price in the short term. As a result, few fund managers bother trying to ensure that portfolio companies are well managed, even though it would benefit all investors if all fund managers did this. Instead, they focus solely on trading. We probe this phenomenon of absent ownership in chapter 3.

Speed Kills

Novelist Richard Harris wrote a book called *The Fear Index* about a hedge fund that uses enormous computing power to detect the mood in financial markets, and thus profit by out-guessing other traders. This computer seems a little less fictional after April 23, 2013, which began as a strong day in the American stock markets. At 1:07 p.m. the S&P 500 index was up about 1 percent, but all at once, the market began to crash. In three minutes, all the day's gains were reversed. It later emerged that someone had hacked into the Associated Press's Twitter account and posted a false report of an explosion at the White House. Instantly, computers that had been programmed to scrape information from the Internet—in this case, social media feeds—sent sell signals to other computers, which saw all the other sell signals, which . . . well, you get the idea.

The hoax was discovered almost immediately, and by 1:10 the markets had recovered.[43] Still, fortunes were made and lost in those three minutes, as $136 billion in value evaporated and then reappeared. "No human believed the story," said Rick Fier, Director of Equity Trading at Conifer Securities. "Only the computers react to something that serious disseminated in such a way. I bought some stock well and did not sell into it. Humans win."[44] Others also blamed the computers but noted how scary that thought is.[45]

It was not the first time Wall Street had dodged a bullet. Nearly three years before, on May 6, 2010, there was the "flash crash." At about 2:32 p.m., a mutual fund entered a sell order for a large amount—$4.1 billion's worth—of a futures contract designed to mimic the performance of the S&P 500 index. The computer program that entered the trade was created to take into account the volume of trading, but not the time frame or the price.[46] It turned out there weren't enough buyers for such a large sale. Within seconds, high-frequency trading computers went into an electronic frenzy, creating what the *Wall Street Journal* called a "hot potato effect": computers sold to other computers, which then tried to sell to other computers to hedge their positions.[47] In just three minutes, from 2:41 to 2:44, the price of the futures contract and the actual S&P trading basket dropped 3 percent; then, in just fifteen more seconds, it dropped another 1.7 percent. Soon the crisis spilled over to individual stocks. According to a joint report from the US Commodity Futures Trading Commission and the SEC, some twenty thousand individual trades on three hundred different securities were made at prices at least 60 percent different from the prices that existed before the flash crash started—even though the market had recovered in twenty minutes and had returned to normal by 3:00. Some stocks were traded at "irrational prices as low as one penny or as high as $100,000."[48]

So the flash crash was warning no. 1, the false tweet warning no. 2. Barry Schwartz, a Canadian portfolio manager, draws a simple conclusion: "Don't let computers rule your investments."[49] But few are listening. High-frequency computer-driven trading is estimated to account for 61 percent of all stock market trades in the United States.[50] If such trading adds value, it does so at a cost to other investors.

The computer programs now trading in financial markets are not designed to create long-term owners like Warren Buffett. They are designed to respond to news by trading shares, a task they can perform far more quickly and effectively than humans can. Because humans still program the computers, the machines are subject to human error. Humans, working at human speed, often recognize their mistakes and correct themselves. But by the time a human realizes a computer has made an error, it has already completed thousands of buy or sell orders. Thus the same dynamic exists with computers as with risk models or diversification: computers are useful tools that work very well in normal situations—and dangerous tools when situations arise that were never contemplated by the people who programmed them.

Opacity

All of the investment products, tools, and techniques described earlier in this chapter are supposed to help savers. But they have been used to profit the producers of financial products. Surely, you might say, if these techniques are so damaging to our long-term savings, we will see the charges being made and ask appropriate questions, just as we check a hotel bill to make sure we don't pay for services we did not use. Knowing what you are being charged is crucial if markets are to work properly.

Yet typically, savers don't know how much they are being charged. The number and amount of the various fees are rarely brought to savers' attention, and when they are, savers often aren't very good at pursuing the arithmetic. As we noted at the beginning of this chapter, 1.5 percent a year may not seem like very much, but over a lifetime it can reduce the value of a person's pension by 38 percent.

Even if customers understand the significance of the annual charge, it is only part of what they end up paying. Lots of other costs are subtracted directly from their savings without their even being aware of it. For example, they will not be told about the cost of trading shares or other investments. Chris Sier of the UK government's Knowledge Transfer Network tried to estimate how high these charges are. He calculated that the hidden charges of fund management doubled or trebled the charge we are actually informed about. So that 1.5 percent charge we learn of might actually be 3 percent, meaning that two thirds of the earnings from your pension may disappear in costs.[51] Studies of other specific types of investments would seem to confirm Sier's viewpoint. CEM Benchmarking is the global leader in fee analysis for large, sophisticated pension plans. Even that firm has been frustrated by the lack of transparency about fees related to private equity investments, a rapidly growing area. It estimates that more than half of the costs that investors bear in private equity funds, 2.02 percent out of 3.82 percent per year, are not reported as fees.[52]

Meanwhile, the fund managers have the use of your assets. As noted previously, some companies make millions of dollars by sending trades to exchanges and computer sites that pay for "order flow." Custodians and others often make money by lending the stock that customers own and then remitting only some of the resulting income back to the customers' accounts.

The Next Good Idea That Could Turn Ugly

By now, the pattern should be clear: tools like risk models, diversification, and computers move from appropriate and limited use to widespread abuse, driving the financial system further out of alignment with citizen interests. But we don't always have to look in the rearview mirror to retroactively find error. A future candidate for misuse may be what is known as "liability-driven investing" (LDI).

There is nothing wrong, in theory, with LDI.[53] It works by encouraging pension and insurance companies to estimate as precisely as possible the payments they will have to make in the future, and then invest in a way that will let them meet those obligations. Since those obligations are payment streams that stretch far into the future, the offsetting investments generally are long-term bonds that will pay interest and mature over time. If the promised pensions have cost of living increases, investors buy special bonds that include some type of inflation protection. These investment choices are determined by formal legal liabilities, hence the phrase "liability-driven investment." Today, more than a quarter of all the defined benefit pension plans in the United States have an LDI program.[54]

That all seems sensible, and versions of LDI have existed for years. So why worry that it may eventually blow up? One reason is simple: LDI is often costly. While the math is still the same, the world has changed since LDI was introduced. In 2002, the yield on a ten-year US government bond was more than 5 percent; today it is less than 2 percent.[55] Whether in the United Kingdom, continental Europe, the United States, Japan, or elsewhere, interest rates are a fraction of what they were in 2002. Fund managers are thus forced to look for riskier investments than T-bills, or else they may not be able to cover their liabilities.

Worse, LDI strategies face the danger of overreaching themselves, replacing common sense with mathematical technique. That is because they aim to mirror precisely the specific obligations an investor might face, in particular those that are set down in law. But there are many situations where the pension fund manager or insurer might not know the precise obligations. For example, to know a pension fund's obligation thirty years out requires that the plan sponsor know how long all its employees will live. It would have to know with certainty what inflation would be and whether the bonds it has bought to offset that inflation will move in lockstep with it. In other words, a strict LDI program needs to model both assets and liabilities many years into the future. That's hard to do; as we have seen, models work best in normal times when variables are known. A mismatch could result in buying bonds that don't cover future inflation. Improvements in health care and life spans could enable entire workforces to outlive their pensions. To be sure, there are many LDI practitioners who recognize this and, as a safety valve, leave some amount of their assets and liabilities out of their strict LDI calculations. But an LDI strategy that tries to be precise is likely to end up being precisely wrong.

LDI was a good idea in 2002; it's a dangerous one today unless tempered by caution and common sense.

Rays of Hope from the Hidden Revolution

Not surprisingly, these misalignments between the incentives of the finance sector and those of investors have eroded trust. A 2013 survey of global investors revealed that while trusting asset managers to do what is right is the single most important factor in their choice of a manager, barely half of investors have that trust. The numbers for the United States and the United Kingdom, where financial markets are most developed, are even worse. Just 44 percent and 39 percent of investors, respectively, think the finance industry can be relied upon to serve the interests of its clients.[56]

Why hasn't anyone done something about this? And how can savers make sure they get a decent deal? Here are a few ideas.

INEXPENSIVE BETA RATHER THAN EXPENSIVE ALPHA

As more and more people realize that trading shares is costly and adds little value, there has been a growing acceptance of "index" or "tracker" funds. These funds attempt to track the returns and risks of an asset class (as represented by a benchmark such as the S&P 500 or FTSE 100) and make no effort to outperform it. The great advantage of index funds is that they generally charge very low fees.[57]

Nearly a quarter of all mutual fund assets in the United States are now in index funds, as are about 17 percent in Europe.[58] Even in the United Kingdom, a redoubt of active management, the market share of "trackers" recently reached a market record 8.7 percent in 2012, up from 7.4 percent in 2011.[59] Many professionals create a "core and satellite" structure, using index funds as the core allocation to any asset class (say, bonds and stocks) and active managers for specialty allocations.

USING COLLECTIVE ACTION

The popularity of index funds has its own consequences. When large numbers of investors are locked into a list of stocks, portfolio companies receive less robust signals of confidence or discontent through the marketplace. Index funds can't buy shares to reward good management or dump them when a CEO has gone awry. But there are other ways of encouraging good corporate performance. Awareness is growing that citizen investors benefit when asset managers address ownership issues in ways other than trading shares, even if doing so does not gain the asset manager any ground over a competitor. We show that in chapter 3.

In theory, if all asset managers bore the costs of engaging on systemic issues, there would be no free riders—but they don't. Still, the more comprehensive the collective effort, the more the free rider problem is minimized. The United Nations' Principles for Responsible Investment (UN PRI), for example, has some 1,260 signatories agreeing to six broad principles headed by a pledge to incorporate environmental, social, and governance factors into investment decision making. PRI signatories then commit to engage on those systemic issues with the companies whose shares they own. Those asset managers, asset owners, and service providers owned, managed, and otherwise oversaw some $34 trillion in capital in 2013, or more than 15 percent of the world's investible assets, by PRI's own calculations.[60] By sharing the costs of engagement broadly, they decrease the costs for any one member. At some point, the extra cost becomes not worth bothering about and/or is compensated for by the reputational or other benefits an asset manager or owner or service provider receives. We have a long way to go, but these pioneering initiatives help show the way.

REDUCING THE NUMBER OF AGENTS

Some large, sophisticated institutional investors have begun to realize that the lengthy chain of specialists creates multiple fees between them and their investments. As a result, they are rethinking their entire relationship with the asset management industry. As much as possible, they are managing their own money rather than farming it out. That effort has long been under way for stocks and bonds, but now these mega-investors are attempting to manage such complex investment strategies as private equities and hedge funds. The giant Canadian pension plan for Ontario Teachers buys significant direct stakes in companies and infrastructure. For example, it owns the rail link between London and the Channel Tunnel. As Michael Williamson, executive director of the State of Wisconsin Investment Board (SWIB), explained, "The market giveth and the market taketh away, and there's not much we can control out there—but fees are one area we can." That is why SWIB has long managed most of its own assets, rather than outsource them to money management firms.[61] Leo de Bever, chief executive of the Alberta (Canada) Investment Management Corporation, which manages $70 billion, noted, "The big investors are saying, 'Wait a minute, we don't have to do this anymore.'"[62]

Others are looking at even more radical solutions that not only eliminate intermediaries like money managers or private equity funds but create entirely new forms of investment. Tim MacDonald of the Capital Institute advocates "evergreen direct investing" (EDI), which we profile in chapter 3. By refocusing on income and cash flow, EDI investors would be relieved of the need to buy and sell in the marketplace to monetize investments.

UNDERSTANDING THE COST

Finally, here is an example of regulators helping to make markets work. Government officials around the world rightly worry that savers will not be able to choose the best investment funds if they don't even know how much they are being charged. Given the tremendous effect even small changes in fees can have on the amount of wealth accumulated over a lifetime, regulators have recently placed the spotlight directly on the fees that agents charge.[63]

In Denmark and Holland, new transparency rules allow savers to see exactly what is being taken out of their pension accounts. Rather than being told some percentage, they are given a schedule that looks like a bank statement, detailing all income and costs. The US Department of Labor issued a detailed set of regulations mandating better disclosure of fees paid by investors in defined contribution pension plans affecting some 72 million people plus their families, and containing about $3 trillion. These reforms force the sponsors of the plans to disclose, each year, individualized information about administrative fees, such as those for legal, accounting, or recordkeeping; and investment fees.

The US Labor Department anticipates that over the ten years following adoption, improved fee disclosure will bring a net benefit of some $12.2 billion,[64] and that is just for the time saved from not having to search for the information. The department's projection does not include the hundreds of billions of dollars that workers will save from making more informed decisions.

Elevating Common Sense

Despite these changes, the system's incentives still do not always help us, either as savers or as citizens. Mathematical models and economic incentives that should help improve performance have themselves become sources of problems.

Nevertheless, the innovations to offset dysfunction provide some grounds for optimism. Solutions lie not in ever-more-complex algorithms but in a return to the basic tenets upon which successful financial systems depend: a return to ownership rather than the trading of assets; a return to institutions that will act in the customers' best interests even where there is no short-term profit to be made; a return to transparency and trust; and a return to common sense.

Takeaways

- Despite its reputation for employing "the best and the brightest," the finance industry is inefficient. Since the time of the railroads, over the past 130 years, when other industries have generated huge increases in productivity for their customers, the finance sector has generated none at all.
- Perverse incentives encourage industry experts to do things that are not in their customers' interests.
- We reveal what some of these incentives are, as well as questionable "tricks of the trade," and the waste of our savings that results from them.
- Sensible investment rules have been abused, creating cost and little benefit.
- Fixes are developing that involve collective action to advance investors' interests and investment vehicles that protect against high fees. But alone, they are not going to solve the problem.

3
The Return of Ownership

s the doyen of shareholder activists, Bob Monks, once observed, "Capitalism without owners will surely fail."[1] This is hardly a radical comment; it is a sentiment that both Adam Smith and the ordinary person in the street would recognize. Capitalism is founded on the principle of private ownership of property and the assumption that people care for what they own.[2] If those who own assets don't look after them, the value of those assets will wither away. Similarly, if we give our assets to others to manage, we need to be sure they are well looked after.

Ownership is so well established a principle that the very word has come to connote stewardship. Organizations constantly monitor who has "ownership" of key functions. The opposite is also true: not having ownership implies a lack of care for an asset. Today, however, ownership is changing. Market institutions seem on a one-way path to divorcing our money from ownership, allowing tremendous misalignments of interest, not just in the finance industry but throughout the rest of the economy.

In this chapter, we explore how the market can return to tested ideas of ownership, wherein capital at risk is aligned with the prerogatives and responsibilities of ownership. But first we need to understand three major ways this basic building block of capitalism is under attack: the chronic short-termism that we describe as an economic attention deficit hyperactivity disorder; the emergence of multiagency capitalism; and the consequences of the growing derivatives markets, which Warren Buffett described as "financial weapons of mass destruction."[3]

How Ownership Has Been Lost
"ECONOMIC ATTENTION DEFICIT HYPERACTIVITY DISORDER"

Lifespans today are the longest, and most predictable, in history. That means that we can be more patient investors, riding out the inevitable market ups and downs, but you would hardly know this from looking at how our savings are actually invested. As a Reuters report noted, "While the average holding period of a New York Stock Exchange (NYSE) traded stock was 10 years in the late 1930s, the trend since 1995 has been down and down, driven by ever more frenetic trading. By 2010 the length of time the average share is held is down to a mere six months, according to NYSE data. To be sure, the rise of high frequency trading has played a role in driving down average holding time. Estimates vary, but the average domestic equity actively-managed mutual fund in the U.S. has an annual turnover rate of between 89 and 130 percent."[4] In other words, the typical fund changes its entire portfolio in a little more than a year. Public equity investors don't seem to have the ability to keep still. Markets are experiencing sugar highs of trading, facilitated by technology that makes transactions easier and less costly, egged on by a business press that needs a constant barrage of headlines to feed its twenty-four-hour news cycle.

That a holding period of a year is considered long term today suggests the magnitude of the problem. What great company can be built in a year? In 1988, Warren Buffett wrote of Berkshire Hathaway that "when we own portions of outstanding businesses with outstanding managements, our favorite holding period is forever."[5] In defending investments Berkshire Hathaway had made a decade earlier, Buffett was criticizing the prevailing practice of trading companies based on short-term stock price movements rather than long-term intrinsic value. Great companies, he was saying, take time to build, and patient investors invest for the long term. Buffett, who stands at one end of the investing spectrum, believes that ownership, stewardship, and time frames should align. He is an active owner, advising CEOs and serving on the boards of some companies he has invested in.

At the other end of the spectrum are those who measure their trades in microseconds and nanoseconds. One high-frequency trading strategy is to electronically race your buy or sell order to a stock exchange or trading pool computer. Fast computers located adjacent to those exchange computers can trade in as little as three thousandths of a second. Because their electronic signals literally have less distance to travel, they can react to developments and leap in before everyone else's buy and sell requests. High-frequency traders can buy and sell the ownership right in a company one thousand times in the time it takes you to blink.

To be clear, this activity is not marginal to our capital markets. The World Federation of Exchanges notes that in

2012, computerized trading programs accounted for an estimated 51 percent of shares traded in the United States and 39 percent of shares traded in Europe.[6]

Thanks to the rise of these high-frequency traders and the glorification of day trading, the activity in buying and selling companies has exploded. That changed context pervades—some would say perverts—the thinking of virtually every market participant. Few share Buffett's favorite holding period of forever. Aaron Cowen, a respected hedge fund veteran, told a gathering of investors in 2013 that the quick trading crowd was so prevalent that he had to "think differently" and that a longer time frame was his competitive advantage. His definition of long-term? "So, OK, we'll hold for a year."[7]

For years, investing gurus urged retail investors not to try to outguess the market on a day-to-day basis. "Buy and hold" was the advice: pick great companies and stay with them.[8] We are 180 degrees away from that. Today, a Google search for the phrase "buy and hold is dead" yields about 100,000 hits, including books like *Buy and Hold Is Dead (Again): The Case for Active Portfolio Management in Dangerous Markets* and *Buy and Hold Is Dead: How to Control Risk and Make Money in Any Environment*; innumerable articles with titles like "Buy and Hold Is Dead and Gone" and "Buy and Hold Is Dead (And Never Worked in the 1st Place)"; video clips; blogs; and stock market tips.[9]

As in less metaphorical forms of attention deficit hyperactivity disorder (ADHD), not all of this activity is intentional. One study showed that about two thirds of institutional money managers trade more than they say they do, and more than they themselves expect to, even though "they were aware that excessive turnover was potentially harmful to their clients."[10]

The market's economic ADHD is compounded by another dysfunction: myopia. The price of a share, as virtually all Finance 101 courses teach, is determined through a "discounting mechanism." It is thought to represent a summary of all the future value the company will deliver to its shareowners. Investors' ability to calculate that price correctly is fundamental to the market's getting the price "right." But in "The Short Long," the Bank of England's Andy Haldane examined how investors discounted future cash flows when valuing some 624 large-capitalization companies listed in the United Kingdom and the United States. Overall, Haldane found that cash flows taking place in the distant future are deeply discounted: those that are five years away are valued as if they were eight years away, and cash flows more than thirty years in the future are "scarcely valued at all."[11] Yet for an investor of forty saving for retirement, a payment in thirty years' time is very important. And for an economy dependent on roads, ports, water mains, and other long-lived infrastructure that may last a century or more, thirty years is almost short term.

Perhaps most disturbingly, errors are growing more common. As the Bank of England officials concluded, "Myopia is mounting." Overall, they estimate "excess discounting of between 5% and 10% per year." While a 5-to-10 percent error may not seem like much, it compounds over time. The authors cite example upon example of investments that should have had positive values but were not made, in contradiction of standard economic theory. "This is a market failure," they write. "It would tend to result in . . . long-duration projects suffering disproportionately . . . including infrastructure and high-tech investments . . . often felt to yield the highest long-term (private and social) returns and hence offer the biggest boost to future growth."[12]

ECONOMIC ADHD IN THE BOARDROOM

In recent years, economic ADHD has evolved to become still more dangerous. Like a number of diseases that can "jump species," it has spread from the trading floor to corporate directors and CEOs. Concern about short-term market price movements has direct and deleterious effects on how our businesses invest, or don't, for the future.

According to one academic study, more than three quarters of senior corporate officials in the United States will not make an investment that would benefit the company long term if it would negatively affect even a quarter's reported earnings.[13] The researchers note that senior managers blame investors for this mindset: "Because of the severe market reaction to missing an earnings target . . . firms are willing to sacrifice economic value . . . to meet a short-run earnings target."[14]

Such thinking has not improved profitability. Quite the reverse. While short-term stock price performance can be influenced by everything from corporate announcements to cost-cutting to balance-sheet actions such as share buybacks, a company's long-term viability is captured by a fairly simple equation. Companies have to earn more than their cost of capital, or else once they run through that capital, they will cease to exist. Think of it as a farm family whose members eat only what they grow. They can splurge occasionally and eat more than they produce. But if they continue to do so, they will eventually starve. Yet 43 percent of the S&P 1500 companies had a negative return on capital for the ten years ended 2012.[15] Another study shows that rates of return on assets and on invested capital for the largest US companies have been declining for decades. "Basically, it's a disaster. Around 1965, those rates were around five or six percent. And now they are down around one percent. A 75 percent decline," wrote Steve Denning, *Forbes*'s expert on leadership.[16] The former Price Waterhouse business consultant Mark Van Clieaf believes one reason is a lack of focus on long-term financial sustainability. He notes that fewer than 10 percent of the 1,500 largest American companies use accountability periods of at least four years for determining executive compensation.[17] Put another way, more than 90 percent of the largest US corporations base the compensation they gave their five highest-paid officers entirely on performance over three years or less. This leaves those executives with no incentive to encourage research and development, infrastructure, or any long-term investment. Fewer than 15 percent of large companies include any such drivers of future value in their incentive compensation programs.[18] As the Bank of England noted, those are the investments most likely to have the biggest positive effects on the economy. Myopia prevails not just among investors but in boardrooms as well.

EXECUTIVE COMPENSATION:
THE DISEASE SPREADS

How did short termism jump from the stock market to the boardroom? As with many of the dysfunctions described in this book, the culprit was a good idea that produced unintended consequences. Here is one example from the United States. In 1992, the electorate was angry that CEOs were, in some people's view, enriching themselves at the expense of shareowners and workers. Presidential candidate Bill Clinton even mentioned it in his campaign book, *Putting People First*, and promised to reform executive compensation abuses.[19] After Clinton won the presidency, it wasn't long before Congress changed the tax laws in an effort to "curb runaway pay for corporate chieftains"[20] by making compensation of more than $1 million non-tax-deductible unless certain conditions were met.

How well did it work? In 1995, shortly after the law was passed, the average CEO in America earned some 122.6 times the compensation of the average worker. By 2011, that ratio had almost doubled, to 231 times.[21] Reasons for the growth in CEO-to-worker compensation are argued ferociously, but as former SEC chairman Christopher Cox testified, "one of the most significant reasons that non-salary forms of compensation have ballooned since the early 1990s is the $1 million legislative cap on salaries for certain top public company executives that was added to the Internal Revenue Code in 1993. As a member of Congress at the time, I well remember that the stated purpose was to control the rate of growth in CEO pay. With complete hindsight, we can now all agree that this purpose was not achieved. Indeed, this tax law change deserves pride of place in the Museum of Unintended Consequences."[22]

The law's biggest flaw, Cox believes, is that it includes an exception for "remuneration payable solely on account of the attainment of one or more performance goals" and approved by shareowners.[23] Regulators ruled that stock options would automatically count as performance related, as they would, in theory, reflect the company's performance in the marketplace.

At first, shareowner activists embraced the measure, thinking that equity-linked compensation would align their interests and those of the executives. Offering share options would give the CEO an incentive to work on the shareholder's behalf—since, after all, much of the CEO's wealth would now be in the company's shares. Also, these were the salad days of the early technology revolution in Silicon Valley. Young, rapidly growing but cash-poor companies that were about to transform the world made a deal with their workers: stay with us for little salary, and we'll give you a bunch of options that will make you rich when the company goes public or when our stock price rises once our products are commercialized. That worked well for many of those smaller technology companies. They minimized their cash outlays while motivating their employees. With Silicon Valley driving American economic growth, why wouldn't everyone emulate its success formula and pay key employees with options?

Problems soon surfaced. Some corporations developed tricks to boost compensation payments. If the stock market had a bad year and the stock options looked like they wouldn't be worth much, it was argued they should be repriced to make sure the CEO still had an incentive. Accounting rules were changed. Options were backdated or otherwise manipulated to stack the deck in executives' favor.

For example, in 2012, Exelon, a Chicago-based utility, added $85 million in nonexistent profits to its compensation calculations, arguing that if not for some pesky regulatory setbacks, it would have earned that money. That mythical six cents a share added millions to the top executives' bonuses. Not coincidentally, the company's executives had "earned" bonuses above their target levels in four of the previous five years. Along the way, Exelon's operating profits and market capitalization were halved, causing losses for investors.[24]

The idea of paying executives some type of equity is ingrained in today's capitalism because it seemingly aligns the executive's rewards with those of the shareholder for whom the executive is supposed to be working. While many commentators have remarked on the lack of true alignment, which creates "pay without performance,"[25] less attention has been given to the implications of the fact that the form of pay makes CEO compensation dependent upon stock price.

Executive compensation is thus what has enabled economic ADHD to jump from investors to directors. This is not healthy for our economy. Perhaps that realization is starting to dawn on forward-thinking board leaders. Speaking to a gathering of one thousand directors, former Merck chair and CEO Raymond Gilmartin noted that "short-termism" has moved from the stock market to the boardroom because "incentive systems really emphasize this system of maximizing near term share price" rather than "intrinsic corporate value."[26]

The reliance on equity-linked compensation has another perverse consequence. The trend toward mechanistic formulaes in the remuneration of CEOs allows directors, CEOs, shareowners, and others to pretend there is a level of precision in compensation that just doesn't exist. Every time an anomaly arises, ever more complexity is added to the remuneration package. Directors are able to exercise ever less judgment. Supporters of this false precision—and they include shareowners, compensation consultants, directors, and intermediaries who advise institutional investors how to vote on compensation issues—claim that formulaic compensation is necessary to reduce subjectivity. But it doesn't. A study by Income Data Services compared executive remuneration to company performance over the first thirteen years of this century. They found almost no relationship between the two.[27]

In any case, trying to eliminate subjective judgment cannot be sensible, since using judgment is what directors are supposed to do. Informed discretion is supposed to be how owners, through their board representatives, exercise stewardship and oversight. Substituting formulas for judgment has allowed board members to avoid the hard compensation decisions that real owners would make, such as rewarding a CEO who invests in new products that will pay off years later but that will depress the stock price for a few quarters, or cutting a CEO's pay for failing to foresee a competitive challenge. Current pay packages require CEOs and other executives to respond to markets that value trading over stewardship. Pay formulas tied to stock prices that are increasingly swayed by high-frequency traders undermine directors, the very people elected by owners to provide oversight. In effect, corporate directors are complicit in their own disempowerment.

Don't Bank on It

Critics of current remuneration practices often identify "misaligned incentives" as the root of the problem. But let's put it more plainly: boards are paying CEOs to do the wrong things, and those compensation packages were deeply implicated in the financial crisis. The official Financial Crisis inquiry commission in the United States concluded, "Compensation systems—designed in an environment of cheap money, intense competition, and light regulation—too often rewarded the quick deal, the short-term gain—without proper consideration of long-term consequences. Often, those systems encouraged the big bet—where the payoff on the upside could be huge and the downside limited."[28] Yet the same compensation systems continue today, and banks are no different from other corporations.

The many articles written about compensation all agree on two things: first, pay incentives really do affect how executives and companies act, and second, the bigger the company, the more the executives are paid.[29] As Harvard professor Lucian Bebchuk and Cornell professor Yaniv Grinstein note,

"The association we find between CEOs' compensation and firm-expanding decisions undertaken earlier during their service could provide CEOs with incentives to expand firm size."[30] It is therefore no surprise that the banks that got into the greatest trouble in the financial crisis were often those that had most aggressively pursued growth.[31]

Growth is good, so long as it is sustainable. The problem was that the banks, like many companies, asked their employees to generate the greatest possible return for shareholders in the shortest amount of time. That makes sense in most companies, where shareholders provide almost all the capital that is at risk. But in banking, most of the finance is provided by depositors and lenders, often with explicit or implicit guarantees from the government. This creates a danger that prudent profit-seeking can morph into imprudent risk-taking. If everything goes well, the executives reap the rewards, but if it doesn't, the troubles are laid at the feet of the public taxpayers. Academics and bank regulators call this situation "moral hazard," but at its heart, it is the same "Heads we win, tails you lose" philosophy that we all recognize as grossly unfair.

The inherent nature of banks makes moral hazard more than an academic concern. The International Finance Corporation (IFC, the private sector arm of the World Bank) explains in its training guide for bank directors that the very business model of banks makes them inherently fragile.[32] Growth, for banks, is a tricky proposition. The IFC compares the situation in which banks find themselves to the Greek myth of Icarus, who dons wings made from feathers and wax. Icarus learns to fly but ignores his father's warning to not fly too high, because the sun will melt the wax and cause him to crash. So too with banks. Banks are most profitable when they lend as much as possible at the highest interest rates possible, but that is also when they are the most vulnerable to a liquidity crisis; a run on the bank. Typically, the borrowers willing to pay the highest rate of interest are those with lower credit, who present the greatest risk that they can't or won't pay back their loans. Judging risk and getting the balance correct is the essence of being a good banker.

But the formulaic way in which bankers are paid and the correlation between company size and compensation give little incentive for prudence. Economic ADHD is built into the structures of institutions whose very purpose is to be safe and prudent and whose business model is leveraged and fragile. As the writer Upton Sinclair famously said, "It is difficult to get a man to understand something when his salary depends upon his not understanding it."[33]

Agency Capitalism

Most of us experience ownership in straightforward terms. If you want a new jacket and can afford it, you go to the store and buy it. Larger purchases may be more complicated, but your essential relationship to the thing you bought remains the same. To buy a car, for instance, you might need a car loan, but then you buy the car. In general, there are few intermediaries. A salesperson may help you choose the jacket, a car dealer may help you navigate the sales process, but in the end, you own it and the intermediaries fade from the picture.

Your relationship, as a partial owner, to the company in which you invest is more complicated. As we saw in chapter 2, the number of institutions and people between you and the corporation can be staggering. These might include a broker or financial advisor who helps you decide what mutual fund or stock or unit trust to buy; your employer's human resources department, which selects mutual funds or other money managers for your defined contribution pension (or the trustees of your defined benefit pension, if you are among the lucky workers who still have one); the advisor who helps the human resources department or trustees make those selections; the portfolio managers of those mutual funds; the investment banks and other analysts who inform those investment decisions; the proxy services that advise those money managers on how to vote on a host of governance issues; and the proxy solicitor who collects their votes.

In theory, this chain of intermediaries should act as your agent, accomplishing each task efficiently and expertly on your behalf. In reality, small misalignments of interest along the way result in those corporations being governed through what academics call "agency capitalism," in which the institutions are, for their own economic reasons, "rationally reticent" to be active owners.[34]

Once a company's shares are bought, of course, a whole other set of intermediaries enter the scene, from the company's directors and executives to the lawyers, compensation consultants, accountants, and others who advise them.

Let us cite two examples of how the chain of agents may not always act in your best interests. One is from the money management part of the agent chain and the other from the corporate part.

As we noted earlier, most fund managers compete on relative performance over short time horizons: they are looking to outperform their rivals from month to month and quarter to quarter. This focus on trading means they are unlikely to devote much attention to even the most basic tasks of ownership, such as voting at the annual meetings of the companies in their portfolios. It is easier for them just to sell the shares if a company is not performing than to intervene in issues that may be critical to us as savers but that can't improve short-term relative performance. Yet those votes have tremendous effects on absolute value. Among other things, ballots elect the directors who select the CEOs, set dividend policy and the strategic direction of companies, oversee management, determine employment and approve executive compensation arrangements, assess environmental and social risks, and even approve the company's capital structure. Robust voting benefits the company generally—all shareowners, employees, customers, and suppliers. Influencing these matters through shareholder pressure would arguably bring more benefits to investors (and, in all likelihood, the real economy and society) than the best stock picker can achieve. But benefits would not accrue to any one asset management company making an informed vote, at least not in terms of relative return compared with rivals; instead, they would be spread among all investors.

For this reason, too many fund industry leaders opt myopically, but with a laser-like focus, to concentrate on beating their competitors. "I want to do what I get paid for," said Tom Jones, a former head of Citicorp's asset management unit. "And to do shareholder activism isn't what I get paid for. . . . If we spend money to do shareholder activism Citigroup asset management shareholders bear the expense but don't get a benefit *that is distinct from other shareholders*" (emphasis added).[35] In other words, Jones didn't doubt that there is an absolute benefit for his investors. But from his perspective, the lack of a *relative* benefit disqualified the effort.

That mindset is reflected in how some money management houses staff their units that are tasked with ownership.[36] Our survey of ten of the largest US-based asset managers showed that while they have literally hundreds of people selling products, they employ an average of about four people each to analyze voting issues. Those four cast ballots on behalf of citizen investors at, on average, five thousand companies.[37] Given that US companies average about nine directors each,[38] those four people are making a decision to vote for or against more than ten thousand directors every year. Averaged over the whole year, that means they are deciding whether to vote for about fifty people every working day. And that doesn't count their votes on merger and acquisition decisions, executive compensation, or approving auditors. What makes the findings more troubling is that we specifically chose to survey the more professionally run mutual funds, with good reputations for ownership.

Of course a few investment houses understand that absolute return is, in the long run, more important to their investors than relative return. Blackrock, the largest fund manager in the world, has made engagement with companies something of a calling card.[39] So too have investment companies such as Hermes in the United Kingdom, APG and PGGM in the Netherlands, and various "socially responsible investors" such as Domini, Trillium, Pax World, and some religious-affiliated investors.[40]

But even Blackrock devotes a tiny proportion of its revenue to being a good owner. It boasts a well-regarded group of twenty or so professionals, but even this seems a modest number for an organization of over ten thousand people looking after $4 trillion of investment. And the fact that the *New York Times* saw the mere existence of that group as worthy of a prominent story shows just how rare such units are.[41] Hermes, which boasts the largest and most effective ownership program of any fund manager in the world, employs fewer than thirty people on that activity, and can engage with only a portion of more than seven thousand companies in client investment portfolios. There remains a huge gap between the incentives of fund management companies and the needs of their clients.[42]

As Columbia University professors Ronald Gilson and Jeffrey Gordon conclude, "The business model of key investment intermediaries like mutual funds, which focus on increasing assets under management through superior relative performance, undermines their incentive and competence to engage in active monitoring of portfolio company performance."[43] This raises the question, can a system that makes it economically "rational" for owners not to act like owners really maximize value?

Even if our agents did begin to act as owners, they would find it difficult to do. The rules of agency capitalism allow misalignments to attenuate the ownership chain between you and the companies you own.

Here is one example, which will seem bizarre to anyone outside the United States. The most fundamental ownership prerogative of investors is to elect directors. Directors, in turn, have great latitude to use what in Delaware is termed the "business judgment rule." That is, boards can consider a range of factors in making decisions, and as long as those decisions are well informed and not subject to conflicts of interest, directors generally need not worry about being legally liable for the outcomes. Businesses, after all, need to take risks to be profitable, and not all risks will be positively rewarded. The business judgment rule requires directors to act in a fiduciary manner and, in turn, allows them to set strategy, hire or fire the CEO, borrow money, or issue stock. The implication is clear: who populates the board of directors of a company is arguably the most important factor affecting the value of its shares.

In theory, electing a board of directors is like electing a legislature. You vote for your representative in the US Congress or the European Parliament or the Japanese Diet, but once elected, your representative is free to vote as he or she thinks best. Few people admire the courage of legislators who vote entirely on the basis of constituent polls. If the constituents don't like what the legislator does, they can vote the legislator out of office. Of course, politicians who lose an election must step down. The same applies to corporate directors. At least in theory.

The facts, however, are different. In the United States, it is perfectly possible, even common, to stay on as a corporate director having "lost" a bid for reelection. Only 5 percent of corporate directors who fail to receive a majority of votes leave their boards.[44] Put another way, in nineteen of every twenty cases where a majority of owners of the company refuse to support a director, he stays on the board the following year.[45] As dysfunctional as many of the world's political systems are, it is difficult to imagine a legislator losing an election yet remaining in office. But in corporate America, it is allowed because many US companies use either a plurality or a hybrid majority system of voting. In uncontested elections, a director is allowed to continue in office even if 99 percent of the shares are "withheld" from that candidate, though sometimes the board must okay that. The continuation of such unelected directors on boards is perfectly legal, but it hardly strengthens the ownership chain. Directors who stay on after being rejected by most shareowners are the most egregious example of agency capitalism, in which the interests of the agents deviate from those of the owners.

The chain of agency capitalism is full of anomalies like this. Agent after agent is encouraged to act contrary to the interests of those whom the agents ostensibly serve.

"Financial Instruments of Mass Destruction"

While agency capitalism and economic ADHD weaken and misalign the links between capital and ownership, financial instruments known as derivatives can destroy them altogether. Derivatives allow someone to "own" the economic return from a company, but not the share. Or to own the voting rights the share confers while having no capital at risk. Derivatives even allow the ultimate conflict of interest: an investor may "own" a share of a company and vote for the board or on a contentious merger but stand to benefit if the company goes bankrupt. Warren Buffett famously called derivatives "financial weapons of mass destruction," adding, "I view derivatives as time bombs, both for the parties that deal in them and the economic system."[46] Derivatives permit economic interests to be completely divorced from ownership privileges.

Derivatives and the way they are employed can be technical and hard to understand. They have legitimate purposes in allowing investors to hedge against risk. But like so many investment innovations, their use has expanded far beyond their original purpose. Fully understanding derivatives may be a challenge even for experts, but understanding how fundamentally corrosive they can be is easy.

Think about allowing someone with nothing at stake to decide a major issue. Would you want foreign agents who wished harm to your country to vote for the president or prime minister? Would you want a stranger to take out an insurance policy on your life? In the first instance, allowing noncitizens to vote for the leader of a hostile country is dangerous. In the second, what assurance do you have that the stranger, who now has an economic interest in your death, isn't above trying to monetize that interest? Yet that type of situation not only can happen but has happened in our capital markets. Speculators have learned how to profit by minimizing, or even destroying, the value of the very thing they own. That motivation is counter to most understandings of how capitalism works, and counter to the social goal of maintaining a growing, functioning, and fair economy.

In 2004, Mylan Laboratories launched a takeover attempt for King Pharmaceuticals at a very high price, a deal that made Perry Capital, a hedge fund run by a former Goldman Sachs trader, very happy. Perry owned seven million shares of King and stood to make a handsome profit. But the shareholders of Mylan were unlikely to approve such an expensive acquisition. Faced with the prospect of the takeover failing, Perry found an ingenious way to influence the election without taking any economic risk. The hedge fund bought 9.9 percent of Mylan's shares, but then used derivatives to hedge out any potential loss from the shares it owned. The hedge fund could vote its shares to urge the possibly overpriced purchase without taking any risk. Even if Mylan overpaid by hundreds of millions of dollars or were even destroyed by the transaction, the fund would not be hurt. As two respected law professors concluded: "The more Mylan (over)paid for King, the more Perry stood to profit."[47] Yet Perry, technically and legally, was an owner of Mylan.

We don't know precisely how often derivatives are used in this way, since these actions usually take place in the shadows. For example, in the highly contested 2002 merger between Hewitt Packard (HP) and computer maker Compaq, HP founder Walter Hewitt vehemently opposed the deal, arguing that the merger would make his namesake company overly dependent on personal computers. Rumors abounded that Compaq shareowners bought HP shares to vote them in favor of the merger, but hedged out any economic exposure. The merger passed on a close vote.[48] There were reports of similar incidents in France with insurer AXA, in Australia at former retailer Coles Myer, in Singapore at MFS Technologies, and in Korea with Hyundai Merchant Marine. Defenders of the current regulatory environment claim that such empty voting is rare. But at least eighty incidents have been documented in which so-called investors have found ways to insulate their own economic exposure even while affecting other peoples. Not all used derivatives, but many did.[49]

One of the advantages and dangers of derivatives is they can navigate into the gaps in disclosure regimes, leaving researchers and regulators in the dark. The eighty documented cases of economic decoupling may be the tip of the iceberg. But it seems clear that the potential damage from empty voting is real. Leaving aside the effect of such manipulative efforts on specific companies, the decoupling of economic interests from ownership rights undermines the basic assumption that the two are inalienable, and that therefore shareholders can be trusted to promote good management of the companies they own. That assumption is not just fundamental to capitalism. It also underlies virtually every law that governs marketplace conduct, from disclosure regulations to who gets to vote to reorganize a company in bankruptcy.[50]

A report from Stanford University's Rock Center for Corporate Governance and the IRRC Institute catalogues innumerable regulations based on the assumption that "voting interests and economic interests are . . . aligned."[51] The report's key conclusion is that "the legitimacy of modern corporate governance rests on the premise that, in shareholder elections, shareholders are economically motivated to vote in a manner that maximizes the value of the corporation's shares."

Solutions: Injecting Ownership Back into Capitalism

If the causes of diminished ownership in our capital markets are multifaceted, so too must be the solutions. In later chapters, we will propose fundamental changes to the way we organize, regulate, and even conceive of capital markets. For now, here are some immediate steps that could mitigate the damage and restore ownership in markets.

PAY CEOS IN CASH

The road to hell is paved with stock-linked compensation plans. Investors, boards, regulators, and executives have spent a quarter century promoting such plans as a way to align the incentives of CEOs and other executives to shareowners' interests. As each measure brought unintended consequences, compensation plans moved on to the next minor tweak, without fundamentally fixing the problem. One article distributed to directors of US companies noted: "When problems arise, companies tweak the mechanics: they move from stock options to performance units to restricted shares; they change grant dates and vesting periods."[52]

It is time to understand that this is the wrong path. "Aligning interests" has failed. One reason is that CEOs are employees—highly paid, highly important employees—and like most employees, they know better than their employers whether they are doing a good job. That is why we don't put most employees on "piece rates": we pay them for their time, and expect their commitment in return. Small bonuses in stock may be merited, but good employees make the commitment to work hard and well.

By paying CEOs primarily in stock, we have encouraged them to play the market rather than build great companies over time. For CEOs and other executives who experience loss in the value of stock, the pain is mitigated by their not having paid for the stock and by the expectation of another grant next year. Also, the time horizons of CEOs, many of whom are at the zenith of their careers and likely to retire in a few years, is shorter than that of investors.[53] More importantly, perhaps, compensation in stock makes CEOs focus on stock price rather than on building sustainable, intrinsic value.[54] As a retiring European CEO once remarked, "In my day being CEO was thought to be a privilege; today it is treated as a prize."[55]

As important but less obvious, equity-linked compensation has minimized the discretion of independent directors. Typically, the formula and assumptions behind equity-linked compensation are designed by the board of directors' compensation committee three years in advance of when it will be paid. This, inevitably, makes compensation schemes fairly formulaic. Directorial judgment is limited to the front end of the process, when directors have less information than they would if they could apply normal business judgment once the results are in. Even the participants understand how disconnected compensation is from reasonable evaluation. As a European bank official admitted, compensation has become a slot machine: directors pull a lever, and three years later, out comes a trickle of coins or a fountain of folding money.[56]

Deciding to pay CEOs and other executives in cash would allow directors to direct, while it would remove the myopic focus on stock price. Of course, virtually every participant who benefits from the current dysfunctional system would have to accept change (an agency capitalism problem in itself). Compensation consultants would have to change their focus; boards would have to get used to making judgments, explaining them and standing behind them; proxy advisory services would have to change how they judge "alignment"; and institutional investors would have to devote resources to understanding, for each company they invested in, why directors were making the decisions they were. Paying CEOs in cash would also expose US companies to tax liabilities for any payments that exceed $1 million. Perhaps it is time to repeal that IRS section that supercharged the trend toward equity-linked compensation. It was designed to slow the growth of compensation, but it clearly has not.

LIGHTEN UP ON USING PEER GROUPS
TO DETERMINE COMPENSATION

It is common practice for companies to benchmark their CEOs' compensation to the amounts peer companies pay their CEOs. This makes a certain sense. If you are buying dry cleaning services or a hamburger or a smart phone, there is a market, and the market prices affect what you are willing to pay. But it doesn't work that way for CEOs. A recent paper by Charles Elson and Craig Ferrere of the University of Delaware demonstrated that there isn't really a traditional labor market for CEOs and that peer grouping ratchets up executive compensation with no commensurate benefit.[57] Perhaps most important, it makes the directors responsible for executive pay look outside the company rather than focus internally. Elson commented, "Even the best corporate boards will fail to address executive compensation concerns unless they tackle the structural bias created by external peer group bench-marking metrics.... Boards should measure performance and determine compensation by focusing on internal metrics. For example, if customer satisfaction is deemed important to the company, then results of customer surveys should play into the compensation equation. Other internal performance metrics can include revenue growth, cash flow, and other measures of return."[58] In other words, boards should focus, as owners do, on what makes the business flourish.

USE THE RIGHT METRICS

As discussed earlier, 90 percent of large American companies measure the performance of their executive teams over a three-year period or less. About a quarter don't have any long-term performance–based awards at all.[59] Fewer than 25 percent incorporate the cost of capital into their executive compensation formulas, and only 13 percent consider innovation—such as new products, markets, or services, research and development, or intellectual property development—in determining compensation.[60]

You couldn't design an incentive scheme better suited to keeping a CEO focused strictly on the short term if you tried. So let's do the opposite: let's evaluate CEOs over a more appropriate time frame. We should consider a balance of metrics so that real economic value (return on invested capital greater than the cost of that capital) is created over time, and we should include metrics that speak to how companies really grow future earnings.

DE-EMPHASIZE TRADING AND SPECULATION, AND REWARD INVESTING FOR THE LONG TERM

Market conditions encourage trading in public stocks based on price, rather than investing in public companies based on value. Here are suggestions for how to reverse that trend.

Tim MacDonald of the Capital Institute has proposed a different form of ownership for long-term investors. In a back-to-the-future synthesis of modern financial engineering and old-fashioned direct ownership, he would have pension funds, endowments, insurance companies, sovereign wealth funds, and other large long-term investors curtail their public market investments, getting away from what he calls the tyranny of the trading tape. MacDonald's idea, which he calls "evergreen direct investing," is that an investor would make a direct investment into a company. Over time, the pension fund's investment morphs from equity into debt, providing long-term cash flows after the period of high risk and need for growth capital has passed. Meanwhile, the equity interest of the operators of the business would increase over the years, encouraging them to think like long-term owners. Unlike traditional private equity, in which the investment is time limited by the terms of the fund that makes the investment, "evergreen" investing has no time limit, and thus no arbitrary need to buy or sell. Because it emphasizes long-term cash flows, evergreen investing is the institutional equivalent of trying to figure out if you can retire based not on how much wealth you have acquired but on how much income you will have.[61]

END THE FAVORITISM SHOWN
TO HIGH-FREQUENCY TRADING

In September 2012, the New York Stock Exchange was fined $5 million for sending out market prices to certain people before others. "Improper early access to market data," the *New York Times* reported, "even measured in milliseconds, can in today's markets be a real and substantial advantage that disproportionately disadvantages retail and long-term investors."[62]

Ironically, less than two months before this ruling, the SEC approved the New York Stock Exchange's request to charge thousands of dollars a month to high-frequency traders to "co-locate" computers at the NYSE's data center in Mahwah, New Jersey.[63] When you are dealing in billionths of a second, the distance from the information source to your computer matters. That high-frequency traders are able to get information before everyone else surely "disadvantages retail and long-term savers." When former SEC chair Elisse Walter was asked about the SEC's role in facilitating high-frequency trading, she admitted that the regulatory response had been "inconsistent."[64]

ENCOURAGE NEW TRADING PLATFORMS THAT
PROTECT INVESTORS

Some entrepreneurs are not waiting for regulators to tackle the high-frequency trading issue but are creating a new exchange, called the IEX, that will build a 350 microsecond delay into its computerized trading so as to frustrate high-frequency traders. Nor will the IEX pay the rebates other exchanges pay to high-frequency traders to get them to boost volumes and liquidity. The IEX is backed by mutual fund companies and other longer-term investors, and the hope is that it will attract enough investors frustrated with the advantages given to high-frequency traders to provide adequate liquidity.[65] It may or may not work, but the basic idea, to find a venue where longer-term investors can be treated fairly, will no doubt be a driving force in other innovations.

REGULATE HIGH-FREQUENCY TRADERS APPROPRIATELY

Some academics make a strong case that when a high-frequency trader can get information before the general market, it functions as something of a "market maker," a legal term that carries with it a requirement to not take advantage of that information asymmetry. Recent work has suggested that math and physics can create a standard for who is a market maker, thereby ensuring a fair trading system for all.[66]

USE COLLECTIVE ACTION TO ALLOW MONEY MANAGERS TO FOCUS ON BENEFITS FOR ALL

As we have seen, citizen investors benefit when asset managers address big systemic issues, even if no individual asset manager gains a competitive advantage. There have been recent efforts to encourage institutional shareholders to be better owners. This was a principal objective of economist John Kay's 2012 report to Britain's Department of Business, Innovation and Skills. The industry responded a year later with blueprints for an Investor Forum designed to pool investor influence behind good long-term management at corporate boards. Other groups in the United Kingdom include NGOs ShareAction and the Carbon Disclosure Project (CDP), and commercial platforms F&C and Hermes Equity Ownership

Service.[67] In the United States, the Council of Institutional Investors has brought big funds together in the United States since 1985; other groups, including Ceres, focus investors on specific issues such as climate change.[68] Similar investor coalitions exist in Australia, the Netherlands, Italy, Brazil, and elsewhere. At the global level, the International Corporate Governance Network and the United Nations' Principles for Responsible Investment (UN PRI) encourage collective shareowner action on policy issues.[69]

All these groups are meant to help asset managers use collective action to mitigate the "free rider" issue. In theory, if all asset managers bore the costs of engaging on systemic issues, there would be no free riders. That's not possible in reality, but by sharing the costs of engagement with companies broadly, these groups decrease the costs for any one member.

USE TODAY'S TECHNOLOGY

If it is difficult for institutional investors to act as responsible owners, it is nearly impossible for individuals. But technology could change that equation.

Argus Cunningham, whose day job is to train pilots for the US Navy, is an individual investor. He is well aware of the difficulties investors like himself have in understanding the issues at companies they have invested in. He found his inability to communicate with those companies particularly vexing; all too often, the investor relations office ignored his queries.

In their spare time, Cunningham and a small team developed a website called "Sharegate" that enables both individual and institutional investors to aggregate their shares for the purpose of getting companies' attention.[70] Sharegate's mission is "to introduce modern communication methods into public company stakeholder interaction."[71] When a user sends a query to a company, Sharegate automatically aggregates the holdings of all its users to let the company know its answer will be shared with a larger fraction of its ownership. While the site is not profitable as of this writing, it has attracted its first large institutional participant, the Florida State Board of Administration, which has more than $150 billion in assets. Sharegate also boasts a number of features designed for an online community built around shared ownership.

Technology may also allow individual investors to reassert their ownership rights. While individual investors account for 27 percent of the average company's shareholders, they tend to be more passive than institutional investors in exercising their responsibilities and rights. Individuals vote the proxies for just 29 percent of their shares, while institutions vote 90 percent of theirs.[72] One reason is that individuals are daunted by the complexity of voting. The information is often convoluted, and the process time consuming. If you own a diversified portfolio of individual stocks, you may have to do it twenty or thirty times or more. But technology has made it possible for individuals to vote their preferences without the need for individual review of each proxy. "Advance Voting Instructions" (AVI) allow investors to vote automatically with or against management, or with a well-known third party such as the giant pension fund CalPERS, or with the recommendations of a proxy voting agency. While widespread AVI is not yet available, it is being examined by the SEC and the American Business Conference, a trade group of midsized companies.[73]

While it is too soon to predict whether Sharegate or AVI will succeed, we think that they are an early indication of an indisputable fact: technology, which has often encouraged speculation and discouraged responsible ownership, can be used to do the opposite.

USE TAX POLICY—GENTLY

While the unintended consequences of the US tax policy designed to slow the growth of executive compensation should serve as a warning, they should not take tax policy completely off the table. We suggest two well-calibrated tax reforms that could amplify an ownership ethos. In a number of countries, long-term capital gains (from investments that are held for more than a set period, usually a year) are taxed at lower rates than ordinary income. But this is a blunt instrument. Pass the time limit, and you get one rate; sell earlier, and you get a different one. Instead, why not have capital gains taxed at decreasing rates the longer you own the asset? That would truly encourage longer-term investing. Also, why not allow investors to deduct capital losses against other income? Those losses can offset capital gains, but deductions against ordinary income are currently capped at a miserly $3,000 per year in the United States. Raising or eliminating this limit would encourage investors to take risk, a common prerequisite to creating wealth. A panel of business, academic, and investing leaders assembled by the Aspen Institute endorsed just such a plan.[74]

BRING DERIVATIVES OUT OF THE SHADOWS

A hundred years ago, US Supreme Court Justice Louis Brandeis observed that sunshine is the best disinfectant.

Derivatives, by contrast, often hide in the shadows, protected by disclosure rules that are complex and inconsistent.[75] For example, someone who wants to influence a company can buy a "call option," that is, the right to purchase the company's shares. That investor therefore has "hidden ownership" of the company, since by exercising the option it will have actual ownership. More importantly, derivatives such as swaps allow so-called owners to hide the fact that they have decoupled their economic risks and may be practicing empty voting. Regulators could, in theory, require disclosure of so-called morphable ownership, or preclude nominal owners from voting if they had disposed of their economic interests by derivatives or if the investors would actually benefit from a decline in the company's stock. In practice, however, enforcing such a rule would require searching through a chain of agents to determine who owns what, and how many shares those investors are allowed to vote. But an answer exists. In the United States and elsewhere, owners of more than 5 percent of the voting rights in any company are required to disclose their ownership. Why not extend that rule to force disclosure of economic interests as well? In other words, if you owned 5 percent of the votes, you would have to disclose not only the shares you owned but also the derivatives you owned based on those shares. Similarly, if you owned 5 percent of the economic interest in the company, you should disclose it. Believe it or not, you could own economic interests equal to 5 percent or even 10 percent in a company today through the use of derivatives, and never let anyone know.

Looking Forward

Most of the world's large companies are owned not by tycoons but by millions of people who have set aside money for their pensions and other savings. But a long chain of agents, competing for relative performance, hobbled by inadequate rights, and using ever-more-complex derivatives, too often results in empty ownership and effectively ownerless corporations. This is bad for our savings and for the economy as a whole. Part of the solution, as we have seen, is to improve the governance of companies. But we must also improve the governance and incentives we offer those who manage our money.

Takeaways

- The first principle of any effective financial system must be to ensure that those we entrust to manage our money do so on our behalf. That may seem like a pretty basic demand, but its implications are profound.
- Our savings are invested in many types of investments, including company shares. Taken together, these savings are so great that it is we, the people, who in aggregate own the majority of large companies. If these companies were run properly, they would be run on our behalf. Imagine if every CEO of every big company acted as though they were reporting to us. It sounds revolutionary, but it is the way today's system ought to operate.
- Over the last generation, there have been numerous forces divorcing companies from the responsibility to serve their owners.

- One force divorcing companies from the responsibility to serve their owners has been a focus on short-term security trading and the hard wiring of this perspective into the boardroom through executive pay.
- Another force divorcing companies from the responsibility to serve their owners has been the proliferation of agents between us, the savers, and the companies that our savings finance.
- There is a growing divorce of ownership rights from our economic interests in the company through the use of financial instruments known as derivatives. Even worse, derivatives allow investors to benefit when companies do badly, even while allowing those investors to exercise power at those same companies.
- Chronic misalignment threatens to leave us with "ownerless corporations."

4
Not with My Money

We have seen that perverse incentives create a gap between the vast population of savers and those we trust to manage our money. This raises a question: can we make the financial system accountable?

The answer, as we shall see, has a major impact on both the amount of wealth we accumulate over time and the performance of the companies whose shares we own. At a broader level, how we address accountability affects public confidence in what we call free enterprise. After all, once hidden failures are exposed, they could prompt an understandable reaction from capital providers: "Not with my money!"

In this chapter, we examine the consequences of different types of governance arrangements among agents handling our savings. Then, we analyze what roles citizen investors actually play once they hand their money over to funds and pension plans. Finally, we posit solutions, including those riding the next wave of change: how social media can contribute to revolutionizing the market and building a new form of "civil economy" while restoring a powerful sense of ownership among savers.

An Information Vacuum

Anyone seeking to learn about the governance and operations of agents to whom we entrust our savings meets a vast information vacuum. In many markets, they will find it tough to determine how savers' money has been invested or their shares have been voted; they will struggle to identify exactly which individuals hold responsibility as overseers of their funds, to assess how conflicts of interest may be addressed, or to discover whether money managers are paid to further customers' interests or their own. As we noted in chapter 2, savers sometimes are not even told what charges have been made to their account. It is scarce wonder that we may not get fair value for our money if we can't even find out what we are being charged.

Some regulation does protect smaller investors. In the United States, for example, mutual funds must disclose many (though not all) of their charges. But for large swaths of the finance sector, charges are simply not known or are not comparable. Even mega-investors smack into a wall of opacity when they try to truly understand all the expenses and fees subtracted from the return on their investments. Pension plans that manage tens of billions of dollars do not receive information on pass-through costs and even on some fees, from private equity funds, hedge funds, and other alternative investments. As one report noted, "These expenses, which certainly have an effect on the net return . . . are often not reported as fees by . . . pension funds and investors, because of the significant amount of manual effort involved in collecting the information and because a number of pension funds consider these costs to be a form of profit sharing that is not comparable to a fixed management fee."[1] If the pension systems don't receive the information, they can't report it to the members.

The irony is that pension plans and the fund management companies that manage money for those funds have pressed for public corporations to reveal more about their governance. Institutional investors have wanted to know how companies pay top executives, how they assess risks, who sits on their boards, and how they structure board leadership. Funds have sought greater board accountability through meaningful elections of directors. They have asked for better audits. All of these demands are founded on the premise that transparency can reduce risk and improve performance. Today, though, only a handful of retirement savings plans would be able to meet the disclosure and accountability standards they demand of companies.

In most countries, as a result of reforms enacted over many years, corporations are now required to supply a kind of governance dashboard, allowing investors to tell at a glance who is in charge, how much they make, and what risks and opportunities they see the company facing. Firms must feature, and tell you about, a board of directors. They must describe how directors are elected, and they must provide information about the directors' skills and professional backgrounds. They must tell shareholders how many directors are independent non-executives, how often the board meets each year, what percentage of meetings each director attends, and whether key committees, such as the audit committee, have the requisite expertise. Boards must detail ways they address important responsibilities such as financial controls and CEO pay. They have to say whether they are led by an outside chair or a combined chair-CEO. Some even have to describe whether the company faces climate risks.[2] And they must provide reams of data on how executives are compensated.

Behind all this disclosure lies a bedrock doctrine of the capital market: because corporate directors are the agents of shareowners, investors are entitled to sufficient information to judge whether boards are doing an adequate job.[3] Yet no similar doctrine applies universally to the many agents who hold shares on our behalf.

Some disclosure rules on the governance, compensation arrangements, and fiduciary duties of savings plans do exist, primarily for commercial enterprises such as mutual funds and banks that deal with retail clients. But retirement savings plans face a fraction of these requirements, even though, arguably, savers are in a similar position to shareowners in a corporation. Just as institutional shareholders expect corporate boards to nurture their investment, employees expect retirement plans to grow their nest eggs as much as possible, and individual investors expect mutual funds and insurance plans to act on their behalf. But individual citizen investors have fewer tools to discover whether agents are doing that job than pension funds have when they monitor portfolio companies.

The global shift from defined benefit pension plans (which provide a fixed monthly amount in retirement) to defined contribution programs (in which the financial comfort of retirement depends on how much and how well each individual has invested) is Exhibit One in the case for accountability. In a defined benefit plan, the company sponsoring the pension fund was responsible for ensuring the pension was paid. The ultimate pension received by retirees was an obligation of the sponsoring company or organization. In this situation, a lack of disclosure about how the money was invested was problematic but often irrelevant. All that mattered was whether the company could pay the pension obligation when it came due, a question on which the company's own financial statements provided relevant disclosure. But with the defined contribution system, how much a saver gets in retirement is the saver's problem. One would think, therefore, that the governance of these schemes would offer the saver more accountability.

In fact, it offers less. Take, for instance, a garden-variety defined contribution plan in the United States. Unlike traditional pension plans, it is not required to have a board of trustees. Instead, a single administrator, normally a human resources executive attached to the sponsoring corporation, is generally in charge. The absence of a governing body opens a gaping hole in transparency, as well as in accountability. For instance, the law obligates the employer to outline the menu of investment choices available to plan members, but not information on how those fund options were vetted and selected. That means that if we want to track whether plans do better when they are more accountable, we have few data to work with. Plans in other countries are little different.

Data Hunters

Still, researchers are a determined lot, and they have been able to throw some light on what this governance gap might be costing us. Mining what information they can find, they have uncovered fragments of evidence about the behavior of investment agents that have long been hidden. One of the most pointed studies, by Keith Ambachtsheer and two colleagues at the University of Toronto's Rotman School of Management, revealed a link between the quality of a retirement plan's own governance and the performance it achieves for its members. The authors used a screen of forty-five tests of governance to draw portraits of a fund's transparency and accountability to its members. They included factors such as whether a board exists and whether it has relevant skills or evaluates its own performance regularly, whether compensation information is available to savers, and whether conflicts of interest are recognized and managed. Ambachtsheer's group concluded that best-governed funds "outperformed the bottom ones by an average 2.4% per annum" between 2000 and 2003.[4] The "Ambachtsheer gap" compounds every year. After twenty years, a saver contributing every year to a well-governed fund would be about 30 percent better off than someone stuck in one that was poorly governed.[5]

Indications that accountability improves results are slowly accumulating. The Cooper Review, a 2010 government inquiry in Australia, also projected substantial benefits when funds have better governance.[6] Scholars have found similar results in sovereign wealth funds.[7] And Morningstar's test of its own stewardship rankings of more than forty US fund companies found a correlation between the governance of mutual funds and their performance over five years.[8] As Oxford University's Gordon L. Clark brutally puts it in reference to both defined benefit and defined contribution plans: "Poor organizational systems combined with a palpable lack of expertise makes many pension funds a soft target for unscrupulous financial service providers."[9]

Why should good governance improve investment returns? The very problem at issue, the lack of transparency in most funds, makes it impossible to say for sure. But one plausible explanation is that accountable governance reminds intermediaries to be accountable to savers rather than putting their own interests first.

Jennifer Taub of Vermont Law School sought a measure to demonstrate whether US mutual funds were acting as investors to advance their beneficiaries' interests, as they advertised, or to protect the commercial prospects of their own fund family companies. To do this, she looked at circumstances where those interests might diverge, namely, how mutual funds vote on shareholder resolutions at public companies.[10] Taub discovered that the more an investment or mutual fund depended on contracts to run company 401(k) pension plans (which are standard defined contribution retirement savings vehicles in the United States), the less likely it was to vote in favor of investor resolutions that reflected criticisms of management—even at corporations that were chronically destroying shareowner capital. That suggests that some mutual funds may quietly put savers' interests second to their own business needs.

Two other scholars, using a very different test, came to similar conclusions. Instead of looking at how mutual funds vote their shares, Lauren Cohen and Breno Schmidt investigated these funds' investment choices and discovered something disturbing: mutual funds buy much more stock in companies whose 401(k) plans they administer, even when these companies are troubled enough to prompt other funds to sell.[11] Cohen and Schmidt concluded that there is "a potentially large benefit to the 401(k) sponsor firm of having its price propped up" by the contracted mutual fund. Moreover, "the resulting loss to mutual fund investors . . . can be large." No economist would be surprised by that finding: it is well known that accountability decreases "rent seeking," the actions an agent might take to extract a benefit from the system. So it stands to reason that a lack of accountability will tend to increase self-serving actions, even if it damaged the interests of ultimate savers.

Two last studies complete our tour of the limited state of knowledge of fund governance and performance. In 2009, Martijn Cremers and three coauthors used still another measure to see if the way mutual funds are overseen could affect returns. They tested whether it made any difference if mutual fund directors personally held stock in mutual funds they oversaw.[12] It did. "Funds in which directors have low ownership stakes, or 'skin in the game,' significantly underperform." Authors found, in other words, that directors with little financial stake in the outcome are associated with firms that lag in creating wealth for investors. Another research duo, Fiona Stewart and Juan Yermo, looked at pension plans in several developed countries and found a host of governance flaws they associated with inferior returns.[13] These included poor representation of stakeholders on fund boards, second-rate training for trustees, and weak controls for conflicts of interest.

Investors have constantly demanded alignment of interest and good governance from companies. Why should we not demand the same from those we trust with our long-term capital? Yet the lack of alignment between us, the ultimate savers, and the institutions investing on our behalf, has eluded widespread attention.

Where does this leave us? A World Economic Forum paper put it best: "Governance, at first glance, might not appear connected to issues around long-term investing . . . [but] the topics are closely related. Not only do governance bodies determine the metrics that are adopted and the ways they are reported, but they also inform the culture and compensation system within which investing activities and strategies are implemented."[14]

Fund Governance

Bob Garratt once titled a book about corporations *The Fish Rots from the Head: The Crisis in Our Boardrooms.* The leadership of financial agents may be looked at through the same lens. When oversight is flawed, the risk rises for financial abuse stemming from conflicts of interest, negligence, misjudgment, misalignment, and incompetence. How can you tell when any of this might be happening to your financial agents? Indicators of misalignment, according to scholar-practitioner Simon Wong, are "financial arrangements that promote trading and short-term returns; excessive portfolio diversification; a lengthening share ownership chain that weakens an 'owner' mindset; [and] misguided interpretation of fiduciary duty that accords excessive deference to quantifiable data at the expense of qualitative factors."[15]

These failings are richly evident in the governance of many corporate pension funds. As we noted earlier, these funds are established by companies for the benefit of their employees. The switch from defined benefit to defined contribution moved the performance risk to the employees, yet control of the fund remains firmly in the company's hands. When a plan is controlled by a plan-sponsor executive, usually the chief financial officer or head of the human resources department, he or she may do the best they can to advance the interests of beneficiaries. But the potential for a conflict of interest is obvious. What is not as obvious is that a corporate official may simply not be as vigilant in overseeing the pension plan if he or she is not overseen by the people with a stake in its performance. In one disheartening case, a corporate pension plan included infamous Ponzi scheme mastermind Bernard Madoff's fraudulent investment program even though the custodian of the plan refused to take custody of Madoff's "assets."[16]

The challenge is to ensure that those with the power to control funds act in the interests of those who are supposed to benefit from them. When those in charge of the plan are not accountable to members, it is difficult to be sure if, when, how frequently, how energetically, and how skillfully this oversight is carried out.

Even when funds are overseen by trustees who owe a duty to fund beneficiaries, there can be huge gaps in skills and knowledge. For example, a study sponsored by the British government showed that among smaller corporate pension funds, two-thirds of the corporate managers responsible for the funds were unaware that charges were being made on the fund and deducted from members' savings.[17] In the United States, public sector and multicompany "Taft-Hartley" defined benefit funds also have trustees, but skill requirements in statutes are minimal, fees for director service are nominal or absent, and many boards are seen as captive to professional advisors or to the constituents, such as political patrons or trade unions, who appoint them. Funston Advisory Services, which performs fund governance audits on a private basis for clients, discovered in the course of a benchmarking effort among select peers in 2011 that none had procedures for removing ineffective board members, nor did most have formal succession plans in place for their fund chiefs.[18] Comparable data are not available on a public, market-wide basis. But features seem no better at UK counterparts. Michael Johnson of the Centre for Policy Studies, when examining Britain's

Local Government Pension Scheme, found "the whole governance framework laughable. Many of the individuals involved lack the ability to ask penetrating questions and demand useful answers [in the face of] . . . deeply entrenched vested interests."[19]

Part of the reason trustee boards may lack juice is that members are not paid or are paid very little. The implicit message, that oversight bodies are not serious or professional, leaves them vulnerable to those who are paid to influence how your money is invested. As Gordon L. Clark puts it, "the fact that pension fund trustees are hardly ever compensated in proportion to their responsibilities suggests that their motives are quite different [from those of] industry service providers."[20] In other words, commercial asset managers are paid to recruit clients, while even well-intentioned trustees are given little incentive to play a robust oversight role. But "plan participants rarely if ever play an active role either in the governance of pension funds or in the scrutiny of administrative and trustee decision-making," according to Clark. "Exit, voice, and loyalty—conventional mechanisms used in governing the principal-agent relationship—are rarely if ever directly available to plan participants. Trustees may be 'representative' of plan participants but are not directly accountable in the sense we associate with representative democracy."

In sum, the accountability features we rely on to improve the governance of corporations do not widely exist among financial agents.

The Solutions Generation

A variety of solutions to the accountability gap have emerged in different parts of the world. Some approaches are the natural province of familiar actors such as governments and institutional investors. Others involve social media innovators and civil society organizations. Together they point the way to the new shape of capitalism. Let's reconnoiter that near future.

GOVERNMENTS

Before we explore what fresh approaches governments might apply to aid citizen investors, we must decide what it takes for government to look out for our interests. This is not a trivial matter; we will see in chapter 5 how regulation misconceived and misapplied can produce damaging outcomes for capital markets and savers. For now, it is enough to note that when regulators are poorly matched to responsibilities, they may look for answers in wrong directions.

One prerequisite for good regulation might be a coordinated approach. In the United States, as well as in other countries, savings oversight is now a regulatory orphan. The federal Department of Labor was handed the job of supervising pension plans in 1974. Since then, however, most retirement savings have migrated from the traditional defined benefit fund to defined contribution plans, where they are largely invested in mutual funds. Mutual funds are overseen by a different agency, the Securities and Exchange Commission. Moreover, the department's fortunes depend heavily on partisan politics. It is typically cosseted under Democratic administrations, starved under Republican ones, and subject to budgetary torque when power is divided. Serial probes by the Government Accountability Office have found it deficient in enforcing rules designed to protect savers.[21] The SEC, another flawed parent, has myriad other securities market priorities—and no specific mandate to look after retirement plans.[22] Congress has been little help; the last major legislative effort to overhaul retirement savings, the "Protecting America's Pensions Act of 2002," was introduced by the late senator Edward Kennedy. It would have established a trustee board with an equal number of employer and employee representatives for all 401(k) plans with more than one hundred participants. It failed in committee.

But regulation in the United States is even more fractured than that. Insurance companies, another important component of many Americans' retirement savings and income security, are overseen by fifty different state regulators. The banks where people save are overseen by a combination of state regulators, the federal Office of the Comptroller, the Federal Deposit Insurance Corporation, and the Federal Reserve. In other words, everyone, and thus no one, is responsible for regulatory policies to protect your and my savings.

Elsewhere, there have been improvements. Australia, which boasts the fourth largest pool of managed funds in the world ($1.7 trillion), has been a pioneer of reforms. Jeremy Cooper's 2009–2010 review paper posed fundamental questions and resulted in a cascade of fund governance directives from the Australian Prudential Regulation Authority (APRA), along with binding rules from the industry's own Financial Services Council. The APRA standards cover everything in fund governance from board turnover and performance reviews to management skills, director oversight of portfolio manager compensation, and whistleblower protection.[23] They mandate that each fund have a trustee board led by an independent chair; that a majority of trustees be independent of members or any plan sponsor; that compensation arrangements be fully disclosed; and that the fund's voting records be released to members. In the Netherlands, also home to a strong pension system, legislators took similar action in 2013.

All retirement schemes in the country were ordered to add governing supervisory boards and to ensure that they included retirees as well as current workers and corporate representatives.[24] The Organisation for Economic Co-operation and Development produced broad principles of pension fund governance in 2009.[25]

In other markets, regulation of fund governance is patchy at best. It is particularly weak with regard to defined contribution plans, where members make individual investment choices and bear personal risk for the outcomes. The Cooper report outlined the challenge this way: "The trustee has a responsibility to apply a greater level of scrutiny to the sorts of products that are offered to super fund members. . . . It should not be possible for trustees merely to preside over a menu of investment options principally selected by . . . external parties."[26] That point is critical. If savers do not actively oversee their finances, and if there is no trustee to ensure savers' interests are put first, then the temptation for providers to benefit at the expense of their customers is enormous.

INSTITUTIONAL INVESTORS

The second source of solutions to the accountability gap is the institutional investment world itself. A corps of pension funds has recognized that commercial conflicts may cause misalignment with beneficiaries and has road-tested state-of-the-art remedies. Here are five strategies for improvement.

Looking in the mirror. As many governance experts have reported, one of the most powerful drivers of improvement on corporate boards comes from directors' looking in the mirror. Periodic, intensive, independent assessments of directors' own performance, both individually and as a group, often provide a wake-up call. Policy in some jurisdictions has responded: in the United Kingdom, bank boards are now mandated to undertake an outside evaluation at least every three years. But in the investor world, full-blown assessments of fiduciaries are rare. Mutual funds boards in the United States have been required to undergo self-evaluations since 2004, but there is room for improvement in the quality of those reviews, which often focus on compliance with policies and procedures, rather than effectiveness. Greater potential lies in the relatively new concept of the "fiduciary audit," which examines how well a retirement plan is fulfilling its obligations to produce value for beneficiaries. Such audits are starting to appear in the United States, with CalPERS, California's civil service pension plan, as the most prominent adopter. In 2011, in the wake of asset losses, "pay to play" scandals, and persistent calls for an overhaul, CalPERS board president Rob Feckner and CEO Anne Stausboll commissioned outside parties to assess the board's governance. They even commissioned a study to benchmark CalPERS governance practices against those of similar US funds.[27] Research was painstaking, as such characteristics are generally not public. In response to the recommendations, the board approved a series of far-reaching governance reforms. A year later, it moved to make independent assessments a biennial practice. Seeing the benefits of evaluation, other US public funds commissioned independent governance reviews, resulting in a myriad of specific recommendations. Some states, such as South Carolina, have made such fiduciary reviews mandatory.

Two-way communication. Pension funds, insurance companies and other fiduciaries for citizen savers generally do not ask members what types of investments they need or even whether they trust the plan. But a few institutions do. Perhaps the best example is the €100 billion Dutch health sector pension fund Stichting Pensioenfonds Zorg en Welzijn (PFZW), covering two million members, and its asset manager PGGM. Starting in mid-2011, the two organizations began conducting a quarterly "Brand Tracker" survey of beneficiaries. These exercises provide regular data on how the fund is perceived and whether it is meeting members' needs.[28] The results influence strategy; PGGM cites findings to support its profile as an advocate of long-term stewardship.[29] Triodos Bank, also based in the Netherlands, also tries to connect clients with the way their savings are invested. According to ShareAction, Triodos "account holders can browse interactive online maps and articles about the businesses and projects their money is being lent to, and even visit them in person. Such innovation can make the abstract and nebulous world of finance concrete and meaningful, increasing people's engagement with saving. Yet it is almost entirely absent in the pensions industry."[30] The Ontario Teachers' Pension Plan, CalPERS, and Britain's National Employment Savings Trust (NEST), the government-created supplementary retirement plan, also solicit members' opinions. But the list of funds that do this is short.

DIY fiduciary duty. Fiduciary duty is typically defined through legislation, regulation, and the courts. But ambiguity reigns, as dated interpretations clash with changing markets. Some funds have, within bounds, taken a "do it yourself" approach, choosing to define what they consider to be their fiduciary responsibilities rather than have these imposed on them.

At a 2012 conference, CalPERS CEO Anne Stausboll said that "the fiduciary duty of pension funds should extend to issues outside the parameters typically understood as being directly related to beneficiaries' financial interests."[31] "As fiduciaries," she told delegates, "it is our job to make sure investors, businesses and policymakers are responding aggressively and creatively to the risks and opportunities associated with climate change and other sustainability issues." That view became embedded in updated CalPERS guiding principles: "CalPERS investment decisions may reflect wider stakeholder views, provided they are consistent with its fiduciary duty to members and beneficiaries."[32] Financial agents must attend to risks understood to affect investment outcomes, even if they were once thought out of bounds for fiduciaries.

Oxford legal scholar Claire Molinari agrees with this approach. She notes that while some financial agents fear sustainable investing as a breach of fiduciary duties, funds can instead consider the approach to "meet the fiduciary obligations of loyalty, prudence, diversification and impartiality."[33] That approach gained authoritative traction in 2015, when a coalition of United Nations entities and the Principles for Responsible Investment issued a detailed legal analysis aiming to "end the debate" on whether it is within the bounds of fiduciary duty for investors to incorporate environmental, social, and governance risks when making portfolio decisions. The report's unequivocal conclusion sought to turn the dispute on its head: "Failing to consider long-term investment value drivers, which include environmental, social, and governance issues, in investment practice is a failure of fiduciary duty."[34]

Pay for performance. A chronic symptom of the mismatch between citizen investors and financial agents is the way asset managers' compensation is structured. Incentives usually reward those who achieve short-term targets that benefit the firm, rather than long-term value creation that benefits the saver. A handful of fund managers have sought to change those terms in the face of industry inertia. Generation Investment Management issued a paper, "Sustainable Capitalism," that called for alignment of pay and long-term interests. According to the paper, "most compensation schemes emphasize short-term actions disproportionately and fail to hold asset managers and corporate executives accountable for . . . their decisions over the long term. Instead, financial rewards should be paid out over the period during which these results are realized, and compensation should be linked to fundamental drivers of long-term value, employing rolling multiyear milestones for performance evaluation."[35] Beneficiaries with money at other financial houses could press for similar compensation standards.

Benchmarks. Institutional investors have often responded favorably to codes developed by national bodies on how funds should act as owners of shares in public companies; they have collaborated constructively, for instance, with "stewardship" principles that now form part of market architecture in the United Kingdom, South Africa, the Netherlands, and other markets.[36] These codes suggest how investors should engage with the companies they invest in. But principles that might address the internal governance of the funds themselves are a different matter. Even advisors to investing bodies are skittish about raising questions about internal governance with clients, perhaps for fear of resistance. One consultant laudably put forward a dozen indicators of a well-governed fund, but these contained no mention of communication and accountability to members. A notable exception is the International Corporate Governance Network (ICGN),[37] the investor-driven professional body with pension funds and money managers representing assets exceeding $18 trillion. In 2013, it adopted a Statement on Institutional Investor Responsibilities.[38] While six principles set expectations for fund behavior in respect of portfolio companies, six others set aspirational guidance for their own governance. These focus in particular on the accountability of an institutional investor to its beneficiaries and individual investors. And they touch on most of the categories discussed earlier in this chapter. The ICGN statement made history as the first set of international standards for fund governance, and the first explicitly to involve that silent third estate, the beneficiaries, in every step.

SOCIAL MEDIA

So far, we have looked at traditional ways of providing accountability: better information and better governance. But other solutions to the accountability gap are bubbling up in social media. In an earlier era, public companies could safely rank investors in importance by the size of their holdings. Executives could be confident of their ability to control proprietary information and to manage aggrieved employees without triggering broader problems for the firm. Social media have upended those assumptions. Today, any lone consumer tapping on a tablet in an Internet café, any citizen with one share of stock, or any disgruntled worker with WikiLeaks in mind has the potential to sway a Wall Street behemoth's fortunes.

Facebook, Twitter, and other social media can turbocharge investor, consumer, or community activism because cyberspace is an unprecedented force multiplier. Social media can be a low-cost, high-impact tool for assertive campaigns in the capital market, and it radically drives down their cost. United Airlines, for instance, suffered a consumer uprising in 2009 that became a case study of the corporation as victim of social media attack. A passenger took a run-of-the-mill complaint about a musical instrument damaged in a baggage transfer and turned it into a YouTube video called "United

Breaks Guitars."[39] The company was caught flat-footed when the video went viral, exacting a nasty reputation hit.

Investors have joined in too, though less often. Yahoo! saw perhaps the best-known example in 2007 when Eric Jackson, a retail investor with a handful of shares, stirred a large-scale shareowner revolt through his Breakout Performance social media campaign. The activist investor Carl Icahn started using Twitter in June 2013 as part of a battle over the Dell buyout and quickly gained 76,000 followers.[40] Then there is retail shareholder David Webb, in Hong Kong, who writes a blog from his home flat. People feed him tips about insider corporate wrongdoing that could never appear in Hong Kong's mainstream media, because they are controlled by either the state or major families. Webb's blog has been widely read by big investors.

But to best understand how potent the combination of social media and frustration at the finance sector can be, look at Russia. In a country where wealth often comes from state favoritism and troublesome journalists have suffered mysterious deaths, one of the most prominent political opposition figures started his career by blogging about capital market abuse and corruption. Alexei Navalny, the lawyer-blogger-turned-politician, gained prominence by advocating for minority shareowners and for fairer capital markets. He built a potent online presence through a blog featuring commentary, news analysis, and corporate documents pried from companies through the courts.[41] His efforts to spread transparency whether companies liked it or not stirred not only investor scrutiny but civic protest. Navalny's canny use of social media turned him into a national figure, but may have prompted charges that landed him under house arrest. His blog continued to attract national and international following.

Even when Russian authorities periodically blocked them, his posts somehow managed to reach social media outlets.[42]

Others also understand the leveling effect of social media in confronting disproportionate power. Social media channels are changing and arising at rapid speeds. Here are a few examples:

- Twitter boasts hashtags that draw robust exchanges and action in the capital market. These include streams on specific companies or on hot topics, such as #corpgov, #sayonpay, #secproxy, #boardroom, #fiduciary, #ethics, #CSR, #diversity, #governance, and #compensation.
- Facebook features dozens of governance commentators who post media reports, video links, and opinions on issues and events. Facebook groups also foster dialogue and collective action.
- LinkedIn, the social networking site pitched to professionals, features groups that host cross-border dialogue on corporate governance. One, run out of Canada, has more than twenty thousand participants.
- Harvard Law School's Forum on Corporate Governance and Financial Regulation has become a prime resource for academic papers and comment on corporate governance in the United States. Sponsors have vastly magnified their outreach by posting regular notices on Twitter at @HarvardCorpGov.[43]
- The granddaddy of social media in corporate governance is www.corpgov.net, founded and edited by California-based James McRitchie. He

has been posting news and analysis and inviting dialogue on the site since 1995, which makes its origins virtually prehistoric.

- Magazines such as *Capital Aberto* in Brazil and *Corporate Board Member* and *Directorship* in the United States have expanded their online presence and encouraged online dialogue on articles.
- A search for "corporate governance" on You Tube returns more than 100,000 videos.
- Other groups mobilize private platforms to stir collective action. The Principles for Responsible Investment, for instance, operates an online clearinghouse for exchanges and collaboration among signatory institutions.

Most social media energy in the capital market has sought to focus institutional and retail investors' attention on the behavior of corporations. Only a handful of instigators put institutional investors themselves in the crosshairs. It seems reasonable to speculate that over time, the accountability of these investors will also become a subject of social media. But it may take a different path. Grassroots campaigns have already surfaced to influence the way US mutual funds vote shares on specific issues.

A likely source for a social media uprising is from the inside. Powerful organizations sometimes breed social media discontent. So one threat is a leak of information or a campaign focused on one investment organization, by either an employee or a customer. Media already exist to cover an organization from within. A popular finance blog, Dealbreaker, has become almost mandatory reading from Wall Street to the City of London, thanks to its combination of sassy, snarky, timely commentary and offbeat coverage of the finance industry's peccadilloes.[44]

As we write this, such a campaign is already under way, focused on the energy industry. The environmental group 350.org has used social media with university students, calling for their institutions to divest themselves of companies and funds that invest in fossil fuels. One major technique 350.org and the Responsible Endowments Coalition (REC) use is to call for student representation on the governing bodies of university endowments and for more transparency in how the endowments are invested. Whether or not you agree with the call for fossil fuel–free investing, it is clear that the techniques pioneered by 350.org and REC can quickly, easily, and inexpensively be applied to a wide array of situations.

Apps, in particular, are underutilized tools, at least for now, in bids to enhance the accountability of investment agents. But examples in related fields hint at how change could develop. For instance, Buycott, a free app launched in 2013, aimed to help consumers align their values with their purchasing. It asked: "Have you ever wondered whether the money you spend ends up funding causes you oppose?" Opening the app on a smartphone, a user could select or start a campaign on an issue such as worker safety in Bangladeshi factories. Then, developers instruct, while shopping, "scan a barcode with the Buycott app and it will look it up in our database and try to determine who owns it. Buycott will then trace the product's ownership back to its top parent company and cross-check this company against the campaigns that you've joined before telling you whether it found a conflict." A glaring risk is, of course, that the information in the Buycott database—supplemented in wiki style by users—may not be accurate.

But we can easily imagine a tool being developed to ask a parallel question: "Have you ever wondered whether the money you *save* ends up funding causes you oppose?" It could compare pension or defined contribution plans on select criteria, providing users with a picture of how well agency arrangements align with citizen investor interests.

CIVIL SOCIETY

Entire bookshelves are devoted to the importance of civil society organizations (CSOs) such as community groups, professional bodies, research institutes, faith-based groups, rights advocates, trade unions, and media, to the health of democratic culture. In 2010, US Secretary of State Hillary Rodham Clinton made support for civil society an explicit priority of American foreign policy.[45] With the State Department asserting that "a robust civil society is necessary for democracy to thrive," Clinton argued that CSOs underpin "both democratic governance and broad-based prosperity. . . . Societies move forward when the citizens that make up these groups are empowered to transform common interests into common actions that serve the common good."[46]

The presence of CSOs in the capital market is growing rapidly. CSOs have long turned citizens' attention to corporate behavior on such issues as CEO pay, boardroom diversity, climate change, political contributions, and workplace safety. The next phase of civil society action, as with social media, may focus on institutional investor behavior. Until now, groups had concentrated on agents as owners of equity shares, property, or commodities. What is new is the rise of groups that gauge investment agents on their accountability and transparency—

that is, on their internal governance characteristics. Already some groups are calling attention to agent accountability to citizen investors.

Proponents of private sector social responsibility have been the first to break ground here. Consider an arresting video that went viral in 2007.[47] A man and a woman are huddled with a financial advisor to discuss their portfolio. The financial advisor walks them through gains in energy and tech stocks as they flip through a binder. "You took a little hit on real estate," the advisor explains, "but more than made up for it in genocide." As the two slowly turn to pictures of slaughtered children, the advisor looks in their stunned eyes and nods reassuringly. "You're really making a killing in Darfur." Fade to black while an announcer asks: "Is your mutual fund funding genocide?" With this unsubtle message, the producer, the Save Darfur Coalition, sought to awaken scrutiny of US mutual funds that invested in companies the group linked to genocide.

Other groups have used similar means to stimulate citizen pressure on financial agents. The Asset Owner Disclosure Project (AODP) tests how institutional investors address climate change that ultimate beneficiaries can identify funds that are awake to the risks and challenge those that are not.[48] After 348 institutional investors called for putting a price on carbon, AODP asked one thousand of the world's largest investors, with $70 trillion in assets under management, what their portfolios held in high-carbon assets.[49] Similarly, Ceres, the US environmental coalition, has published periodic comparisons of mutual fund voting on climate change issues, hoping to provoke citizen engagement on the issue with the funds that manage their savings.[50] And 350.org has already persuaded several university endowments to divest from fossil fuels.[51] The AFL-CIO trade union federation has a related approach to the question of excessive CEO pay at US companies.[52] The AFL-CIO argues that its members should insist on investment agents who handle their money in alignment with their goals.

Other groups, rather than focus on a single issue, tackle the accountability gap as the overriding challenge. UK-based ShareAction, founded in 2005 as FairPensions, says it "believes strongly in connecting pension savers with the management of their money and in making the investment industry more transparent and accountable in its dealings with pension savers and retail clients."[53] The group encourages grassroots savers to "petition your pension scheme to become a responsible investor, showing your pension scheme that their members want them to be environmentally, socially and financially responsible. Seen another way, this is about you taking responsibility for the way your capital is being used to shape the world you—and future generations—live in." US-based ProxyDemocracy takes a related approach: it posts mutual fund voting records on a range of issues and derives an Activism Score for each fund based on quantitative criteria.[54] "Our job is to help you understand whether your mutual fund represents you well," the group's website explains. "If you think it doesn't, let your fund know or switch to a new fund that does." Canada's Shareholder Association for Research and Education (SHARE) serves as a watchdog on how investment managers vote on behalf of citizen investors, particularly on governance, environmental, and social issues.[55] Britain's Trades Union Congress tackles broad fund governance by sponsoring a labor-based Trustee Network.[56] And the venerable CFA Institute, which certifies financial analysts, plays a role by circulating a Pension Trustee Code of Conduct.[57]

University students are making their mark here too, as they did in supporting the disinvestment movement in the

1980s against apartheid South Africa. We have already mentioned the Responsible Endowments Coalition, which not
only calls for more responsible investment practice but also
demands governance reform. "The broader campus community, especially students and alumni, must also have a say on
some level in how the endowment is managed."[58]

A more assertive student group, based at Oxford University, opened a different civil society front in December 2013
with a campaign labeled "Push Your Parents."[59] The working
title of the project, floated before launch, was more expressive:
"Hey Mum and Dad, Did You Know Your Pension is F***ing
Up My Future?" The group's founders hope to alert parents to
the accountability gap with agents handling family savings.
They want mothers and fathers to demand a say in how their
funds are managed.

New CSOs will undoubtedly take new approaches to the
challenge of agent accountability. Policy entrepreneur Marcy
Murninghan, for instance, floated the idea of "Civic Stewardship Leagues," with local chapters that would enable citizens
to deliberate on the environmental, social, and governance
impact of public and endowment fund investments, underwritten by taxpayers, in the same way the League of Women
Voters prompts discussion of US politics.[60] Other thoughtful
plans surface regularly.[61] Perhaps the surest sign of a growing
field is the rise of companies that see prospects of profit from
working on investor accountability. Market analysts Morningstar and BrightScope, for instance, offer tools to compare
US mutual funds on governance criteria, and the consulting
firms Mercer and Towers Watson feature units that advise on
fund governance. More specialized commercial services are
likely on the way.

Many of these ideas to empower citizens sound like plain common sense: of course we should have clear information to help markets work, and regulators should be assiduous in making sure that the finance industry works productively on its clients' behalf. But these conditions have been rare. We have allowed malign incentives to encourage behavior that does not help customers, we have allowed our capital markets to become suffused with trading, and we have neglected the rights of citizen investors to influence investment agents. We have also, as we shall see in chapter 5, got the wrong end of the stick in the way we regulate markets.

Takeaways

- Responsible ownership under capitalism means that the financial system needs to reflect the interests of the saver. And that needs to apply to all the agents in the "investment chain."
- A gaping hole in that chain of accountability exists between perhaps the most important of those agents, the fund managers, and the savers they should serve.
- Thanks to substandard governance, the investment industry does not reflect the interests of those it is there to serve. Those who control our savings are rarely representative, are sometimes conflicted, and occasionally even lack the skill to oversee our savings.
- Solutions lie in regulation, voluntary moves by the fund management industry, and innovative citizen action that may be facilitated by social media.

5

The New Geometry
of Regulation

The 2008 financial crisis wiped value from economies around the world, but it also created a boom in financial regulation. In the aftermath of the collapse, vast numbers of laws and regulations were passed with the aim of ensuring that such a crisis would never happen again. The scale and complexity of this activity are mind boggling. In the United States, the key piece of legislation, known as the Dodd-Frank Act, ran to 848 pages and mandated four hundred new rules, which in turn are expected to generate another twenty thousand pages of regulation. In Europe, one analyst calculated that banks would have to hire seventy thousand new staff just to be sure they were complying with the new laws.[1]

So when the heads of the world's central banks met in August 2012 at their annual jamboree at Jackson Hole, Wyoming, they were keen to hear the results of a study by the Bank of England's director of financial stability, Andy Haldane. Haldane had asked a simple question: would these new regulations have better predicted and thus helped avoid the financial crisis? He looked in particular at the international rules used to calculate a bank's "solvency," and hence whether a bank had adequate reserves to withstand future crises. In the 1980s, these had been calculated using simple rules of thumb, set out in the convention known as Basel I. By 2012, the Basel III convention had laid out a much more sophisticated system, aimed at ensuring that loans that were more likely to go bad required greater reserves. After all these years of work, how much better was Basel III than Basel I?

Haldane brought two pieces of bad news. First, neither of the Basel rules was very good at predicting failure.[2] Second, despite its sophistication, Basel III was actually a *worse* predictor of bank failure than Basel I, and Basel I was worse than simple accounting ratios. In other words, the boom in financial regulation had not improved the predictability and reliability of the financial system but had done the exact opposite.[3]

The ineffectual response of regulators, both before and after the crisis, has left the financial system—and by extension every citizen—vulnerable to future economic shock. We need a new framework for regulation that focuses not on rules for their own sake but on encouraging the best possible outcomes from the system as a whole. Before we can begin to sketch out that framework, however, we need to step back and ask another of those bedrock questions: what is regulation for?

What Is Regulation For?

Most of us would say that we work in "market economies," that is, economies in which the buyer and the seller decide what things are to be produced and at what price they will be sold. Yet these market economies are affected by vast amounts of regulation. When you pour a glass of water from the tap, its quality is subject to regulations. So are the pipes through which it comes to you. When you start your car, every component of it, as well as the fuel, will have been subject to regulation. If you want to build an extension to your house, it must pass zoning and building regulations. And, of course, most financial transactions are governed by contracts, which require contract law to make them valid and enforceable.

It is not just the products and services we buy that are subject to regulation; so are the processes by which they are made and sold. Regulations determine the information we are given about the processed food products we purchase. If we take out a credit card or buy a pension, the way in which it is sold, and the often complex and lengthy information provided along with the transaction, are mandated by regulation. Regulations prevent producers from taking advantage of their customers, for example, by prohibiting monopolies.

The market economies in which we live are thus highly regulated. What, then, is the purpose of this regulation?

We regulate markets for the same reason we regulate car engines: to make sure they work properly. The promise of markets is that they allow each of us, as consumers and businesspeople, to decide what we want to buy and what we are willing to pay. Similarly, they allow producers to decide what they will supply and what price they will ask. With adequate competition, this autonomy enhances the possibility that consumers will be able to choose the best deal for themselves and, provided there are enough competing producers, that there will be supply at a price that reflects the cost of production.

This can happen only if certain conditions hold. One is that production and consumption do not affect others; for example, that manufacturing does not pollute someone else's water supply. If markets create such "externalities" (costs and benefits that are not included in the price of goods), then they won't work as well, since neither the manufacturer nor the consumer is charged for the loss of other people's clean water supply. Similarly, if buyers don't know what they are purchasing, they may be sold a poor product. Again, the market will not work well.

In theory, we could create market solutions for these problems. Take regulation of the pharmaceuticals industry. Most of us don't really know how the chemicals we are swallowing to cure our illness actually affect our bodies, and so we could be poisoned if we buy a poor product. Hence we have legislated to have the industry regulated. It doesn't need to be. We could allow the charlatan to compete with the ethical drug producer, and individual patients could all ask to review the clinical studies on competing drugs before deciding whether to follow their doctor's prescription. But the cost for each of us to find and to assess those studies would be huge. An economist would say that the "transaction costs" would be high.[4] It is less costly to pass legislation to require that when a drug maker makes claims about a drug's benefits and safety, those claims have passed a certain level of scrutiny.

Some, of course, argue that we should regulate less. As we write this, the British government has a significant program to lessen what it terms the "burden" of regulation.[5] Often regulations can seem foolish and trivial. They incur costs not just in complying but in documenting and reporting. Furthermore, where regulation is limited, markets have a way of filling the gap. Reports from friends, consumer magazines, and websites such as Yelp or TripAdvisor or Edmunds often help us buy the best product or get the best deal. Companies brand their goods, promising that they will live up to expected quality standards, and they make great efforts to protect their brand and avoid reputational damage. Mobile computing is revolutionizing such nonregulatory approaches, allowing not just instant comparison shopping but crowd-sourced reviews of products and services in real time.

Naturally, one central question about regulation is, what should be left to the market, and what to the regulator? After the financial crisis, the pendulum swung toward more regulation. But regulations don't replace markets; they help them do what they ought, which is to give consumers the goods and services they desire, at the lowest cost, in a way that brings the least negative impact to them and others.[6]

Even if we agree on this basic point, that regulation should make markets work better, there are other questions about how regulation should be structured. How do we decide if the market is behaving as it ought, and at what level should intervention take place?

How We Regulate Today

Today's dominant approach to regulation is to identify and isolate a specific problem and then regulate to prevent its happening again. Each transaction and each entity are considered, and if something goes wrong or is deemed likely to go wrong, a regulation is put in place to prevent the problem. We can call this approach "atomized regulation."

In the case of the banks, on which Haldane's paper focused, the danger is that banks can make a lot of money in the short term by lending at high interest to people who are poor credit risks. For a time, that may look quite profitable, because in the early years of the loan there may be few defaults. But if there is a recession, borrowers won't be able to repay, and banks, in turn, may be unable to pay their depositors. In response, the international regulator in Basel has developed ever-more-complicated classifications of risk for different sorts of loans. Each type of loan requires a different level of reserves to compensate for the risk.

This atomized approach, focusing on each product and service, is typical of financial regulation. For example, regulators have decided that in order to get a fair deal on their credit cards, consumers need to know all the terms and conditions associated with it. As a result, someone buying a US credit card will receive thirty-one pages of detailed legalese. That is up from one and a half pages thirty years ago. How helpful has that been? Senator Elizabeth Warren, an assiduous campaigner for consumer rights, has said that although she used to teach contract law at Harvard, she couldn't understand her own credit card contract.[7]

It is easy to see how this atomized approach creates a growing body of regulations. Every time there is a crisis, a new set of statutes is passed, each designed to fight the last war.

There are other problems with this approach.

First, it assumes that if every part of a system is well designed, the system as a whole will be effective. It is a bit like designing a car by having one person choose the best engine, a second choose the transmission completely independently of the first choice, a third choose the chassis, a fourth the brakes, and so on—and then for the team to assume that in the end they will have designed the best possible automobile. This is often called "the fallacy of composition": that if all the parts of a system work, then the system itself will also work. Think of it this way. We often say a chain is only as strong as its weakest link—and regulators often try to strengthen "weak links." But if we bulked up every link, there is a very good chance the chain would lose its flexibility. Each link would be strong, but so large that it could not interact properly with the adjacent ones. In fact, the chain would become brittle, and if we tried to bend it, it might well break, though all the links were strong. In finance, even if every financial market is atomically regulated to make it "safe," that does not mean the financial system is safe, or that it can flexibly react to unanticipated situations that arise between the individual participants.

The second flaw in atomized regulation is that it requires that we measure the future with some accuracy using mathematical risk models. But as we saw in chapter 2, these models simply don't work: they fail in precisely the unusual and stressful economic times when we most need them. And if they don't work for a single entity, like a bank or a savings account, how can they forecast conditions in a complex system of borrowers and lenders? They are no more likely to predict the next crisis than previous regulation was able to stop the last one.

Third, regulation that focuses only on an entity level, using a "Do this; don't do that" approach, does not address the reasons individuals and institutions behave badly in the first place. Instead, it encourages regulated entities to try to unpick the regulations, or to find a way around them. As Senator Warren observed of the twenty-nine new pages of information credit card suppliers must now provide, it was there that the "tricks and traps" lay. And if one entity finds a profitable trick or trap, others quickly copy them. Over time, more and more people find and exploit loopholes.[8]

Fourth, as regulators take on increasing responsibility, there is a tendency for individuals within the system to feel that the limit of their responsibilities is to meet the letter of the regulations. This phenomenon, in turn, can degrade the checks and balances that make the system stable and effective. It tends to encourage executives to excuse themselves of responsibility for the behavior of the regulated entity, providing that they simply comply with the law.

Which feeds the fifth problem: the atomized approach to regulation grows less effective over time because rules are, by their nature, rigid, while markets are dynamic and constantly evolving. That means regulators must quickly determine whether new products and services are safe, toxic, or somewhere in between. If there are issues, regulators face a dilemma. They can try to propose new regulation, but political realities make this either impossible or time consuming, meaning regulations chronically lag behind markets, often by years. Alternatively, regulators can try to extend existing regulation to new situations that the authors of the regulations never contemplated, resulting in a bad fit and unintended consequences. As Michael Daniel, President Obama's special assistant for cybersecurity, said of another field where evolution takes place quickly, "It is very difficult to move fast enough [to keep up with] the bad guys."[9]

Could we construct a system better suited to maintaining a fair and dynamic economy? Rather than just focus on command and control of the entities that comprise the system, could regulators also look at their construction and the interactions among them, to create the sort of systemic architecture and ethos that will spur positive and self-correcting behavior?[10] We believe they can.

A Better Approach: "Systemic Regulation"

Such a system must be designed as a whole entity, not a patchwork. Imagine a water engineer who is responsible for flood control in a river valley. Upstream, the adoption of new farming techniques means that after each storm, the river bursts its banks, flooding the valley. The first thing the engineer does is to build flood defenses around all the houses, but these are still inadequate against the really big storms. So new levees are built, but they only divert the flood waters farther down the valley. The engineer's job is endless. More and more flood-control projects are commissioned, but they are simply palliative. At the end of the day, if the valley is to be protected, the new farming technique needs to be adjusted to diminish the downstream side effects. The engineer must consider the whole river system, not just the flooding of each individual property.

So it is with financial regulation. Rather than just focus on specific problematic transactions or on particular companies within the system, regulators need to consider the financial system as a whole; the purpose of regulation is to make that whole work effectively. That, in turn, raises another question: what do we mean by "effectiveness"? The success of the financial system cannot be judged by how many transactions have taken place, any more than the drug industry is measured by how many vials of medicine are sold. Ultimately, we measure the success of the drug industry by how well it has treated illness. The industry's ability to generate income for itself is not the measure, but it should be the consequence of success. Success is judged by the value the industry has delivered to society—in other words, by outcomes. We must surely do the same for financial markets.

Some may object that such a starting point implies even more regulatory intervention than we have today. In fact, it is likely to require much less, given the explosion in legislation over the last thirty years. Further, this reasoning should be particularly compelling for those who believe in free markets, since its aim is to reproduce the characteristics that justify free markets.

How do we measure the effectiveness of the financial system? In chapter 1, we discussed the purposes of the system. They are to match people with savings to those who wish to borrow, and to do so in a way that maximizes the return to the saver and minimizes the cost to the borrower; to defray risk for both savers and investors; to ensure safe custody and provide a payments system; and to oversee the governance of companies, ensuring that the law is respected and the power entrusted by shareholders is properly used. The system should be judged the more effective if it provides those services at a lower cost to customers, without allowing externalities to shift costs onto the public. Thus a financial system that takes up 5 percent of GDP is preferable to one that provides identical services but absorbs 10 percent of GDP.

So a well-regulated system is one in which the financial services industry performs its functions well at the lowest possible cost. This does not mean that any failure to live up to that goal requires a new regulation. It may, but this should not be a reflexive assumption. In other words, a market failure is a necessary but not sufficient condition for regulation. There are costs to regulation; we should not lightly restrict markets any more than we should restrict any individual human action. Nor should we restrict innovation or competition. The regulator must clearly articulate the purpose of any policing, and design the incentives so that they encourage entities to do the right thing in the first place, not to police the breach after it has taken place. And they should measure the success of regulation by the success of the system: does it deliver the right behaviors and outcomes? We call this holistic perspective "systemic regulation."

Furthermore, the regulator's choice is not simply between "the market" and "regulation." Markets behave very differently depending on the nature of their participants; how they compete; the sophistication of customers; and the relevance, reliability, and availability of information. Regulation can be used not just to constrain behavior but to shape market institutions that can guide outcomes. To extend the analogy of the water engineer, the task is not simply to build flood defenses. Rather it is to consider the effects on the whole river system: what farming techniques are appropriate? How can protections be built into the environment that prevent damage? How can the system be managed to both allow for individual initiative and encourage people to maintain its sustainability?

These points may seem obvious, but the regulatory response to the crisis has paid scant regard to them. Atomized command-and-control regulation is still the overwhelmingly dominant form. A complex system of principals and agents is matched to a complex set of regulations. And, as Andy Haldane reported to the bankers gathered in Jackson Hole, it simply doesn't work.

How might regulators design a system that allows "commonsense" banking and investment institutions to become established, to flourish, and to innovate?[11]

Three Critical Disciplines

Three important disciplines underpin the regulatory tool kit: a fiduciary legal system, well-designed institutions to promote responsibility and accountability, and attention to the behavioral aspects of economic systems.

THE FIDUCIARY FIX

A well-designed financial system will deliver value to customers *outside* the financial system. When those customers, their agents, or their agents' agents decide how to manage a customer's money, they should do so in the customer's best interest. In a classical free market, that would happen as a matter of course, because the customer is always able to choose the best deal. But as we discussed in chapter 2, agents in today's financial markets have the ability to reward themselves in ways that are not to the customer's benefit.

This characteristic is not unique to the financial system. Agents have that ability in all sorts of situations. Doctors can benefit at their patients' expense; teachers can exploit their pupils; parents can exploit their children. But most do not do this because they feel bound to act in good faith in another's interest. In legal terms, that is known as a "fiduciary responsibility." We give our money to investment managers because we trust that they will manage it on our behalf, not on their own.[12] For the system to work as it ought, financial managers must accept a professional obligation of loyalty, to put client interests first, to avoid conflicts of interest, and to keep the costs of services reasonable and visible.[13]

This system of good faith relationships has been at the heart of many financial institutions' success. Many savings and banking institutions began as mutual companies where all shared in the profit, so there was no advantage from the entity benefiting at the expense of its customers. Other institutions were established around religious and professional groupings. That agents would act in good faith was essential to the establishment of a successful financial system.[14]

Not surprisingly, therefore, there are legal duties designed to help regulate those who are asked to undertake business transactions in good faith. These legal protections, which have been with us for centuries, allow an asset that is owned by one person to be controlled by another. They were used in feudal times, when a child who was too young to inherit the throne would have a regent appointed, who would then step aside when the child grew up. In the same way, we depend on our agents to act on our behalf when we give them our pension assets to manage and ask them to return to us a fair income when we retire.

Some financial activities require fiduciary standards more than others. People who own shares in a company, whose value depends on the company's performance, require a broad fiduciary obligation from the directors and from anyone else who has discretion on how the shares are managed. When we give our money to a pension fund to invest on our behalf, we give it discretion, and so require a broader obligation than we do from the bank where we hold our savings account.

But both of them owe us a duty of loyalty, to act on our behalf, and a duty of care or prudence, to act with adequate expertise and balance. Note that fiduciary duties do not mandate any specific behavior. If they did, they could be replaced by contracts. Indeed, contract law rather than fiduciary obligation governs the relationship between companies and those who lend them money. Anyone who has ever received a mortgage knows how much documentation is required and how specific the provisions are. But fiduciary duty is not like that. It doesn't mandate but rather *guides* behavior, allowing agents who owe the duty to make their own minds up about the best course of action, within the broad obligations they have accepted.

Although fiduciary systems have strengths, they also have weaknesses. The first is that there is limited market incentive for people to establish themselves as fiduciaries, since they cannot profit by it as much as if they did not have to be loyal to their clients. That is why so many of our original financial institutions were established by faith groups, and why so many pension funds were established by employers wishing to give a benefit to their employees. Their founders had motivations that went beyond personal gain. Today, in a society with more mobility and less loyalty, many of these institutions have severed their traditional ties and are now for-profit corporations, indistinguishable in purpose from their competitors.

The second problem is one we have already described: the tendency after every failure to enact a regulation. Such rules can ossify behavior even as markets and expectations evolve, and this has occurred with fiduciary obligations. The legal imperatives governing fiduciaries have fallen well behind modern trends in capital markets, encouraging fiduciary institutions to be more myopic than they should. Designed as the law's secret sauce assuring alignment of interests, fiduciary duty laws are now so watered down that they allow agents to siphon value that rightly belongs to citizen investors.

Equally, fiduciaries tend to seek advice to ensure they never fall foul of the law. For instance, in order to ensure that they fulfill their "duty of care," trustees are often advised to make sure they do what every other similar trustee is doing. As pension expert and legal scholar Keith Johnson has put it, this creates a "lemming standard": it is legally permissible to behave foolishly provided everyone else does too.[15] This has led to the idea that it is acceptable to "fail conventionally" but dangerous to try unconventional solutions that have a better chance of success.

Today's debate on fiduciary duty was begun by members of the UN Environment Program's Finance Initiative and the Principles for Responsible Investment (UN PRI). They were concerned that pension trustees were being given advice that they could only look at short-term financial performance when thinking about how they invested.[16] A landmark study, undertaken by the legal firm Freshfields, showed this to be entirely wrong.[17] Nevertheless, narrowing interpretations of fiduciary standards can create sclerosis in financial management, where those who manage our money respond to narrow legal interpretations, not to the needs of their customers.

In 2009, such concerns prompted Australia's minister for superannuation and corporate law to commission an inquiry into the governance and efficiency of retirement plans. Were they, the inquiry asked, "individually or as a class, sufficiently accountable to members?" Its final report proposed a detailed menu of fiduciary recommendations. One year later and on the other side of the world, the British government commissioned economist John Kay to explore whether dysfunction or breaks in the investment chain might be causing harmful short-term behavior among investors and companies. Kay sought to discover "whether the current legal duties and responsibilities of asset owners and fund managers, and the fee and pay structures in the investment chain, are consistent with asset owners' long term objectives."[18]

Kay's final report, issued in 2012, called on the Law Commission of the United Kingdom to review the concept of fiduciary duty. When it did so nearly two years later, its conclusions echoed those of reformers. Fiduciaries had broad powers to act in members' interest; these powers and obligations should remain even if the fiduciaries delegate to or contract to others to act for them, and fiduciaries should not feel that they risk legal action if their judgment suggests they take a different approach from others.[19]

Other reforms can strengthen fiduciary responsibilities, too.

Rediscovering the duty of impartiality. Financial institutions often claim that meeting fiduciary standards means generating maximum profit in the short term. But while some citizen investors need to draw cash from their accounts every month, others won't require access to it for decades. A revised policy should resurrect the long-ignored "duty of impartiality," which obligates an institution to weigh the interests of these different beneficiaries.[20] Some call this "intergenerational equity": younger investors' need for patient capital must be balanced against retirees' need for short-term payouts.[21] The duty of impartiality could emerge organically through the courts, if cases asserting breaches produce judgments that reemphasize it, but most advocates believe the vacuum may require legislation or regulation.

Apply fiduciary duty to intermediaries. Statutes designed to safeguard retirement savings were written long before the advent of today's complex market, where intermediaries with many functions touch on the value of savers' assets. Yet these middlemen normally do not fall under fiduciary duty standards and have no obligation to act in beneficiaries' ultimate interests. Vanguard founder John C. Bogle has long called for a fiduciary duty "establishing the basic principle that money managers are there to serve . . . those whose money they manage."[22] In Britain, the Kay Review urged extension of fiduciary duty to intermediaries. Prompted by the Obama White House, the US Department of Labor proposed extending aspects of fiduciary duty to financial advisors and brokers. The draft regulation, once announced, generated a full-scale backlash by parts of the finance industry, which wants to limit obligations to clients to those expressed in contracts.[23]

Widen fiduciary duty to include risks and opportunities that are difficult to quantify in the short term, but no less real. So long as environmental, social, and governance (ESG) factors are excluded from portfolio managers' generally accepted investment responsibilities, many will feel not only free but legally obligated to steer clear of them. Yet these factors can have real impacts on returns. Saker Nusseibeh, the CEO of Hermes Investment Management, who oversees nearly $50 billion in assets under management, estimates that taking them into account adds as much as 5 percent a year to the firm's returns.[24]

An industry body in Australia, the Financial Services Council (FSC), has shown a path to reform. It urges boards of savings funds each to develop, approve, and disclose a policy addressing ESG risks affecting investments. Because ESG factors can have a "major" impact on financial performance, the council asserted that monitoring them "is an important aspect of trustees' discharging their duties [to] members." Such a policy "should document processes regarding engagement with companies on environmental, social and corporate governance activities and ensuring that voting rights are managed with due care and diligence."[25] The FSC stance echoes the Australian Treasury, which helped funds kick-start attention to ESG risks by investing public money in a Responsible Investment Academy. Now part of the UN PRI, it offers online training for asset managers in ownership skills.[26]

Finally, regulators should make sure that those who sell financial services do not abuse the word "fiduciary." The word has a pleasant ring to it, and so in the United Kingdom, for instance, it is now common for financial agents to call themselves "fiduciaries" when they owe no greater obligations than the letter of the contract they sign with you. That misleading practice should be policed.

The first step in creating a better regulatory environment is to reassert fiduciary obligations. But for such a system to work, it will need institutions that support good practice.

WELL-DESIGNED INSTITUTIONS

Economic systems resemble political systems in that successful ones feature checks and balances, robust information, and a culture of accountability. Political regimes, of course, get off-kilter from time to time, but they can self-correct. While laws are important, there are more basic, ingrained tenets without which citizens do not trust government. These include the following:

- *Responsibility.* Lines of responsibility are sufficiently clear that individuals can be identified with outcomes.
- *Accountability.* There are mechanisms to hold agents accountable.
- *Relevant and unbiased information.* Accountability mechanisms require relevant, reliable information from a free and unfettered media and from independent, accurate sources of statistical information.
- *Vigilant oversight.* Citizens must care about the system and employ these accountability mechanisms.

Economies need the same characteristics. If fiduciary obligations compose the legal skeleton for a financial system, these tenets provide the muscle. A focus on these aspects of the system offers regulators a constructive way to assess their effectiveness and a means of self-correction.

The idea that a well-regulated system requires well-designed institutions would have been clearly apparent to economists of a century ago. They often described their subject as "political economy," and they studied the effects of both institutional structures and culture on the functioning of a market economy. The aim of political economy is to design institutions that generate constructive outcomes, reward good behavior, and deter bad behavior.[27] The motivation of the market participants is intimately connected to the effectiveness of the system. Since few systems are totally self-regulating, the question is how to craft regulation to nourish institutions that encourage trustworthy behavior.

In this, we are enormously assisted by the fact that the ultimate beneficiaries of the financial system have similar interests to citizens as a whole. In most Western countries, the ultimate shareholders, depositors, and customers of our banks, insurers, and investment management companies are millions of citizen savers, through their pensions and other investments. The question for the regulator is how to create a framework in which these shareholders, lenders, and customers are well served. How do we create an effective constitution for capitalism? One place to look for an answer is in the combination of psychology and finance called behavioral economics.

BEHAVIORAL ECONOMICS

If the purpose of regulation is to create better behavior, another discipline also needs to be considered: the relationship between written regulations and actual practice. For example, we know that posting speed limits does not prevent people from driving faster than the regulations permit. What does?

A traditional economist might answer in this way. When we are deciding whether to exceed the speed limit (leaving aside the issue of safety), we think about the benefit we get from breaking the law, we think through the penalty we will have to pay if caught, and we calculate the probability of being caught.[28] If the benefit is greater than the penalty times the probability, we break the law.[29] We are, in other words, amoral and rational creatures seeking to maximize our own benefit, so the traditional economist's solution is to change the terms in the equation: either increase the probability of being caught by putting more police on the road or increase the penalty. How can we test whether this works?

The psychologist and behavioral economist Dan Ariely undertook an experiment that explored exactly these issues.[30] Subjects were asked to take a test where they would be paid $1 for every question they got right. They marked the test themselves, put the exam paper in the shredder, and claimed their reward. In other words they could cheat as much as they liked. The experimenters had previously tested other groups and hence knew what the average score should be. Needless to say, the group who reported their own scores did better than average. One question the experimenters hoped to answer was whether this was because a few people cheated a lot or because many cheated a little.

Before continuing, readers might want to reflect on this, since it is important for the way a financial regulatory system should be designed. Does it need to change the behavior of the average market participant, or just focus on a few bad apples? Ariely found the former: lots of us cheat a little. The experiment was carried out in China, Italy, Turkey, Canada, Israel, and Great Britain, as well as in the United States, with little variation among countries. The analogy to speed limits is obvious: when the limit is 30 mph, almost everyone drives at 40 but almost no one does 90.

Regulators need to design systems that discourage people from cheating. One means of discouraging cheating is supervision: when people know they are being observed, they cheat less. The purpose of institutions that foster responsibility, accountability, and transparency is to ensure that supervision is visibly in place.

Ariely found that other methods reduced cheating as well. One was simply to remind people of their moral obligations. When participants took a pledge and signed it before taking the test, Ariely found that they would cheat less. Even if they were asked only to remember as many of the Ten Commandments as they could, the mere process of reflecting on moral values reduced dishonesty.

What encouraged dishonesty? One influence was seeing others act dishonestly or benefit from dishonesty, particularly where these were people whom subjects thought of as part of their own "group." Another was being part of a culture that condoned dishonest behavior. People also cheated more, Ariely found, if they were distanced from the act of taking money. Many who would take paper from the company stationery cupboard would never dream of stealing money from petty cash. Creative individuals were more likely to cheat, as was everyone when they were tired. People would cheat more if they could rationalize that it was benefiting others. And unsurprisingly, they cheated more where they had a conflict of interest.[31]

Ariely's findings give a sense of why bad behavior was so common on the trading desks of banks and in the selling of pensions and investments.[32] In such situations, there is often a highly competitive culture of bonuses and incentives among a small, close-knit group of people. Often they have little relationship, or none, with the customers whose money they are managing, and they have huge financial incentives to cheat. They often suspect others are benefiting from cheating. This is a breeding ground for dishonesty that would tempt even the most saintly. Part of the regulators' job must be to create conditions that satisfy both the traditional economists and the behavioral economists: regulations must create the proper incentives and also promote a culture of honesty.

Better Regulation

What would regulation look like if it took into account the way individuals really act, rather than the way economic models say they should behave?

First, it would abandon the idea that there are two distinct and separate entities called financial institutions and regulators. The nature of regulation changes depending on the institutions to be regulated. If rules are designed to deliver good outcomes, they will require less "Do this; don't do that" interference. Financial institutions need to be regulated and accountable, but they also need to serve as quasi-regulators of the marketplace. Markets, institutions, and regulators all exist to make sure the customer gets a good deal.

Second, regulators must have regard not only to law but to institutional design, and to the likely behavioral consequences of rules, supervision, and sanctions. Some fairly straightforward ideas along these lines could improve on today's practice. For convenience, they are grouped under the four tenets of well-functioning systems: responsibility, accountability, information, and civil society oversight.

RESPONSIBILITY

The central responsibility is that each entity operates in the interest of those for whom it ultimately works. For financial institutions, that means the ultimate providers of capital: customers and shareholders. Banks and the like should keep themselves free from conflicts of interest, give an account of what they have done, and be able to demonstrate that they have properly served their clients.

As mentioned above, one way regulation could promote such responsibility is that regulators could reinforce mechanisms that strengthen fiduciary duties. For a start, they could apply fiduciary duty to intermediaries so that these duties cannot be subcontracted away. Further, they could clarify that fiduciary duty requires independent judgment and does not automatically equate to short-term stock price performance, since focusing on this sole measure is not always in clients' interests.

Then there is transparency. We know that oversight discourages cheating. So regulators should require full fee disclosures: financial intermediaries should have to tell their clients all the ways in which they get paid and what they pay others from clients' funds.

Further, why can't financial institutions borrow a notion from the medical establishment? Just as doctors sign and police the Hippocratic oath, those who manage others' money should make an explicit commitment to their clients. As behavioral economists have shown, reminding people of their moral obligations really does change behavior for the better. That is why many schools now require students to sign an honor code statement when they take exams. Such promise-making is most effective if the pledge is made before action is taken. Rather than have an investment salesperson sign a form after the sale is made, declaring that the customer has been fully informed, it would be better if the promise were made before the transaction began.[33] Virtually every major financial firm in the United States has an ethics and compliance policy that key employees must acknowledge annually. Why not make those who manage others' money reaffirm every year that they are acting as fiduciaries?

ACCOUNTABILITY

If agents are going to be responsible, they must be supervised. That means not only that they must provide a true and fair account of what they have been doing but that someone must receive that account and be authorized to take remedial action if the agent is not behaving properly. Audit standards are critical.

The legal requirement that banks undertake annual audits was introduced to make sure they did not overextend themselves and that they had regard for the interests of their shareholders and depositors.[34] One principle of these standards was that calculations of value should be made "prudently." Some years ago, that notion of prudence was set aside out of concern that it might cause a bank's profits to be understated, and therefore its shares might not be properly priced by investors.[35] That is fine if the primary purpose of accounting is to help set share prices, but it is not. Before the 2008 crisis, many banks fooled themselves into believing they were making profits, and that their managers were entitled to bonuses, when many were barely solvent. Had it not been for government bailouts, depositors would have lost their money. Some argue that if auditors focused on the banks' accountability to their creditors, and hence the need to determine profits prudently, the financial crisis would have been substantially mitigated or even avoided.[36]

Moreover, a focus on share price creates a focus on short-term trading rather than long-term value creation. No less a personage than James Doty, the chief audit regulator in the United States, acknowledged the issue, in slightly different language. He has said he would like audits "to return . . . to their original fiduciary role, as opposed to compliance."[37]

Doty is not the only regulator trying to refocus auditors on the big picture. In the United Kingdom, audit reports were expanded in 2014 to provide a broader assessment of the health of the company and the basis of that judgment. By providing more qualitative information about the risks a company faces, the audit reports become more than a compliance exercise.

Finally, regulators could add accountability to executive compensation. Why is a CEO's performance measured only as short-term return to shareholders? This is not an academic question. As noted in chapter 3, executive compensation above $1 million is tax deductible to a US company if the compensation is "performance" related. But few have examined the definition of "performance." It should mean more than stock price appreciation, which is influenced by everything from global politics to the state of the economy, making the linkage to actions taken by management tenuous, at best. Performance should be defined to encourage behaviors that improve a company's long-term outlook and thus help grow the economy. And it should be measured over rolling three- or five-year periods, rather than twelve months.

RELEVANT AND UNBIASED INFORMATION

There is a close relationship between accountability and information. Not only do outsiders use the information but the reporting itself changes behavior. If someone has to report every time they do something questionable, they will be far more hesitant to do it in the first place.

How could regulators use information to improve the system? An overarching principle would be to ensure that there is maximum transparency in situations where the system might be abused.

Here is one example. At present we have a huge market in securities known as credit default swaps (CDSs). These are effectively life insurance contracts on a company, which pay out if a company defaults on its debt. Like human life insurance, they can be useful for anyone—say, someone who had lent the company money—who would be in trouble should the company fail. But unlike life insurance, CDSs do not need the permission of the party whose life is being insured. No one knows who holds a CDS or even the exact size of the CDS market. Estimates are in the trillions. Precisely because it is dangerous to allow people with bad intentions to take out insurance on your life, we should at least know who it is who holds a CDS. Having regulators know exactly what CDSs are outstanding and where they are can only help in their efforts to maintain a stable financial system.

Other financial instruments can also, in Warren Buffett's memorable phrase, become "financial weapons of mass destruction." Public disclosure of terms and conditions should be a requirement before any financial instrument can be tradable or transferable.[38] While CDS terms are becoming standardized, thanks to the International Swaps and Derivatives Association, there is no central clearinghouse of such instruments.[39]

We could also use information to keep our regulators on their toes. If we want financial markets around the world to be effective, why isn't there a global rating of regulators? Since investors can be expected to gravitate to the most trustworthy financial centers, such a rating might help create a race to the top, rather than one to the bottom. The Financial Stability Board has already identified "Key Standards for Sound Financial Systems."[40] What is missing is a commitment from the FSB to publish a market-by-market assessment of how well each market adheres to the standards.

VIGILANT OVERSIGHT

"The price of freedom," as Thomas Jefferson supposedly said, "is eternal vigilance." The same could be said of effective financial markets.

As we noted in chapter 3, fund managers need to be the owners, not just traders, of shares. Yet for years their trading activity has increased. The average annual turnover rate among US mutual funds is between 89 and 130 percent, meaning that many funds hold the average share for less than one year, even though core stakes remain for far longer.[41] Globally, institutional accounts have an average turnover of 72 percent per year.[42] Short-term buying and selling can encourage investment managers and asset owners to believe that they can trade their way out of danger. They are thus less likely to be vigilant participants in policing a responsible and accountable financial system. Market practices enable frequent trading in a number of ways. For starters, we have lowered the cost of trading. We have allowed exchanges to profit from co-locating high-frequency traders' computers adjacent to the exchange's servers, so as to save milliseconds on computer-driven trades.[43] While such actions benefit traders, they also decrease market vigilance. And the ability of high-frequency traders to benefit from ultrafast trades raises fundamental issues of fairness and market confidence.[44] It is time for regulators and legislators to start considering whether ever-more-rapid trading is really a good thing for the system as a whole.

Vigilant oversight could also be ramped up in other areas. Vast amounts are spent on broker research about whether to buy and sell companies. Why not encourage brokers to report on the long-term strategy and governance of the companies we invest in? We could focus a little more on the critical role played by the financial media. Ironically, while the resources of the World Bank are used to train journalists in emerging markets about the importance of corporate governance so that they can provide appropriate monitoring through the media, no such effort is made in the United States, the European Union, or Japan.

Making Systemic Regulation a Reality

Our current system of "Do this; don't do that" atomistic regulation doesn't work, and the continual addition of new rules creates an increasing burden. We need a new approach aimed at creating a self-correcting financial system that concentrates on delivering value to its customers instead of principally to itself. This is hardly a new idea. It is essentially a call for a return of "political economy," to a focus on designing economic systems to deliver constructive outcomes.

The irony is that even without regulation, such systems can emerge because they are so valuable. Observers often note, for example, that the United Kingdom has strong laws to protect shareholders. Among other powers, they can sack corporate directors with less than four weeks' notice. Companies listed on the London Stock Exchange often have many shareholders, each with a small holding in the company, which might otherwise give little individual influence over the conduct of the company's affairs. It is often assumed that the existence of tough legal powers for shareholders is what has allowed the diversity of ownership. But in a fascinating study, Julian Franks and two coauthors showed that dispersed ownership predates any legislation. Why did directors not take advantage of their dispersed owners? It seems it was because originally the dispersed shareholders all came from the same region as the company and its directors, or from the same religious faith. The reason directors didn't cheat the shareholder was not because the law prevented it but because they all shared a culture of ethics and honor.[45]

Some policymakers' statements suggest that they seem to understand this. The Basel rules on banking are based on three pillars: the minimum capital requirements that Haldane investigated, supervisory oversight, and market discipline. Like most financial regulations, Basel rules conceive of market discipline as no more than the production of information. In fact, the regulator needs to think about how the market can create fiduciary behavior through responsibility, accountability, information, and vigilance.[46] This does not seem such a radical demand, or one that our regulators should have difficulty in understanding. So why are these values not embodied in our regulations?

One reason is simply that it is not clear who should take the lead. The plan we have described requires someone to define what is wanted from the financial system and coordinate a regulatory response. This requires political vision and authority. Few politicians have been bold enough to define what we want from the financial system; it is easier to criticize. No individual regulator has the authority to step into this vacuum; hence they tend to continue, each in their own area, with an atomistic approach.

The finance industry's titanic lobbying efforts also pose a major roadblock to change. When individual firms and industry bodies seek to exercise political influence, which they have in ample supply, their aim is almost always to stall, fend off, or severely restrict any new rules.[47] Where there is an atomistic structure of regulation and the issues can be made to seem complex, industry lobbying makes coordinated, purposeful reform very difficult. Civil society organizations and other platforms designed to represent citizen investors and to champion market accountability are often outgunned.

Another reason solutions have been lacking is that our economic models have become too narrow. Under certain assumptions, any transaction between a willing buyer and a willing seller will benefit both. But in the real world, those assumptions don't always apply. As we shall see in chapter 6, "externalities," principal-agent problems, and behavioral biases all combine to create a more complex world than exists in most economics journals.

We do not mean to suggest that atomized regulation should be abandoned. But by combining it with a systemic approach, we could allow traditional command-and-control regulation to address major abuses and stop bad practices, while designing the institutions of market-based self-policing for continuous self-correction. Together, they should allow regulators to steer between the poles of being overly restrictive or rigidly laissez faire as markets continuously evolve. The aim is not to create a perfect system, but to be approximately right rather than precisely wrong.[48]

Takeaways

- One reason for the flaws in the financial system is the way it has been regulated.
- Regulators have written thousands of rules covering the minutiae of financial practice, but they have not stepped back and asked, "How do we create a finance industry that fulfills its purpose?"
- Our regulations have been atomistic, not systemic.
- The law could make suppliers responsible, promote institutions with better checks and balances, and employ lessons from behavioral economics to get agents to act in our best interest.
- No regulator has ever proposed, let alone implemented, such a plan.
- New approaches could improve the financial sector's productivity, resiliency, and the benefit it provides to society.

6

The Queen's Question

On November 4, 2008, a short, eighty-two-year-old woman in a cream-colored suit found herself in the same room as some of the world's top economic thinkers. The global financial crisis was roiling, and in her anxiety at the suddenness of the crash, she took the opportunity to pose a frustrated question to the group: "Why had no one seen it coming?"[1] The economists were largely stumped. They weren't much more knowledgeable four years later when the same pensioner, this time clad in violet but just as puzzled, walked into another room full of economists. "People had got a bit lax, hadn't they?" she tried. Was the problem "complacency"? Was it that those overseeing the market "didn't have any teeth?" The bank's electronic background hum almost swallowed the sounds of shuffling feet.[2]

That pensioner happened to be Elizabeth the Second, Queen of Great Britain, but she was voicing questions ordinary citizens had been asking for years as the crisis scythed jobs and savings. While better off than almost all of those affected, she herself had lost £25 million. Explanations of what happened, and why, have since mushroomed into a virtual subindustry. But it was Luis Garicano, director of research at the London School of Economics, who tried to answer her in 2008. "At every stage" he said, "someone was relying on somebody else, and everyone thought they were doing the right thing."

The Queen might have replied, how could this be so? Britain alone produces about eight thousand new economics graduates each year.[3] Most are bright; many are inquisitive. Worldwide, some twelve thousand university departments and research institutions are dedicated to the study of economics.[4] The IDEAS economics database, which collates economic research and evaluates scholars, cites over one and a half million economics articles, and is adding tens of thousands more each year. Admittedly, not all of the world's economists study the financial system or the stability of banks. But many do, and until it was too late, no cohesive body of opinion had arisen to suggest that the system was about to malfunction.[5] Everyone, according to Luis Garicano, thought he or she was doing the right thing. In the world of financial services, there was a received wisdom that allowed bankers, academics, regulators, and journalists to develop a blind spot.

The existence of such blind spots is well known. If we focus only on one way of seeing and thinking, we can overlook things that seem obvious in hindsight. In the financial crisis, bankers, regulators, academics, and journalists all looked at issues of risk from a particular perspective that limited their view and prevented them from seeing the looming crisis. Yet that same perspective forms the backbone of almost every introductory economics class today.

In this chapter, we will sketch out the economic model that everyone had in mind and where it came from. We will also try to show its strengths and why it was so influential. But we will also point out its weaknesses and the dangers of letting it go unchallenged, and we will describe some alternative models that might prove useful in explaining how financial systems work.

Before embarking on this narrative, we should point out that many of the elements we discuss are being researched. The economists doing that work deserve great credit; the problem is that their research is not generally being applied. The dominant model of finance that currently holds sway gives only a partial view, but many in the financial world fervently, even militantly, treat it as though it gives a complete explanation of how the system works.

Some History

One way in which countries pay respect to their leaders is by putting their likenesses on currency. The Chinese Renminbi portrays Mao Tse Tung; American bills have pictures of notable presidents such as Washington and Lincoln. A Bank of England twenty-pound note is graced by a portrait of Adam Smith, who was actually Scottish and whom many consider the founder of modern economics. Across the Channel, the ten-euro note used to portray the notable German mathematician Carl Friedrich Gauss. Both Smith and Gauss, each in his own way, profoundly affected how we think about the world, though perhaps not in a manner they would have entirely approved of.[6]

ADAM SMITH AND ECONOMICS

Throughout most of human history, questions that we now call "economic" were regarded as moral questions. According to ancient Jewish tradition, the first question God asks you in heaven is, "Were you honest in your business dealings?"[7] In the Middle Ages, writings on economic matters could be found in manuals for confessors, who were concerned that prices charged by merchants were "just." Adam Smith was a professor of moral philosophy who believed his most important book to be one entitled *The Theory of Moral Sentiments*.[8] But he became most famous for a follow-up work in which he applied his mind to the world of commerce: *The Wealth of Nations*. Even in his own time, it was profoundly influential. Prime Minister William Pitt declared to the House of Commons in 1792 that Smith's work would "furnish the best solution to every question connected to the history of commerce and with the system of political economy."[9]

The Wealth of Nations contains two profoundly important observations, the first of which flew in the face of society's preference for thinking about money in moral terms. "It is not," Smith insisted, "from the benevolence of the butcher the brewer or the baker that we expect our dinner, but from their regard to their own self interest. We address ourselves, not to their humanity, but to their self love."[10] This observation defined what came to be known as *homo economicus*, economic man, whose actions could best be understood, and his behavior modified, by reference to his self-interest.

Smith's second observation concerned productivity. He describes a pin factory in which each worker handles a different aspect of pin manufacture: one draws the wire, another cuts it to the proper lengths, another attaches the heads, and so on. This specialization, Smith claimed, yielded vastly more pins than if each worker made all his pins from start to finish.[11] But such specialization required that people trade with one another: they could swap their specialized labor for cash and use that cash to buy food, clothing, and other necessities.

As a corollary, Smith pointed out that the larger the market, the more specialization, and hence productivity and wealth, it could generate. Therefore free trade and open markets were conducive to greater wealth. The price at which goods were bought and sold was not a moral question but would be discovered in the interplay of supply and demand. Provided there was an open market, prices would be kept down to the cost of the land and labor that were required to produce them. Thus Smith is closely associated with those who believe in free trade, open markets, and competition.[12]

Smith's work became the foundation of economic thinking. If prices and markets were no longer subjects only for moral discourse, perhaps there were logical and scientific explanations for such phenomena as the setting of wages and prices. Creating a framework for this scientific approach was the life ambition of a French economist named Leon Walras.[13] In 1858, having failed as a novelist and as an engineer, Walras listened to his father's advice that there were two great challenges facing the intellectual world. One was to find a complete theory of history (a topic then occupying Karl Marx); the other was to craft a scientific theory of economics, including a mathematical formulation of the laws of supply and demand. Fourteen years later, now as professor of economics at Lausanne, Walras published *Elements of a Pure Economics*, an attempt to do for economics what Newton's laws of gravitation had done for physics. Walras sought a "pure theory of economics . . . which resembles the physico-mathematical sciences in every respect."[14] "We all accept" he wrote, "the current description of the universe of astronomical phenomena based on the principle of universal gravitation. Why should the description of economic phenomena based on the principle of free competition not be accepted in the same way?"[15]

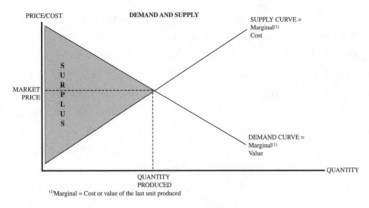

Figure 2. Demand and Supply

The system Walras and others were to describe evolved into what we now term classical economics, which is still taught as the foundation of the subject. The price of goods is determined by the interaction of their "marginal value," the value to the consumer of the last unit sold, and their "marginal cost," the cost of the last unit produced.[16] As prices rise, demand will fall and supply increase until they are equal. Thus the economy is brought back to "equilibrium." This is what has come to be known as the law of supply and demand.

The law of supply and demand had other interesting qualities. Most particularly, it promoted efficiency, since production will continue until the marginal cost of making another unit is exactly equal to the benefit gained from its production, and no further. Competition between producers will ensure that economies are always brought to equilibrium at a point where costs equal prices. The diagram of demand and supply is shown in Figure 2, with the surplus from production (the benefit minus the cost), shown by the shaded triangle, representing the economic welfare generated. It is an elegant model, familiar to anyone who has studied economics, and it underpins almost every course in the subject taught today.

GAUSS AND MODELING RISK

In physics, the world is predictable in the sense that all matter obeys physical law. If some observation fails to conform to the law, then either the law is wrong or the observation is— something has gone wrong with the measurements. Usually, of course, it is the latter, since measures are rarely 100 percent accurate. But scientists have certain statistical methods by which they can determine how accurate their measurements, and therefore their predictions, are likely to be.

One of the key figures in developing those statistical methods was the mathematician who graced the ten-euro note: Carl Friedrich Gauss. Gauss, born the year after Adam Smith published *The Wealth of Nations*, is recognized as one of the world's greatest mathematicians. His most direct contributions were in mathematics and physics; he did not turn his attention to economics, which at the time was not considered a mathematical science. As director of the astronomical observatory at Göttingen, Germany, however, he was interested in astronomical measurements and, in particular, the distribution of errors in measurement.[17] Simply put, he wanted to know how wrong he could be, how often.

Gauss developed a distribution that is now ubiquitous in statistical analysis, represented by the familiar bell-shaped or "normal" curve. Statisticians call this a Gaussian distribution. One feature of the normal curve is that the likelihood of an estimation error gets ever smaller the further it is from the true result. Furthermore, if we know what proportion of measurements lie within a certain distance of the true result, we can work out how many lie within twice that distance, three times. If the true result is 100 and half the measurements lie between 99 and 101, a normal distribution predicts that 82 percent will lie between 98 and 102, and 95.5 percent will lie between 97 and 103. The key point is that the likelihood of different outcomes is predictable, and the likelihood of significant errors diminishes as the error increases; so in our example, there is a 50 percent chance of a measurement error between 0 and 1, a 32 percent chance of an error of between 1 and 2, and only a 13.5 percent chance of one between 2 and 3. The chance of an error above 5 will be around 0.08 percent.

The new subject of economics began to make measurements of economic phenomena. Since these were subject to variation, it was all too natural for economists to plot out these variations using a Gaussian distribution, to calculate how accurate economic predictions might be.

Imagine, for example, that I hold a portfolio of shares in the stock market. Over the years, the value of those shares has moved by less than 1 percent per day on 50 percent of occasions, and between 1 percent and 2 percent on 32 percent of occasions. On that basis, if results are normally distributed, there is a 0.08 percent chance that they will move by more than 5 percent in a day.

Experts often use a normal distribution to measure risk. So although markets are risky, the probability of extreme events is predictable. Furthermore, such events are unlikely, and the more extreme they are, the less likely. As noted in chapter 2, this basic assumption, the belief that the future is predictable, underlies the finance industry's risk models.

Here, in a nutshell, is the economic mindset that led the financial establishment to believe it was "doing the right thing" in the run-up to the global financial crisis. Participants thought that even if they could not predict phenomena precisely, they could estimate the range of likely outcomes. Further, the laws governing economics had certain characteristics. For example, competitive, open markets would tend to move to an equilibrium in which supply and demand are balanced. Markets, therefore, should be left to themselves, and if they did go wrong, they did so for simple reasons that could be solved by regulation. If customers were buying products that were not in their best interest, this could be addressed by giving them more information. Finally, insofar as markets had been volatile in the past, the risk of future volatility, as well as its scale, could be estimated. Risk could be understood.[18]

Our students, taught in that intellectual tradition, employed it to manage our banks, treasuries, and regulators. As Luis Garicano said, everyone thought they were doing the right thing, and everyone was relying on someone else. It wasn't that they were bad people, but that the models and instruments they used to steer the economy provided a very imperfect description of the world as it actually is. The bankers and regulators knew there had been a huge expansion in credit, far out of proportion to the growth in the economy. But mathematical economics and statistics suggested that this was a good thing. That was the view of the IMF, the global institution charged with warning of instability, whose "banner message was one of continued optimism within a prevailing benign global environment." In evaluating why it had made such a gigantic mistake, the IMF subsequently reflected, "To a large extent this was due to the belief that, thanks to the presumed ability of financial innovations to remove risks off banks' balance sheets, large financial institutions were in a strong position, and thereby, financial markets in advanced countries were fundamentally sound."[19] In other words, banks' borrowing and lending had increased dramatically, but their understanding of risk was thought to reduce the threat of a breakdown.

While those financial instruments worked in theory, they didn't take into account the phenomena one finds in the real world. Just as the laws of gravity don't explain magnetism or subatomic forces, so the disciplines of economics that held sway in our financial institutions paid little attention to the social, cultural, legal, political, institutional, moral, psychological, and technological forces that shape our economy's behavior. The compass that bankers and regulators were using worked well according to its own logic, but it was pointing in the wrong direction, and they steered the ship onto the rocks.

History does not record whether the Queen was satisfied with the academics' response. She might, however, have noted that this economic-statistical model had been found wanting before—in 1998, when the collapse of the hedge fund Long-Term Capital Management nearly took the financial system down with it. Ironically, its directors included the two people who had shared the Nobel Prize in Economics the previous year.[20]

The Queen might also have noted the glittering lineup of senior economists who, over the last century, have warned against excessive confidence in predictions made using models. John Maynard Keynes, no mathematical slouch, warned eighty years ago that "too large a proportion of recent 'mathematical' economics are mere concoctions, as imprecise as the initial assumptions which they rest on, which allow the author to lose sight of the complexities and interdependencies of the real world in a maze of pretentious and unhelpful symbols."[21] Friedrich von Hayek, accepting his Nobel Prize in 1974, argued that "the failure of economists to guide policy more successfully is closely connected to their propensity to imitate as closely as possible the procedures of the . . . physical sciences." He called this false imitation "decidedly unscientific."[22]

John Kenneth Galbraith would indignantly describe this form of economics as a convenient way to avoid addressing challenging real-world economic questions. "The pretention of economics that it is a science," he wrote, "is firmly rooted in the need for an escape from blame for the inadequacies and injustices in the system with which the great classical tradition was concerned. And it continues as the defense for a quiet, non-controversial professional life even today."[23]

None of these economists ever intended to suggest we abandon technical rigor where it is appropriate, and neither do we. As our colleagues have pointed out, among the 1.3 million papers economists have published, many touch on economic history, sociology, and psychology. But we do suggest that the economic models used to manage and regulate finance suffer from a "lack of intellectual degrees of freedom."[24]

So what is missing? How might we reform economics so that it handles the critical questions to which we need answers? How can we think about the financial system in a way that might give us early warning of the next crisis and help the system improve its productivity and hence its contribution to our welfare?

Economics with Purpose

One obvious place to begin would be with "purpose." Just as we have asked what is the purpose of the finance industry, so we could ask what is the purpose of the economics through which we seek to understand the industry's operations. On this Adam Smith was very clear. The aim of economics, he wrote, was "to provide a plentiful revenue or subsistence for the people, or more properly to enable them to provide such a revenue for themselves, and . . . to supply the state with a revenue sufficient for the public services. It proposed to enrich both the people and the sovereign."[25] In other words, we study economics to understand how we might create a more prosperous society.

Where Are We Falling Short?

Recall that we discussed the financial services industry's role in generating prosperity. It creates safe custody and provides a payment system, it takes money from where it is to where it is needed, it helps mitigate risk, and it manages a proper system of governance. These are very important functions, but the financial services industry does not perform them particularly well. Not only have there been many financial crises, there has been no improvement in the industry's productivity for more than one hundred years.

This is not because of insufficient effort devoted to researching or teaching financial economics. It has to do with the sort of financial economics we study and how we apply it. Theorists in the field have sought to emulate physics in trying to describe economic phenomena according to mathematical rules. There is no problem with that, except that the picture it provides is incomplete. If the purpose of economics is to help us understand how we generate prosperity, this involves disciplines that are not readily susceptible to mathematical inquiry.

This was the conclusion of the Chinese Academy of Social Sciences. It had been asked what accounted for the preeminence of the West and why, until the last three decades, China had slipped behind. At first the academy's researchers thought the answers must have to do with military technology, or political or economic systems. But ultimately they abandoned these explanations. The reason, they decided, "is your religion: Christianity. That is why the West has been so powerful. The Christian moral foundation of social and cultural life was what made possible the emergence of capitalism and then the successful transition to democratic politics. We don't have any doubt about this."[26] Their approach echoes the work of the sociologist Max Weber, who attributed Europe's economic success after the renaissance to the moral values imbued by Protestantism; hard work and accumulation became legitimate moral goals.

More recently, economists have tried to discover why some Eastern European countries have made a successful transition to capitalism following the dissolution of the Soviet Union, while others have not. After testing a litany of potential explanations, they concluded, in the words of the journalist David Brooks, "Finally, and most important, there is the level of values. A nation's economy is nestled in its moral ecology. Economic performance is tied to history, culture and psychology."[27]

This analysis creates a problem for those who try to describe economics in purely mathematical terms. The issue is not whether the Chinese or the observers of Eastern Europe are right in their conclusions. (We suspect both are oversimplified.) Instead, the critical insight is that nontraditional economic factors such as religion and culture have major effects on economic behavior. If the purpose of economics is to help generate prosperity, and prosperity depends on such factors as religious belief, history, and culture, then the influence of morals, politics, technology, and other institutions becomes a necessary part of the study of economics. What generates prosperity, indeed what prosperity is, becomes a complex question whose answers lie well outside the sort of explanations that mathematics can provide.

To be clear, mathematical models are often relevant and essential to rigorous analysis. But if they are our only approach to the subject—if, rather than keeping the subject broad, economists narrow it, so that it can only be described in precise mathematical models—then we have a big problem. As one leading British economist noted, "I am continually frustrated at the economics profession's insistence on technique, such that it prefers good answers to uninteresting questions."[28]

Imagine that an economist is asked to project what will happen if two islands, one of cattle farmers and one of sheep farmers, suddenly discover each other's existence. The economist will tell us that this is a good thing, and depending on each population's preferences for beef and mutton, a rate of exchange will be determined between the animals, and that everyone will be at least as well off as before. She will note that because of shipping costs, sheep will remain cheaper on Mutton Island, and she will also be able to give a sense of what will happen if one or other of the island's farmers forms a cartel to control prices, and so on. All of this analysis is helpful.

But the scenario our economist describes is not likely to take place in the real world. Anyone who has reflected on the history of the native tribes of America or Australia understands that the new European discoverers brought with them disease and conquest, not equitable trade. In China and Japan, they produced what are referred to as "unequal treaties." History shows us that even the simplest trading requires some approximate parity of power and information, as well as numerous shared understandings of the proper relationships between trading partners. For instance, what constitutes "fair trade"? What can be owned? Land? Water? Air? What obligations come with ownership, or with employment? All of these complex social questions are profoundly important to a working economic system. Yet economics tells us little about them.

Even in the simple case of our two islands, the economist has told us little about how the farming industries on each island arose and will develop. Are they efficient? Are they developing new technologies? Are they sustainable, or do they threaten to despoil their environment? One can go on. The point is this: as economics has sought to emulate the physical sciences, it has maintained a form of intellectual purity— but at the cost of abandoning the study of certain factors that are surely relevant to the way prosperity is generated.

Adam Smith noted humans' ability to trade with one another. "The propensity to truck, barter or exchange one thing for another," he wrote, "is common to all men."[29] But our ability to do so requires, at the least, that "transaction costs" be kept low. These are the costs involved in ensuring that the buyer gets the service he requires and that the supplier receives proper compensation.

Where transaction costs are high, it is difficult to get markets to work. For example, lighthouses find it hard to charge passing ships for their service. Traditional economists had bundled these into a separate sort of product, known as "public goods," where markets will fail and the goods must be purchased by the state. But as the Chicago economist Ronald Coase pointed out, the difference between the transaction costs involved in the provision of lighthouses and other goods is one of degree, not of quality. He noted that the first light-houses were privately provided by the operators of nearby ports, and concluded that by dividing the world into "private goods," where markets would regulate prices effectively, and "public goods," where they would not, economists had posed the wrong question.[30] The issue was not about whether there should be state or private provision, but how best to manage transaction costs so that the buyer and seller could easily strike a good deal. For example, if you buy a pension or take out a loan from a bank, how can you know that it will provide you with what you want? How you can be sure that the seller will deliver? These are profound issues.[31] If we knew the answers to them, it would give us some important clues about improving the productivity of financial services.

Coase is known as an "institutional" economist. He was interested in how we frame the institutions of the market to ensure that it works effectively. Yet much modern economic analysis simply assumes that the right economic institutions will exist. Coase thought that in making this assumption, economics had become so "remote from the real world" that it was "incapable of handling many of the problems to which it purports to give answers." For Coase and other institutional economists, the principal issue was not about creating markets that would, like the force of gravity, move prices to "equilibrium." It was about how to structure institutions so that transaction costs were kept as low as possible, buyers could get what they wanted at the lowest cost, and sellers could maximize profit.[32]

But while institutional economics is actively studied, the design of effective financial institutions is not a major focus for financial economists. Those who do study institutional design tend to concentrate on its theoretical rather than practical aspects.

Modern financial economics does not begin by looking at how the world is and asking how to make it more prosperous. Rather it begins with a "model world" and tests how far the real world accords with the model, from time to time relaxing its assumptions to make a better fit. People trained in this way are masters of sophisticated analysis. But they sometimes lack wisdom about how the real world behaves, and the skills to understand how it can be made to behave better.

When challenged, economists point out that most economics is about market failures and problems. To say that financial economics is about simple market mechanisms is a "straw man and a textbook model." But that model gets used, and misused. As the economist Andrew Scott told us, "We teach it as a benchmark, of what is the best you can do thanks to Adam Smith's invisible hand, and then everything is about how you get back to that first best given an imperfect world. And of course most people with limited economics remember just that very clear result—competition is good and markets work well."[33]

But whether the economics profession is to blame, or its pupils, or its interaction with the finance industry, is a moot point. The way we think about the management and regulation of the finance industry has become one sided. Competition and markets work well, but only if participants are rewarded for fulfilling the purpose for which the markets were established.

Gaps in Risk Management

It's not just the economic model we use that is inadequate. So is the way we have been encouraged to think about risk. The models with which we manage the financial system often assume that the distribution of events will follow a Gaussian bell curve or some other distribution pattern. This is a world susceptible to mathematical evaluation, with a predictable frequency of extreme events. But if the economic model gives a narrow view of the world, the risk model does a poor job predicting how it functions. This happens for two reasons.

The first has to do with the difference between risk and uncertainty. Donald Rumsfeld, the former US defense secretary, made this distinction when he talked about "known unknowns" and "unknown unknowns."[34] We might think of known unknowns as representing risk. If we throw a pair of dice, we don't know what the outcome will be, but we know that it will be between two and twelve and that each outcome will come up a predictable percentage of times. But some outcomes cannot be predicted, even probabilistically. For instance, the dice might be loaded. As Rumsfeld stressed, it is in the nature of military operations that you cannot predict what the enemy is going to throw at you, so you can't predict the outcome of a campaign. There are too many possibilities, and too many uncertainties.[35]

The second point has to do with whether the normal curve and its variants describe the distribution of real world phenomena. Even if we set aside the problem of "unknown unknowns," evidence suggests that economic phenomena are not normally distributed, because extreme events are much more likely than the Gaussian bell curve predicts. Nassim Taleb concludes that analyses based on bell curves tell you "close to nothing" because "they ignore large deviations, cannot handle them, yet make us confident that we have tamed uncertainty."[36] Andy Haldane, director of the Bank of England, opined that although "normality has been an accepted wisdom in economics and finance for a century or more . . . in real world systems, nothing could be less normal than normality."[37] Part of the problem is that Gauss never intended his distributions to be used in economics. His aim was to predict error in the measurement of physical phenomena, such as the distance from the earth to the moon. He never imagined that analysts might use his curve to check the variation in asset prices in one period of history and then project them forward into the next.

To take observations of past events and use distributions to predict future events is a bit like living on the slopes of a dormant volcano and insisting that it will not erupt. Insofar as we are able to predict unlikely events, the evidence suggests that they are more likely than a normal curve would suggest.[38] In part, this occurs because in real life we face uncertainties, things that we just don't know about, and can't therefore predict. We also face the problem that if there are risks that we could estimate in theory, often risks do not follow a normal distribution, which makes them impossible to measure in practice. Finally, the world is a complex place where risks and uncertainties often interact. Unlike rolling dice, one outcome in the financial markets often affects the next, so that small events sometimes become avalanches. Often it is these avalanches that we most need to understand and avoid.

Why do we use risk measures that don't predict the things we need to know? One reason is that we have few other effective measures of risk and uncertainty. Most of the time we don't experience extreme events, so the model seems to work. The risk models discussed in chapter 2, which failed so miserably in the crisis, actually work quite well in normal times— when they are least needed. But if we try to predict catastrophic circumstances using a normal curve, we may be like the drunk who is discovered searching for his wallet under a lamppost.

A passerby asks if he is sure that this is where he dropped it. The drunk man replies, "No, but the light is better here."

Queen Elizabeth asked why no one saw the financial crisis coming and was told that "at every stage someone was relying on somebody else and everyone thought they were doing the right thing." Maybe they were looking under the lamppost, where their intellectual models felt comfortable? But the drunk man is unlikely to find his wallet; similarly, the risk measures we were using were never going to detect the rare systemic failures that bring about financial crises.

Missing the Gorilla

Dan Simons and Christopher Chabris are experimental psychologists. In 2004, they won the Ig Nobel Prize for "achievements which first make people laugh, and then make them think."[39] Here is what they did. They asked their subjects to watch a game of basketball and to count how many passes were made by one of the teams. (You can find this experiment on YouTube by searching for "The Monkey Business Illusion.")[40] Most subjects count the passes pretty accurately. But half of them fail to notice that during the basketball game, someone dressed in a gorilla costume walks onto the screen, beats his chest, and walks off again. Because they were focused on counting the number of passes, they missed the gorilla.

Perhaps because the models we are using are so ingrained, those who should be managing and regulating our financial markets have missed the anomalies: the really big questions about how to avoid crises and how to ensure that finance contributes to prosperity. They were so intent on explaining the world in terms of the economic and risk models they had been taught that they continued, and still continue, to adhere to the ways of thinking that failed us last time. This book is filled with examples of where this has happened.

In chapter 5, we looked at the Basel III rules that have been put in place to regulate banks. We noted that they were not a good predictor of whether a bank would fail and that there was little reason to believe they would be effective in preventing the next crisis. One reason is that they used the risk measures we have just discussed. Regulators reasoned that the 2008 crash happened because the banks made too many risky loans. Basel III therefore requires that banks place their loans in different risk categories and hold more reserves against the risky ones. But that implies that we can predict the likelihood of loans going bad, and in a financial crisis, such predictions fail. The Basel rules might work if the aim was to alert an individual bank that it had inadvertently made a series of poor loans and was courting trouble. But what we principally fear is not the failure of one bank but of the entire system. This is a problem of uncertainty, not just risk.

Here is another example. In chapter 3, we noted how financial intermediaries and CEOs of large companies were given big incentives where they benefit if the shareholders do well. That approach to contracts is consistent with our economic models; to get *homo economicus* to do the right thing, he or she needs an incentive. But these incentives sent CEO pay through the roof, with no evidence that companies were better run. In creating these arrangements, we ignored an institution that has proven remarkably effective in ensuring that companies and workers both owe obligations to one another grounded in trust, good faith, and best efforts.[41] It is called "employment." Most employees do not venally seek the greatest possible personal advantage at their employer's cost, but work with their colleagues to create good outcomes. Those who enjoy their jobs see employment as a personal fulfillment. Some view it as a vocation. Even those who don't enjoy their jobs understand the implicit bargain with their employers: come to work on time, work hard, be honest, try to add value. It is hugely to society's advantage that they do so, because the transaction cost of contracting for every element of performance rather than simply trusting one another is very high, particularly when the employee knows more about what he is up to, and how the contract can work to his advantage, than the employer. Yet these detailed, performance-based agreements are precisely the deals we strike with our top executives, who are "incented" through huge issues of shares, options, and bonuses, as if we otherwise didn't trust them to do the job well. The predictable outcome is a legitimization of what to outsiders looks like outrageous greed.

Trust is a central feature of any successful financial system. Well-justified trust keeps transaction costs low and allows the financial system to work. It is the oil that allows the engine to run without overheating and destroying itself. Yet questions about what constitutes trust and how it is promoted and maintained are largely absent from the typical finance course.

One of the legacies of Adam Smith's followers is that they simply assumed that these systems of trust would exist. This is extraordinary, because if Smith were alive today, he would marvel at the degree of trust that exists within our financial systems. He thought it was foolish to give your money to others to manage because if you did, "negligence" and "profusion," by which he meant wasteful squandering, would result.[42] People looking after other people's money would use it to their own benefit. The extraordinary thing about today's financial system is not that it confirms Smith's predictions of market efficiency but that it is trustworthy enough to work at all.

Alfred Marshall, the great classical economist, writing at the turn of the last century, recognized that despite Smith's predictions, financial organizations where shareholders and customers had little direct power had prospered. "It is," he concluded, "a strong proof of the marvelous growth in recent times of a spirit of honesty and uprightness in commercial matters, that the leading officers of great public companies yield as little as they do to the vast temptations to fraud which lie in their way."[43] That spirit of trade morality is what underpinned prosperity. Yet the nature of that morality and the institutions necessary to promote it lie beyond the scope of most of the economics that is studied today.

How might we rebuild our economic studies so that they address these issues? We need not abandon market economics. Nor should we graft a few ethics courses onto a curriculum that otherwise avoids addressing values. Rather we should return to the purpose of economics, which is to understand how we can best generate prosperity.

A New Finance Curriculum

The study of the real economy must start from the recognition that for any sophisticated financial system to exist, a degree of trust is required, plus common values between buyer and seller. Such a study would do the following:

- Train students to think about theory not as an absolute model but as multiple, often competing perspectives on how economic relations can be understood.

- Give explicit consideration to human desires, how they affect our behavior, and how this in turn affects economic decisions.
- Focus on an understanding of institutions, the checks and balances that regulate economic relations.

A market of buyers and sellers needs some degree of trust if it is to thrive. The economist and Nobel laureate Kenneth Arrow pointed out that "ethical elements enter in some measure into every contract; without them no market could function." He also noted that "trust and similar values, loyalty or truth telling, are . . . not commodities for which trade on the open market is technically possible or even meaningful."[44]

In finance, we would do well to note this. We are all aware of fundamental human needs where economics doesn't help. We all know the old line about "money can't buy me love." Indeed, when money does buy love, it's usually considered something else. The same is true of ethical standards. But Arrow is going further, pointing out that markets can function only if they are based upon these ethical standards.

Our economies therefore sit on a foundation of human values. What these are, how they change, and how they affect outcomes must therefore be part of the study of financial economics. Economics is a social science dependent on social institutions, and as these institutions change, so must our approaches to economics. John Hicks, another Nobel laureate, reminds us that "a theory which illumines the right things now may illumine the wrong things another time. . . . There is . . . no economic theory which will do for us everything we want all the time."[45]

If Hicks is right, it implies an economics that does not much resemble physics. Yet when people talk about financial economics, they often speak as though there were, for good or ill, one uncontested view of how the economy works. Some also speak as though that theory could accurately predict complex economic outcomes. On both counts they are wrong.

At least two schools of economic thought are already taught in our universities: microeconomics and macroeconomics. They predict different outcomes. In the textbook microeconomic world, competitive markets tend to move to equilibrium with all resources efficiently employed. In the macroeconomic world, widespread underemployment of resources is not only possible but likely.

Microeconomics has proved more influential in the way we manage and regulate our financial institutions, and few would dispute that the perspectives it provides have helped us predict how markets will behave. One of its starting points is simple: if people are given an incentive, they are more likely to carry out a task. Where consumers know what they want to buy and are fully informed about all the features of the products available to them, free markets and competition will tend to drive good outcomes.

These observations are important, but they rest on a simplified set of assumptions about legal and other institutions that is not warranted by the conditions of the real world. Economies exist only in a social and institutional context. They are created by humans, who are social animals. Therefore we cannot fulfill the purpose of economics, which is to promote prosperity, unless the subject is also rooted in an understanding of how social and institutional considerations interact with incentives.

Here is one example of social forces working against economic ones to produce bad outcomes. Economic theory teaches us that in free markets, employers will hire the person best qualified for the job. Yet for generations, women, whose talents are quite equal to those of their male counterparts, have been denied access to jobs for which they were qualified. This took place even where no laws prevented female employment. It just wasn't the done thing. Even if we ignore the unfairness of discrimination against women, its effect on prosperity was huge, since the labor market turned its back on half of the workforce. Social forces trumped economic ones.

Our social institutions require that we all know the "rules of the game," which require us to behave in ways that are not based only on overt self-interest. Such behavior is necessary for a successful society. Adam Smith may have been right that the butcher, the brewer, and the baker provided our dinner because it was in their self-interest to do so. But either their interpretation of self-interest or their genuine good will prevented them from providing food that would poison their customers, even if they could have gotten away with it.

In short, a model based only on market incentives reflects but a subset of the conditions we must understand in creating an effective economic system. If we seek to promote prosperity, we must focus on this dynamic. The difference between the prosperous life that many of us live today and the frugal existence of our forebears is partially explained by the existence of free and competitive markets. But to ignore the change in technologies, in scientific knowledge, and in social institutions is economic malpractice. These are the forces that underpin our growing prosperity.

In an open challenge to classical economics, Eric Beinhocker, executive director of the Institute for New Economic

Thinking, claims that static models of the economy are misleading. A more accurate description would view markets and economies as evolutionary, adaptive systems, constantly in flux, changing with different environmental pressures.[46] As in evolution, the fit survive and prosper; the weak fall by the wayside. Those who study economics as a complex adaptive system suggest that this theory is more accurate in describing the development of economic systems than current market economics. They also note that the world is very difficult to predict, particularly over the long term. This challenge is serious—first because it offers a different explanation of how economic systems work and, second, because it focuses on the evolutionary factors that are among the most important in generating prosperity.

It is not our purpose to decide which approach to financial economics should be favored. But these competing frameworks do help us understand the forces that shape economic relations. All economists need to understand the relationships of trust, what some call "social capital," that allow markets to work. They must recognize that technology, invention, and human relations are in a state of constant change; so are our economic relations, and these changes in relations contribute to our growing prosperity. So far, as we have seen, the financial services industry has not yielded anything like the gains in efficiency that have been apparent in almost any other industry, particularly given the enabling technologies in information technology and communications that should have assisted them in doing so. Yet we have no clear answer as to why, and therefore no clear remedy.

Traditional microeconomics has its place. But if we are to address the question of how we create a prosperous, sustainable world, it is a more modest place than that which it is currently accorded. Outcomes depend more on human motivation and behavior, and on the institutions through which those motivations are regulated, than a textbook approach often will admit.

Human Motivation and Behavior

A striking example of the power of culture in economics dates from hundreds of years ago. In 1488, Bartholomew Diaz became the first European to sail around the Cape of Good Hope. He was followed by many other explorers in search of fame and fortune. European enterprises thus came to dominate trade in the Indian Ocean.[47]

There was no technological reason why this should have been the case. More than half a century earlier, Chinese fleets—one an armada of over three hundred craft and twenty-eight thousand men—had explored the coast of East Africa.[48] But thanks to an abrupt reversal in policy, the Chinese decided to abandon their overseas opportunities. The reason for the different behavior of the two civilizations may have had something to do with economic incentives, but it was also determined by what each saw as valued and valuable. Human motivation makes a big difference to economic outcomes.[49]

We see the effect of human motivation throughout our economic system. Silicon Valley is full of would-be inventors and innovators, people who are fascinated by technology and keen to take a risk, and who want to emulate Bill Gates or Steve Jobs. That is one factor that makes it a center of development for the electronics industry. Other parts of the world, even other parts of the United States, lack the same social alchemy. Again, some of this may come down to economic incentives, but much has to do with values.

Entrepreneurship, innovation, and leadership all make a difference to our prosperity. When economic historian David Landes reflected on the characteristics of economically successful societies, he wrote that among their qualities are "knowing how to operate, manage and build the instruments of production, and create, adapt and master new techniques," and the ability to pass these skills on from generation to generation. People would be chosen for employment on the basis of merit. An economically successful society would reward initiative, it would be characterized by gender and race equality (otherwise it could not be meritocratic), and it would value scientific explanation. The political system would ensure that effort was rewarded. The government and society would be honest because "people would believe that honesty was right (also that it pays)."[50]

These characteristics are not principally about free markets but about beliefs, values, and institutions. If Landes is right, and if the purpose of economics is to help generate prosperity, these factors should be central.

Economic Institutions

If you listen to any political scientist for any length of time, you will hear about the importance of political institutions. She will tell you about the roles of the executive, the legislature, and the judiciary; the roles of lobbyists and pressure groups; the importance of elections, free speech, and the rule of law. She will say that political institutions are dynamic: the powers of the executive, the role and ideology of political parties, and the way campaign techniques change all are hot topics for research in politics and political science. It is these institutions through which power is exercised to make the government work properly. That is why political institutions are part of the core curriculum in undergraduate political science. If you don't understand the respective functions of the executive, the legislature, and the judiciary, you can say very little about the workings of any government.

Exactly the same lesson applies to our economic institutions. By institutions, we mean not only organizations but all the "rules of the game" that govern our economic relations.[51] For example, textbook economics assumes the existence of clear property rights. Where these do not exist, it is difficult for markets to exist. But property rights are not limitless. If you own a plot of land, you have certain rights over it. But in most places you cannot, without permission or reference to a building standard, construct a building on it. If you own a car, it needs to be insured. And many of the goods we own are "ours" only if we pay tax upon them.

The same applies to the rule of law and the enforcement of contracts. Of course, contracts are usually legally enforceable. But anyone who has taken a contract dispute to court knows that not all parts of a contract may be enforceable, and that they are open to sometimes surprising interpretation.[52] We have developed a set of institutions that, from a pragmatic point of view, help our economy function; but they are not absolute. Even property rights and contracts are conditional, and open to interpretation.

Over time it has been possible to establish new institutions. But they only work if the rest of the system, including legal, cultural, and other institutions, supports them. Take, for example, the limited liability company, otherwise known as virtually every public and many private companies in the world today. In Adam Smith's day, the limited liability company was considered such a dangerous institution that establishing one required an act of Parliament. Yet we have managed to make the limited liability company a key instrument of economic policy. For example, directors today know they can be held individually responsible if they continue to run the business when it will not be able to pay its debts;[53] they cannot pay dividends unless they have reserves to do so; they have their books audited on a prudent basis. After a while, directors' duties became custom and practice. To paraphrase Landes again, most "directors believe that honesty is right (also that it pays)." Far from being a vehicle for cheating investors, limited liability companies have today become the basic legal entity through which production takes place.

The same is true for employment contracts. Today, typically, people don't get paid for their individual output. Instead they are taken on as employees, and this relationship implies responsibilities for both the employer and the employee to act toward one another in good faith.

Within the financial system are complex forms of governance meant to ensure the accountability of companies to their owners and other stakeholders. We have developed accounting standards by which we measure business success. We have vast tomes of regulation that state what is and is not permissible action. And just as we have checks and balances in the political system, so we have them in the economic system. They may vary from country to country, but they all have a similar goal: to ensure that the economic and financial system continues to generate prosperity. Accounting, auditing, employment, regulatory compliance regimes—these are just a few of today's economic "institutions."

The complex ecosystem of money and finance is, to some extent, explainable by economic theory. But a complete description of it must encompass human behavior and motivation, and the institutional checks and balances that keep it functioning. The science of economics we need is a broad, multidisciplinary field of study that includes theory, psychology, and institutions. Much of it may not be subject to mathematical rigor. But it will be more relevant to the problems we face—including how we can make our financial markets work better.

Why Is It Important That We Rethink Economics?

Over the past generation, the world's financial markets have become ever more globalized and specialized. If we want them to continue to serve our interests, the institutions that guide those markets' behavior must also evolve.

Make no mistake: globalization offers huge benefits because of the productivity gains to be had from specialization. The computers on which we type were sold by a US company and assembled in China, and ongoing support is located in India. The software and design that give the computers their unique features employed expertise of extraordinary complexity. The contribution of this process to human welfare is enormous. By allowing each person to specialize and by encouraging global competition and innovation, we are now able to foresee a world where all can have a level of access to food, shelter, education, and health that early economists would have thought impossible.

That achievement has been brought about not just by technical innovation or by trading but by the creation of social institutions that allow those who trade and work together to trust one another. Think of the global multinational company, where tens of thousands of people are employed in scores of locations around the world, all working to a set of norms

on highly specialized tasks, from physical labor to engineering design to bookkeeping. Through those relationships,
employees are able to support one another in completing a
common task. These firms change over time; their scale, na-
tionality, and ownership are certain to evolve. Sometimes they
will organize their production internally, sometimes through
the market. But if they are to operate globally, they depend on
a huge level of trust that the products, subcomponents, and
software that they put together will be supplied on time and
to standard; that they won't include components that might
ultimately damage users' health; that the accounting department will pay suppliers' bills as well as employees' wages; and
much else.

Trust is even more important in financial services. In
part this is because when we commission someone to look
after our money, we may not know whether they have done
their job well until after the event. Indeed, we may never know.
It may be impossible to find out whether the poor payouts we
receive in retirement are due to economic circumstances or
the poor deal we received from the pension provider, and in
any case, it will likely be too late to do anything about it. Thus
we have to trust the supplier to ensure that we get a fair deal,
just as we trust a doctor to prescribe only the correct medi-
cines and only when we need them. This cannot be done
when buyers must be on high alert that the product they are
purchasing may be inappropriate for, or even dangerous to,
their financial health. If our global capital market is to avoid
financial bonfires, then it needs institutions to encourage suppliers to offer only services that meet the test of fairness and
suitability.

Therefore, the practical question that faces financial
economists is this: how do we construct a combination of

motivations, incentives, and institutions to allow our finance industry to deliver services better and more efficiently, something it has not done over the past century?[54] The costs of failure are high; the crash of 2008 and the subsequent recession have taught us that. But the benefits are also enormous; witness the difference in efficiency between the Dutch and the UK pension systems.

This book has suggested some ways forward. It suggests we begin by understanding what the financial system is ultimately for, and then encouraging simple systems to deliver those goals. It suggests we focus on good governance rather than excessive rules. It argues for open, independent information, for debate and criticism, rather than overreliance on experts. It suggests that the role of regulation is to help markets work well; rulebooks should aim at outcomes that better align with the interests of citizen investors.

And we need to rethink the models by which we understand commercial life. Financial economics must once again become a practical science. It might better be called "purposeful economics," a multidisciplinary study with the aim of understanding how best we can promote prosperity. Students of economics must do more than understand textbook theory; they must also encompass competing theoretical perspectives. The field must take into account human motivation, and the "social context within which transactions are embedded."[55] It needs to address, and help design, appropriate institutions to help us generate prosperity. It is as much art as science.

Making It Happen

How might we bring about such a transformation in the way we think about economics?

Funding fresh thinking. One place to start would be reform of the economics discipline itself. That is what George
Soros intended when he founded the Institute for New Economic Thinking, which aims to "nurture a global community
of next generation economic leaders . . . and to inspire the
economics profession to engage in the challenges of the 21st
Century."[56] Soros is clear about the institute's goal. "Economic
theory needs to be rethought from the ground up," he says,
and it needs to stop trying to discover universal laws like those
of Newtonian physics, since "that is an impossibility." Other
thinkers are engaged in similar missions, but none of it will
happen overnight. Few of the world's economic departments
are likely ready to agree with Soros that their subject is
"bankrupt."[57]

How, then, could we accelerate this change? One idea is
to "follow the money." Much of the research done in our economic faculties is funded by governments and foundations.
How about if those funding research, while allowing ample
room for intellectual exploration, steered more resources
toward work that explicitly met Adam Smith's requirement
that it would help us better understand how we "enrich the
people"? And finance faculties seeking private sponsorship
must be careful that they do not bias their research to provide
outcomes favorable to the sponsor. The authors of this book
have attended many meetings where important research topics were suggested but abandoned because the likely findings
would have reflected poorly on those who would have to provide data or funding for the work.

New career paths. The careers of those who teach in our
academic institutions are often determined by whether their
work has been published in peer-reviewed journals. Many of
those journals demand a mathematical methodology. This

should not be the only criterion by which work is judged. Some additional ways of evaluating our economic research must surely be merited, for example, by assessing its likely impact on the outside world. Or simply by how much the research helps us to think of new risks, opportunities, and possibilities.

A new curriculum. We need to educate our future leaders differently. An informal poll we conducted at the 2013 International Corporate Governance Network meeting, attended by approximately five hundred investors, business leaders, regulators, and academics from around the world, revealed a stunning gap in graduate-level business teaching. Virtually every business school the attendees knew, from Tokyo to New York, had an extensive finance curriculum. Not one had a required course on the role of the corporation in modern society, and few even covered the topic in an elective course. Even at the undergraduate level, the mathematical approach dominates. For example, the flagship course at the University of Oxford for those who might wish to pursue a career in policy or politics is Philosophy, Politics and Economics, or PPE. (At the time of this writing,[58] both the current prime minister and the leader of the opposition hold that degree.) Yet even to apply for the course, students must not only have studied mathematics as one of only three or four subjects they have taken in their final two years at high school but also have gained the very highest grade. Otherwise, it is argued, they will not be able to understand the required economics. It is surely crazy to believe that such expertise is necessary, yet its requirement bars many qualified candidates from the course.

The Aspen Institute, based in Washington, DC, is one institution that tries to broaden the typical business curriculum to confront the nuances and contradictions of the real world. It sponsors a host of programs for business school faculty, including peer-to-peer learning, awards honoring pioneers who teach business from a more holistic viewpoint, and teaching tools. Not coincidentally, its website prominently features a page entitled "The Purpose of the Corporation."[59]

Notwithstanding Aspen's efforts, if our business schools and economics departments largely train brilliant technicians who have no sense of the effects of their actions on the economy generally, we have done the world a disservice. At best, we will reduce our graduates to the level of workhorses told to plow a certain well-paid furrow. It will not be their fault. If we teach students only to focus on the short-term numbers, the ability to see into the distance will certainly diminish. But we may also be creating other, troubling effects. Researchers have looked at whether students studying economics, with its assumption that most phenomena can be explained by people acting on the basis of self-interest, might actually shift their moral outlook in response to such study. The evidence suggests that it does; it makes them less cooperative, and encourages them to assume others are similarly uncooperative.[60] Sumantra Ghoshal, formerly professor at the London Business School, warned of the danger that such a view of economics could become a self-fulfilling prophecy. "By propagating ideologically inspired amoral theories," he said, "business schools have actively freed their students from any sense of moral responsibility."[61]

It is no accident that management schools have had increasingly to add courses in ethics, as their curricula are divorced from any framework suggesting a complex model of study and a larger social purpose for business.[62] Adding a free-floating business ethics course is putting a Band-Aid on a self-inflicted illness. Better to restructure the curriculum to help students understand business in a societal context.

Ethical concerns should then become self-evident as an organic element of economics.

Takeaways

- In this book we have described some obvious faults and some obvious remedies to make our financial system work better. So the question arises as to why these are not in place already.
- The answer lies deep in the way we apply the lessons of economics to finance.
- The purpose of economics should be, as Adam Smith said, "to provide a plentiful revenue or sustenance for the people," that is, to help enhance human welfare and prosperity.
- Instead, in the field of finance, we have promoted a narrower model of economics.
- We need to return to Adam Smith's mission. And we need to do so because the models we use to think about economic efficiency and financial risk don't work when we need them to.
- If we continue to use them as though they did, we can expect the same results: no increase in productivity, and repeated crises. More important, we may miss out on the huge benefits a more productive system could achieve.

7
People's Pensions, Commonsense Banks

Shining a spotlight on our financial system reveals a number of imperfections. It is no more efficient than it was a century ago. It is subject to serial crises. It is uneven in providing good long-term governance of corporations and other assets. It is disconnected from the needs of its ultimate capital providers—meaning us. And the economic theories that are embedded as its operating assumptions reflect only one facet of the world in which the industry operates. Taken together, these failures contributed to a bonfire of citizen savings in the 2008 financial crisis—and the slow destruction of wealth that goes on today. The question we turn to in this chapter is what our financial institutions would look like if they were designed to fit their purpose.

Retirement Savings

We look first at retirement savings. Our blueprint for people-centered pensions is hardly complete, but it is designed to accelerate debate about creating savings institutions that are different from those that exist today. We should be promoting a better-calibrated direction of travel for the pension industry. We then apply a similar logic to reform of banks. A comparable focus on shaping services to purpose could equally be applied to stock exchanges, insurance companies, and other bulwarks of today's financial infrastructure.

A COMMONSENSE PENSION FUND

What is the purpose of a pension fund? It is to provide confidence to savers that no matter how long they live, they and their dependents will have an income after full-time employment ends. They will be able to buy groceries, pay the rent, keep themselves healthy, clothe and entertain themselves, and so on.

One way to achieve that is simply to save a lot, so that even if you live to a hundred, you don't run out. That, of course, means setting aside an awful lot of money for a very long retirement—a plan that for most people is both unattainable and wasteful. They can't save that much alone, and even if they did, the money would probably not be needed since most will not live that long.

The more efficient way to provide a pension is for us all to save together, and to share what is known as "longevity risk." Individually, we don't know how long we will live. If you are twenty-five and plan to retire at sixty-five, how many years will you need the income for? You might fall under a bus, or you might live to be a centenarian. Since you don't know how much to set aside, you have to defray the risk that you might live a long time and run out of savings. But if we all save together, then those who die early will still receive an income, and their excess savings can be used for those who live on for many years. By saving in this fashion, for a pension rather than just on your own account, you can enormously reduce the amount you need to set aside for retirement.[1]

The first feature of a commonsense pension, therefore, is that it would allow people to save collectively, or to find another way to share longevity risk.

Where would such a fund invest? It would tend to choose assets that generate real returns, that is, returns that will not be wiped out by inflation. Corporate shares make an appropriate investment, as do property and other assets that are less likely to lose value to inflation.[2] Since pension savings may not be needed for some years, they would be invested for the long term, and their managers would not be too troubled by day-to-day fluctuations.[3] That would allow for truly long-term investments that pay dividends or interest over time, such as infrastructure projects, or the evergreen style of direct private equity investing we described in chapter 3, where the pension plan itself invests directly into an enterprise. Understanding this time frame would mitigate the frenetic trading activity some investment plans engage in today.

Common sense suggests that a pension plan would avoid putting all its eggs in one basket. Rather it should diversify: maybe hold shares in a few companies in different industries, together with some bonds and some property. All these make sense for a pension plan, as they would for any long-term investment.

Costs need to be kept low, because even small increases in fees can make a big difference to pension outcomes. For a twenty-five-year-old with a life expectancy of eighty-five who saves every year and retires at sixty-five, a 1 percent charge—which sounds reasonable until you consider that this charge is levied every year and compounds over the life of the pension—will slice a whopping 25 percent off the income he or she would otherwise receive in retirement. A 1.5 percent charge will cut it by 38 percent, and a 2 percent charge will reduce it by nearly half.[4]

The same is true for returns. A 1 percent higher return each year will yield a 25 percent higher pension for that twenty-five-year-old who plans to retire at sixty-five. It is important that a pension is not invested so conservatively that it wipes out returns.[5]

The manager of a commonsense pension plan would have to be skilled in choosing investments and in administration and have actuarial expertise to know how to set expectations of future income. But above all, he or she would be required to use the money in the common pension pot *only* in the interests of the beneficiaries. Like good doctors, those who oversee the pension fund must have its members' interests at heart; otherwise they will be too tempted by conflicts of interest. That doesn't mean that private contractors won't be commissioned to do the job, any more than a doctor will eschew buying diagnostic equipment from a for-profit company. But the key choices about how the pension is managed must always be made in the interests of the saver.

Given today's employment patterns, a pension should be portable. You should be able to stay on the same plan if you switch employers or if you lose your job or take time off, and all contributions over your working life would count toward your retirement income.

If we agree that the purpose of a pension is to give us an income in retirement, all of these features are plain common sense. Sadly, they are not typical in today's pension world.

HOW THINGS GO WRONG

In the Introduction, we described a set of triplets, Beth, Cathy, and Sarah, and showed how even though they all paid identical amounts into their pension accounts, Sarah, who worked in the Netherlands, ended up with a 50 percent higher pension than her sisters in the United States and the United Kingdom. The reason is that the pension system in Holland, though far from perfect, conforms more closely to the structure we have just described.

Ironically, in the middle of the twentieth century, British and American companies also maintained pension funds for their employees that had many of the same characteristics.[6] Each year, both the employer and the employee put some money into the pension pot, and the government lent a hand by making the contributions tax deductible. Each employee would expect, but not be guaranteed, a percentage of his or her final salary for every year he or she had contributed. The pension wasn't guaranteed because returns are uncertain, and so making such a promise could prove foolhardy. But for many years, expectations were met. Indeed, sometimes they were exceeded.

But both the United States and the United Kingdom turned their backs on this commonsense system. In the 1990s, the British funds were doing well, with more set aside than they needed to meet their obligations. Returns had been good, and those who retired in the 1960s and 1970s hadn't wound up living all that long after work ended. So, in the 1980s and 1990s, many British companies asked for a holiday on their payments into the funds. The trustees agreed only on the basis that the pension expectation became a hard promise, what has become known as a "defined benefit."

But demographics and economic developments inter-
vened. With new technologies and more intense global
competition, companies got more efficient or outsourced abroad,
leading to downsized workforces. At the same time, health
advances allowed lifespans to lengthen. To complicate matters
further, returns in the market were diminishing. British sponsoring companies worried that they would be unable to meet
their pension commitments.

In the United States, these issues were further complicated by tax regulations that penalized firms if they wanted to
overfund their pension plans when business was good. As a
result, they did not contribute when they were most able, and
their plans had little margin of safety when markets declined
or when actuarial estimates needed revision. Furthermore,
since company plans had made hard promises of how much a
pensioner would be paid, accountants insisted that any pension deficit had to be shown in the financial statements.
Sometimes these deficits were enormous. Many companies
responded by closing their defined benefit funds to new members and replacing them with defined contribution plans.

Under defined contribution plans, companies and employees put money into an individual savings account, such
as the US 401(k) plan, that pays out a lump sum or a portion
of the balance periodically, on retirement. The problem is that
individual savings are costly, and they shift all the risk to the
individual saver rather than sharing it through a collective
pension plan. Those who live to be one hundred can run out
of money.

There is a way around this: savers can buy an "annuity,"
a pension payment that lasts until they die. Until recently,
annuities were mandatory for pension savings in the United
Kingdom. But annuities tend to be expensive and yield very

low incomes. This is because in order for the annuity market to work, pensioners need to trust that those who are selling them will live up to their promises. That means that savers need to know exactly what the promise is and that whoever is offering it has enough secure investments to deliver. Annuities end up being backed by ultrasafe bonds, which give low incomes and often little protection against inflation.[7]

In the Netherlands, none of this happened; collective pension plans are still in place. That is one of the reasons why among our imaginary triplets, Sarah can expect to receive a 50 percent higher pension than her sisters. Dutch people have seen their retirement income reduced in recent years, but to nothing like the degree suffered by those saving for a defined contribution pension in Britain or through a 401(k) in the United States.

The reward for designing a better pension system is huge—and if it is based on common sense, that design will produce better outcomes, truly fulfilling the purpose of the pensions industry. To put it another way, if we fail to exercise common sense, millions of working people will pay a very high cost.

Here is the remarkable thing. If we look back at the establishment of our savings institutions, we find that most were created not by clever financiers using complex engineering, but by motivated non-experts deploying common sense.

The Commonsense Pension: A Bit of History

The first significant funded pension plan was established not by bankers but by two largely unheralded Scottish clergymen, the Reverend Robert Wallace and the Reverend Alexander Webster, in the middle of the eighteenth century. Few have ever given better expression to common sense within our financial institutions than Wallace and Webster.

Here is the problem they wanted to solve. From time to time, Scottish ministers would die, leaving widows and children who were unable to take care of themselves. Because the houses the ministers occupied were tied to their jobs, their families would also be left homeless. Of course, many set aside some money for their dependents, but most young ministers could not save the money needed to provide for their families should they die young, which in those days was not an unlikely event. How could they protect their dependents?

Wallace and Webster came up with a straightforward answer. If all ministers put a small amount of money into one savings pot, funds could be built up. If a minister died, those funds could be used to look after his dependents. Of course, you needed to do the calculations carefully. If the dependents received too much income, the fund would run out. If they received too little, they would starve. But if the payments were just right, the widows and orphans would be fed and housed while the fund remained available to the next needy family.

So the ministers gathered their evidence and did their actuarial arithmetic. They wrote to every presbytery to figure out how many ministers died, whether they left dependents, how long they lived, and so on. In 1743, they launched the first modern pension fund.[8]

What Wallace and Webster did was not hard to understand, although the math involved was sophisticated and they got help from the professor of mathematics at Edinburgh University. What distinguished their effort was that they started with commonsense questions about what customers needed—to be able to make a simple, affordable payment and know that after they died their dependents would be cared for—and went on to design the fund on that basis.

In response to this need, the clergymen came to recognize that pensions contain two bedrock elements. One is savings: money must be set aside against old age or some other contingency. The second is insurance: the pension pays out only when a particular unpredictable event occurs—in this case, the death of the family breadwinner. In many modern pensions, the event is reaching a certain age and/or retiring. Distributions occur for the number of years the widow and dependents need support or, today, for the duration of retirement.

Wallace and Webster realized that the best way to deal with unpredictable events is for large groups of people to band together. You may not know whether an event will take place within a certain time period, but if you know the *probability* of its happening, then a community of people can act together to mitigate its effects. In the finance-speak of today, you can "diversify the risk" by sharing it.[9]

For such systems of mutual obligation to work, you need to be sure that those who promote them will fulfill their promises. In the 1700s, few people would have been foolhardy enough to place their money in commercial ventures. Within Wallace and Webster's lifetime, people had seen fortunes wiped out in the manipulations known as the South Sea bubble. The widows of Scottish clergymen would hardly have trusted financial markets to meet their needs in any future crisis. But Wallace and Webster were clerics who offered their service in good faith to other ministers of the Church of Scotland. They could not have been seen as more trustworthy.[10]

Here was the formula for success. Wallace and Webster's pension was run by people who could be seen as having both technical skills and the absolute integrity to work solely in the interests of the saver. In all successful societies, individuals care for others in need and expect that, should they themselves be in need, they too will be cared for. Wallace and Webster's hugely successful pension was a formal system encapsulating those same mutual obligations.

The People's Pension

Today, with the benefit of 250 years' worth of new knowledge and technology, we have the tools to design an even better private pension system. We call it "the People's Pension."

To see what such a plan would look like, let's return to the first question Wallace and Webster posed: what do people expect in a pension system? For most, the answer is simple. They want to entrust their money to an agent who is knowledgeable and honest and who would aim to invest their money responsibly in order to pay an optimum pension for however long retirement lasts. They would want the plan to be understandable and accountable. Most savers don't want a huge and complex choice of providers (a handful do), but they want to be sure that the one they use has these characteristics.[11]

The challenge is to persuade modern institutions to replicate the integrity of those Scottish clergymen. Here is where the business experience of the last half century comes in handy. As entrepreneurs and tycoons have given way to corporations and institutions, much attention has been paid to methods of instilling the proprietary behavior we associate with careful owners in what are essentially market-based bureaucracies. This is what the field of governance is about. We can transfer lessons from the corporate world to long-term savings.

Better governance in funds, as we saw in chapter 4, is associated with better wealth protection. A People's Pension Fund would have a board at the top composed of individuals with a reputation for expertise, integrity, and judgment. Many US private sector retirement plans have no boards at all, and the boards that exist often lack expertise, making them susceptible to capture by advisors. Moreover, only a fraction of boards presiding at investor bodies feature some form of election or representation by members. The first step in designing a twenty-first-century retirement plan is a capable, accountable, and representative board.

The second step is to ensure that, like Wallace and Webster's pension plans, the pension would aim only to advance the interests of beneficiaries or clients who give it money to invest. Any other objectives—such as furthering a fund manager's commercial gain—would be a by-product of having achieved that primary goal. Such a fiduciary duty is not itself new. It is, for instance, embedded within statutory and regulatory regimes such as the ERISA law (Employee Retirement Income Security Act) in the United States. But institutions have strayed from that principle and allowed their own profits to dominate behavior. The time is ripe for muscular reforms to fiduciary duty.

The third indispensable feature of a People's Pension Plan is transparency. Every significant payment made to manage the funds would be plainly reported. The way the money was invested would be absolutely clear, as would other decisions and judgments. Any pensioner who wishes should be able to know where her money was invested, and why.

For Wallace and Webster, accountability and transparency were difficult to achieve; there wasn't even a reliable post office in 1743. Today, the Internet and social media enable vast amounts of two-way communication between a fund and its beneficiaries. It should be simple for a saver to look at the charges on a pension fund and the assets it is invested in and to observe what the board has done to optimize beneficiary interests. Yet today, too many pension managers and investment managers seem to try to make complex investments as opaque as possible. In Iowa, for example, the public pension fund refused to release information about the cost of its investment in a fund managed by the private equity firm KKR. And KKR threatened to bar pension funds that reveal such information from future investments.[12]

A People's Pension Plan would do the kind of reporting investors have long asked of corporations. It would issue a statement at least annually to stakeholders on critical product and governance features, much like the ones auto manufacturers generate about their cars, or like the nutrition labels now mandated for many packaged foods.

Such a statement should, first of all, cover the basics like the costs savers are charged. These include not only the fees levied by the fund manager but the cost of services commissioned from others, such as those for trading securities. To give a sense of the poverty of information available today, the US SEC now mandates that mutual funds reveal a "total expense ratio," or TER. But that ratio does not include all the charges made to a saver's account; it omits trading costs, for instance. Pension funds generally don't even declare the TER; some don't even calculate it. In a People's Pension, fund managers should know all their costs and report them. They should also allow savers to know how their funds are invested. As fundamental as this information is, much of it is not now available from most long-term savings plans.

The People's Pension should explain to beneficiaries what governance arrangements ensure that decisions are made in alignment with their interests. Some jurisdictions already offer templates spelling out precisely how this may be done. Australia, for instance, has required each retirement plan to feature a trustee board composed of sponsor-corporation executives and plan members, and chaired by an independent non-executive. Regulators elsewhere could provide guidance on accountability principles without dictating specific structures. Alternatively, market participants could together craft voluntary, but authoritative, national codes of plan governance that embed such guidance in a People's Pension.[13] One minimum standard: beneficiaries should be given knowledge of not only who are serving as fiduciaries on their behalf but also the fiduciaries' professional backgrounds, skill sets, potential conflicts of interest, independence, and how to contact them to express confidence, views, or concerns.[14] Member elections of People's Pension trustees may be appropriate means of compelling alignment. The International Corporate Governance Network, which represents more than $18 trillion in capital, has adopted guidance on plan board accountability to achieve this.[15]

A People's Pension Plan would subject its governance arrangements to regular independent review to ensure that they meet best-practice accountability principles. This represents another exercise borrowed from the modern corporate governance world. In chapter 4 we observed that it is common (and in some places required) for directors to undertake periodic assessments of their own performance. US mutual fund boards, which often serve retirement savings plans, already have to perform annual board evaluations, though to be fair, their quality and the disclosure of them vary. Fiduciary evaluations are spreading among US public sector funds and prompting accountability reforms. Civil service retirement systems in six US states have adopted the practice.[16] The process was so useful that the Retirement Commission of South Carolina is making more than one hundred improvements following its review.[17] In the United Kingdom, the retirement system Railpen created perhaps the masterpiece of all such self-portraits in 2014. It spent eight months, created sixty working papers, and suggested 442 ways to improve. The architect of that effort, Towers Watson consultant Roger Urwin, noted that there was one overridingly important focus. "We spent a surprising amount of time on . . . the mission and role of the organization, revisiting our values and beliefs." It was crucially important, he said, to "get a common understanding of what it is we're here for, a common sense of purpose."[18]

A People's Pension would reflect the investment interests of beneficiaries. Surprisingly, funds generally do not ask members what types of investments they need, the ownership profile they prefer, or whether they trust the plan. A few institutions do. Perhaps the best example is the €100 billion Dutch health sector pension fund PFZW, which covers two million members. Starting in mid-2011, PFZW and its asset manager, PGGM, began conducting a quarterly "Brand Tracker" survey of beneficiaries to study how the fund is perceived and whether members believe it is meeting their needs.[19] PGGM cites the survey's findings to support its advocacy of long-term stewardship.[20] The National Employment Savings Trust (NEST), the UK national workplace pension scheme, also conducts an annual survey of members.[21] While ultimate fiduciary responsibility rests with the board, beneficiaries' views are a key data point for trustees in making strategic decisions and instructing agents.

A People's Pension should have feedback channels appropriate to the era of social media. It should be easy for members to offer ideas and opinions on aspects of the plan's operations, just as shareholders of corporations and mutual funds may offer resolutions on strategic direction. Two-way communication is essential to modern accountability, and it can be accompanied by offering a way for members to exchange views with each other. Dedicated e-mail inboxes for board members, fund Twitter accounts, chat rooms, and electronic surveys of member satisfaction are now not only possible but easily accomplished.

A People's Pension would pay portfolio managers appropriately. One common conflict is time frame. Pension funds typically claim a long investment horizon, but the advisors and portfolio managers it selects are evaluated and compensated on short-term criteria. This practice demands explanation. Simply having to supply such information could alert fiduciaries to the issue and help beneficiaries and regulators gauge a plan's quality.

Finally, the plan should disclose every year how it or its agents use stewardship tools to protect assets—and not only by the narrow-gauge measure of how they vote shares at portfolio companies. Ballot records certainly have a place: as shareholder champion Nell Minow says, they allow beneficiaries to "see who is voting to enable dysfunctional [corporate] board behavior."[22] But there is much more in the stewardship toolbox that can affect asset value and influence corporate behavior on our behalf. Funds can enroll in the United Nations' Principles for Responsible Investment (UN PRI). They can collaborate with other investors on market-wide initiatives such as the Diverse Director Datasource, created by the two giant pension funds in California, CalPERS and CalSTRS,[23] to improve corporate boards.[24] They can integrate governance and extrafinancial risks as part of portfolio management, performing due diligence research on companies before deciding to buy a stock, periodically while they own shares, and as part of decisions to hold or sell. Those funds that delegate buy-sell decisions to external investment managers can ask if the managers do any of this and can disclose the results.

Beneficiaries might also want to know how much the portfolio managers and investment professionals have themselves invested in the funds they manage, how investment risk management is organized, and to whom the management reports. The US mutual fund research company Morningstar considers whether individual portfolio managers have "skin in the game" as part of its stewardship grading methodology.[25] Some mutual funds even require directors to invest in the funds they oversee.

Disclosure of all these features should be made in plain language. This isn't just a cosmetic concern. The UK's NEST discovered through surveys that technical jargon was a barrier to communication with prospective members, and it developed a glossary of commonly understood pension terms to use.[26] Governance disclosures, similarly, should be written for easy comprehension. Further, any data required should follow a common format, so that individuals can readily make comparisons between institutions.[27]

The People's Pension would be simple to enroll into and open to all. The most effective pension systems are based on "auto-enrollment," meaning that the employer automatically deducts, and often contributes to, the pension payment unless the employee opts out. Savers who are self-employed can establish similar systems through a bank or brokerage. This makes "marketing" of the fund simple, and that in turn helps keep the People's Pension cost low, so value stays with the saver.

This is a long list of characteristics for a People's Pension Plan, and a lot of information that it should make available. Although all of the information is essential and none of it requires higher mathematics, it is unlikely that most savers will read or understand it, any more than all car purchasers understand their car's technical characteristics. Yet the market for autos works well because some buyers are expert and make recommendations, and consumer groups campaign for higher quality and standards. As a result, the quality of automobiles has improved while costs have fallen. We should aim for a similar effect in the investment industry.

Note that these structures for creating accountability and trust do not require participants' day-to-day attention. Investors typically neither need nor want to micromanage ultimate decisions on every issue. Still, it is critical that they have the option to ask questions and make their opinions felt if they wish.

Some say that the structures we suggest are impossible to achieve. We reply that much of what we recommend is carried out in different parts of the world. For example, in the Netherlands collective pensions are the primary model for private pension provision. They have been established both for individual companies and for entire industries. In both cases, beneficiaries are represented on the board. Similar arrangements are found in Denmark, and in Canada. Indeed, as noted earlier, the People's Pension is similar to the model used by Wallace and Webster. If we could manage successfully to run such a pension in the eighteenth century, it should surely be

possible in the twenty-first. We do accept that the market incentive to set up a People's Pension is modest. The business
would likely be a steady earner rather than a high-octane
profit-maker. But that is where policymakers can play a role.
Given the powerful benefits of such a program, they could
choose to encourage or arm twist the development of large fiduciary pension institutions. The reward would be great for
citizen investors, who are also voters.[28]

To recap, a People's Pension plan would do the following:

- Feature an accountable and knowledgeable
  governing board, including some who directly
  represent participants. That board would ex-
  pressly adopt fiduciary duty, and require all its
  contractors to similarly acknowledge their fiduciary obligations. It would periodically evaluate itself.
- Report on costs, benefits, stewardship efforts, and
  decision-making practices in easy-to-understand
  language and in a manner that allows easy comparison between pension funds.
- Enable communication with and among beneficiaries.
- Be easy to enroll in.
- Be large enough to diversify risks among its participants and be portable so that people can continue to contribute throughout their working
  lifetimes.

The prize for building such a system would be higher
and more secure long-term savings. It is up to citizen investors to press policymakers and industry participants to think

through the purpose of pensions and to design the system to meet that purpose.

A Commonsense Bank

If a purpose-based, commonsense approach is right for retirement savings, the same approach could inform the design of banks. We learned the cost of ignoring common sense when the banking system went into meltdown in 2008. Afterward it transpired that many of our largest financial institutions, previously lauded as successful, responsibly run enterprises, were in fact near insolvency. Some did, in fact, go under. Many others survived only thanks to government bailouts.

So let's reflect on the purpose of the banks, and see if we can again draw lessons from the past. One pioneering bank of modern times was the Bank of Amsterdam, founded in 1609, which fulfilled the primary service people need from banks: it kept their money safe. That may seem like a limited objective, but in those days when coinage was often adulterated with cheaper metals, the Bank of Amsterdam would weigh and ascertain its true value, "and give the owner an honest rendering as a deposit."[29]

Today we simply take it for granted that there is a safe place where, at minimal cost, we can keep our money secure. That security underlies the stability of the banking system, because if there is any doubt about a bank's ability to repay, we will simply take our money out and put it under a mattress. If our confidence collapses for all banks, the financial system falls apart.

Once money has been deposited, the bank can fulfill its second purpose: to facilitate payments from the account. It can then go on to play its third, hugely important but very simple role: to lend the money it has on deposit to those who want to borrow, the process known as intermediation.

As we saw in chapter 1, these three primary services—safe custody, payments, and intermediation—are central to any country's economic development.

Looking under the Hood

If these are the services we ask of banks, what characteristics should they have? First, banks need to manage themselves so as to ensure that depositors' money is always safe. Banks therefore need to hold adequate reserves and to maintain accurate and low-cost systems for transferring money. And they need to be very skilled in comparing the promises they have made to those who have supplied them with money, with the risks they have taken in lending to others. If banks are not careful about whom they lend to, defaults will eat into their reserves and ultimately risk their depositors' money.

Banks face several sorts of risks in lending. The most obvious is that the borrower might not repay. The second is the matching of interest rates: a bank needs to beware of borrowing at variable rates of interest and lending at fixed rates, because if the variable rates rise, the bank may be stuck supporting loans that don't support the interest it is paying to depositors. The final and perhaps most distinctive risk is that of a timing mismatch between depositors, whom the banks have often promised to repay on demand, and the loans they make, which are repaid over long time periods. This process is known as "maturity transformation." As long as borrowers do not all decide they want their money at the same time, this process works smoothly. But if there is a run on the bank, it will be unable to repay its debts. Special provisions are therefore needed. Either the bank needs carefully to match the maturities of its loans and its deposits, or it needs to be able to borrow from another source if it starts to run out of cash. This is one of the roles given to central banks: to provide a lender of last resort if a private bank gets in trouble. Of course, no central bank should lend unless the bank that is receiving the funds is solvent and will be able, over time, to repay. Otherwise, banks would be profligate, knowing that they would always be bailed out.

Therefore, if one were to look under the hood of a bank, one would expect it to hold more than adequate reserves so that it has the capacity to fund losses. Like an engineer designing a bridge, it will do its calculations very carefully and then add a considerable margin of error.

The most efficient banking system would keep its costs low, so that it could offer the highest interest rate to depositors and the lowest to borrowers, commensurate with their ability to repay. The problem is that costs are not easy to calculate because the level of default on loans varies over time. As Brian Pitman, a senior British banker, reflected, "it is perfectly possible in the short term to decide to be more risky than your competitors. That will get everybody to beat a path to your door, and you will wind up, short term, with very big profits."[30] In times of plenty, when everyone is able to repay, the bank looks profitable and is tempted to lend more. But if there is a recession, more borrowers default, and a bank that has made too many risky loans may have nothing left when depositors want their money. Therefore, the bank needs to be cautious, to maintain adequate reserves, and not to get carried away.

How Things Go Wrong

The model described in the preceding sections suggests that banking should be a very conservative business, and a couple of generations back, in many countries, banks were indeed very conservative institutions. But their investors, particularly equity investors, were keen that banks become as efficient and profitable as possible, and they began to measure bank success on the basis of the return they made on their equity, and to encourage incentives to bank employees on that basis. Banks were encouraged to minimize the equity they hold in reserve, so that they could make the highest return on it.

The problem is that that equity is the major line of defense ensuring that customers' deposits are not at risk.

If equity and liquidity reserves are low, one might hope that banks are at least prudent in the way they value the loans they have made, and have made provision against any possible loss. So do banks value their loans prudently? Some do, but in many jurisdictions, prudence in accounting has been abandoned as a basis for calculating profit and therefore executive bonuses. This feels like the wrong incentive system for a conservative business.

Common sense would suggest that banks should err on the side of having more equity than they need. Rather than borrow a large amount on the basis of a small amount of equity, they could raise more equity and borrow less. Shareholders might get a lower return on their investment, but it will be much safer, and depositors will be protected.

The ultimate cause of the 2008 crash was that banks did not have enough reserves—that is, enough equity—and they lent too much to borrowers who were credit risks. They did this because they had been encouraged to minimize equity and lend more at higher rates.[31]

But as we noted, a bank can look like it is doing quite well, at least for a while, by taking on extra risk, especially if its profit calculation doesn't take into account the likelihood of future losses. But when the bubble bursts, as it did in 2008, banks do badly, pension funds lose value, the beneficiaries of pension funds lose their savings, and many people across economies lose their jobs.

We could do with a simple, commonsense banking system such as that suggested by Anat Admati of Stanford University and Martin Hellwig of the Max Planck Institute for Research on Collective Goods.[32] Banks should hold enough equity to ensure that everyone's deposits are safe and that they have the ability to lend to the rest of the economy. They would account for their profits on a prudent basis to make sure they were not being encouraged to make profligate loans. Investors in the bank's equity and debt would accept a lower return in the short run but would be more than repaid in the long run, since banks would have less risk of failing. And the economy would have adequate, safe, and permanent supplies of capital. Instead, our banks have huge borrowings (often from one another), justified by complex risk models that must be overseen by an army of regulators. As John Sutherland, who heads banking regulation for the Bank of England, noted, some banks have only three to four cents of equity for every dollar they lend (this is known as the "leverage ratio"), and the British banking system requires some one thousand people to supervise it. If they kept twenty cents in equity for each dollar of lending, he mused, "you would only need about ten of us. . . . Funders would be a lot happier and savers would be more protected. If you wound back thirty years, . . . it would be inconceivable for a bank to be working on a leverage of 3 to 4 percent."[33]

We could, at a very low cost, create banks that are much better at keeping our money safe. Other commonsense reforms could foster safe banks focused on serving their customers. They would be conservative in valuing assets; they would abjure paying highly leveraged salaries to directors and their employees; they would make sure to ring-fence depositors' money, so that ordinary savers would not lose out should other parts of the banks' operations get into trouble.

A commonsense bank would have other qualities as well. It would refrain from using tricks of the trade to take money from its customers in subtle ways, for example, through hidden fees or unannounced reductions in interest rates on deposits. Its documents would be in plain English, and when extensive, they would be given to borrowers, depositors, and other customers in advance so that customers didn't feel pressured to sign long documents filled with legalese while sitting in a cubicle waiting for a loan approval. It would firewall conflicts of interest. It would be open about its trading practices. It would support regulatory mechanisms to expose those who were not trading appropriately, just as a nurse or doctor is supposed to report colleagues for poor practice.

We can imagine governance arrangements that would help ensure that such banks stand true to their purpose, and regulations that would help them succeed. But our point is not to offer a detailed blueprint for banks; it is simply to demonstrate that if one were to design a bank with its fundamental purpose in mind, one would end up with a very different institution from the banks we have today. Had such banks existed in 2008, they might have prevented the meltdown. It is too late to change that now. But it is not too late to introduce common sense to our financial system to avoid the next crisis.

We, the capitalists, have a huge stake in wanting common sense to prevail, in both pensions and banking. After all, citizen investors are beneficiaries of the pension fund, customers of the bank, and taxpayers who will be asked to bail out the system if it goes off the rails. Our financial institutions need to be reshaped so that they are not only fit for their purpose but designed purposefully, with incentives, structures, and governance that drive them to deliver. Part of the solution is returning to the simple logic that Wallace and Webster would have understood, that is, to be clear about the purpose of finance and to build a system that can achieve that purpose.

Both of the reforms we have described, the People's Pension Plan and a more prudent banking system, would give great benefit without being particularly costly. One could also apply this approach to other financial institutions. All would begin by thinking about the purpose of the institution we wanted to create. For example, stock exchanges would be places where securities could be bought and sold, with conditions ensuring that all buyers and sellers were treated fairly and that they had the same relevant information and the same access to the orders of other buyers and sellers. The exchange would act as a guarantor of those trades and provide the information technology to match the buys and sells. In other words, the exchanges would focus on being safe places to trade shares, not ones where the abuses we described in chapter 3 are allowed to flourish.

The key point is this. The financial system we have today deviates from one in which each part is focused on fulfilling its purpose. We have shown what direction reform might take if we were to design "fit for purpose" pension funds and banks that would serve us better than existing institutions. After all, it is our money that they manage. We are the owners. To make the machine work, we need to understand its design and fix it. We need an "Owner's Manual" for the financial system.

Takeaways

- The first low-cost, efficient, collective pension fund was established in the eighteenth century. Today, that structure is being abandoned in favor of individual savings accounts that give poorer returns.
- A return to commonsense pensions, together with twenty-first-century innovations, would make a substantial difference in wealth savings.
- Similar observations could be made about our banks. In the past, excessive borrowing by banks was discouraged. Today, bank directors have an incentive to borrow more, threatening stability in a crisis.
- A return to commonsense pensions and banks would improve our returns while making the financial system more stable.

8

Capitalism
A Brief Owners' Manual

We depend on the financial system to safeguard our savings and to fuel jobs, growth, and prosperity, but rather than focus on those goals, the system has transformed itself into a financial black hole, too often serving its own interests ahead of ours. The great bonfire of nest eggs that it helped kindle in the global financial crisis continues to burn through citizen wealth and corrode the economy.

The financial system will not reform itself on its own. It is citizen investors—"We the capitalists"—who must push for a reboot of the financial system to make it once again safe for users. So at the end of this chapter, we offer a final proposal: a twenty-first-century Magna Carta for citizens living in capitalist economies.

Before we come to that, let us recap where we believe the solutions to our present malaise lie. They involve a return to fundamentals and accountability, but hitched to today's innovations. Taken together, the measures we have outlined in previous chapters amount to a six-step "owners' manual" for the repair and maintenance of the financial system.

Troubleshooting
STEP 1: START BY BEING CLEAR ABOUT THE PURPOSE OF THE SYSTEM: UNDERSTAND WHAT "GOOD" LOOKS LIKE

To solve the problems of the finance system, we must begin with a vision of what a "good" system would look like. Absent that guiding principle, it is hardly surprising that remedies fail. When we don't have clarity as to the purpose of banks, long-term savings arrangements, and other institutions, it dilutes the imperative that intermediaries should serve our interests, not their own. When that happens, they are not being dishonest; instead, they are responding to incentives that are focused on the intermediaries rather than on the ultimate beneficiaries and risk-takers. There is nothing wrong with profits, and intermediaries should be paid appropriately. But they should be compensated for taking care of our needs, not theirs. Unfortunately, we now have something of a tyranny of the experts, and a system partially run for their own benefit. The result, as Thomas Philippon has shown, is anything but efficient in providing essential services to the wider economy.

A return to first principles would require us to recall the industry's chief purpose, which is to offer a safe spot to store wealth (custody), an efficient method for transferring money (payments), reliable channels to borrow and lend so that capital is optimally deployed (intermediation), and the feasibility for users to manage their exposure to risk.[1] Concentrating on these vital services well should generate healthy profits for enterprises within the financial universe and comfortable wages for employees leading them, while improving the efficiency of the entire sector. Practically, that means every financial institution should have a charter and mission statement focused on serving the ultimate provider of capital or the ultimate customer, not just the next intermediary in the chain.

STEP 2: RESTORE ACCOUNTABILITY TO ASSET MANAGEMENT

As chapter 2 showed, managing money can be complicated, and that complexity can hide many tricks of the trade. But investing can be made understandable. Great investors such as Warren Buffett and John Bogle think complexity is the enemy of good investing. US pension giant CalPERS even abandoned its hedge fund program, saying the cost and complexity weren't worth it.

So what can you do? For starters, determine whether your advisor is covered by a fiduciary duty to put your interests first. If he or she is not, be wary. Second, don't invest in something you don't understand. Make your advisor explain it to you, or don't invest. Third, pay attention to fees. Your future returns are a projection; the fees are a hard and fast guarantee of a diminution in those returns. Fees are, of course, necessary. But why pay more than you need? Fourth, remember that you are running a marathon, not a sprint. The point is to accumulate wealth over a lifetime, not to finish ahead of someone else this quarter. Ask about the investment manager's policies with that in mind. Fifth, find out how analysts and portfolio managers are compensated. If your time horizon is long term but they earn extra for short-term performance, you are not in alignment—and may wind up paying more fees than you need to. Similarly, if analysts and fund managers gain bonuses for accumulating clients for their investment house rather than growing the value of your portfolio, they won't be working above all to optimize your interests. Sixth, if you are using a consultant to help select investments, ask how the consultant is paid. Amazingly, many sophisticated consultants who tell multibillion-dollar pension funds how to invest get revenues from the very asset managers they are paid to judge. Finally, does the investment manager pay attention to issues that will affect us all over the long term, such as those reflected in the Principles for Responsible Investment? Or does it think it can ignore the governance of companies in which it invests because it thinks it can trade out of the way of systemic risks such as climate change?

In short, understand whether the institution to which you entrust your money is acting in your best interest or its own. And then insist on periodic, plain-language reports so that you can monitor what your advisor actually does for you.

STEP 3: PROMOTE A CULTURE OF OWNERSHIP IN INVESTMENT

Institutional investors need to install practices that reanimate ownership skills at companies in which they hold stock. Short-term (even millisecond) trading and commercial habits accumulated over decades have displaced much long-term investing and ownership, attenuating the link between the ultimate investor and the companies in which they invest. Savers can wind up paying more and receiving less value while companies sacrifice long-term investments, shoulder higher risks, and pay senior executives with insufficient regard to economic performance. We end up with rudderless corporations.

Publicly traded companies ultimately belong to us. We might begin reforming them by demanding that the boards who run them shift to a simplified compensation model where CEOs are paid not through complex, manipulable option schemes but like other employees, in cash. Bonuses should be linked to real long-term growth rather than stock price; reference to peer groups should be deemphasized in favor of metrics relevant to the ways the business grows. What can you do to promote this? If you own shares of public companies in the United States, United Kingdom, Australia, Canada, or any of thirty-five other countries, chances are that you, your broker, or your fund manager gets to vote on your portfolio companies' CEOs compensation framework. It's a practice known as "Say on pay." So you can help effectuate that change.

Of course, altering the playing field to emphasize long-term economic growth is a massive shift requiring everyone's participation. Stock exchanges and their regulators should end practices that advantage high-frequency traders (or anyone else) over the market as a whole, and they should support exchanges that treat all investors fairly. Institutional investors should pool their efforts to protect the interests of citizen savers; collective action has proven a powerful tool in pressing companies for greater disclosure and accountability. Technology is being deployed to boost retail investors' participation in proxy voting so that with virtually one click in an annual meeting season, their interests can be expressed rather than silent. Much more can be done to expand options for retail voting, for instance, by allowing individuals to order their ballots cast in line with an institution they trust. Finally, tax changes carefully crafted should encourage long-term investment, while disclosure rules should shed light on opaque instruments such as derivatives. We should be wary of unintended consequences, but we should both encourage accountability and mitigate systemic risk.

STEP 4: APPLY GOOD GOVERNANCE TO INVESTING INSTITUTIONS

For nearly three decades, market reforms have refashioned corporate boards of directors into more professional bodies overseeing management. But comparable effort has not gone into the governance of financial agents. It is long past time to make pension and investment funds observe an equivalent to the kind of transparency and accountability standards that have spread throughout the corporate world.

Fixes include disclosure standards on asset owners and asset managers, equivalent to a nutrition statement, so that beneficiaries can compare to what extent their agents are configured to act in their best interests. Transparency could prompt improvements in fund governance that, if research is to be believed, could lift returns. Regular fiduciary audits can be required, to test whether funds are truly serving their citizen investors. Crucially, funds need to overhaul internal compensation arrangements so that rewards go to long-term value creation rather than stock churning and asset accumulation. Members of a retirement plan should have means to weigh in on major issues, through representation on trustee boards, annual meetings, surveys or focus groups, or social media. Civil society organizations should scrutinize funds as rigorously as they do corporations for their commitment to sustainable, long-term value creation. And with the rise of social media, grassroots savers will have a vast and expanding

array of apps and communication channels to monitor their
agents.

You can get started now. More major markets feature
Internet or social media sites focusing on the money management industry; some have entities that rate money managers.
Civil society organizations such as ShareAction do this; from
a commercial perspective, Morningstar grades mutual funds
on stewardship. If you invest through a collective vehicle such
as a pension or mutual fund, ask how it is governed and who
selects the trustees. Then use those channels, or if they don't
exist, press for them.

STEP 5: RESET REGULATION BASED ON PURPOSE

Statutes, regulation, and voluntary standards should be har-
monized to get the system as a whole to achieve its purpose.
Today there are different, sometimes clashing, often obsolete,
and frequently ineffective rule books covering separate parts
of financial machinery. Twenty-first-century rules should be
synergistic and focused on the interests of citizens rather than
those of the finance industry. Moreover, capital market policing should be done, whenever possible, by citizen investors
and their accountable agents rather than via statute.

The place to start is with reforms that support fiduciary
duty. Measures clarifying who owes first loyalties to whom, up
and down the investment chain, can help anchor intermediaries' behavior to the interests of ultimate capital providers.
Then, regulation should shift from trying to anticipate and
outlaw every specific act with potentially negative consequences to articulating broad principles that stimulate self-
correction. That means ensuring that market bodies have the
capacity to make well-aligned judgments, and then giving

them the tools and authority to do that. Regulation that ad-
dresses the system as a whole, not just individual parts,
would concentrate on infusing good governance from top to
bottom. Citizen investors can best add their voices for these
policy changes collectively through advocacy groups or by
communicating individually with their elected representatives.

STEP 6: REBOOT FINANCIAL INSTITUTIONS

The architecture of our financial institutions needs an up-
grade. One useful step would be to construct a People's Pension based on simple, low-cost collective savings. In recent
years there has been a steady drift of retirement savings toward
defined contribution plans that offer members a menu of investment options. But such menus may include investment
funds that siphon excessive fees and put commercial interests
ahead of savers' interests.[2] These may undermine the bedrock
purpose of a pension plan, which is to be a trustworthy guardian of hard-earned savings.

A commonsense alternative would involve default en-
rollment in collective savings pools focused solely on protecting
the interests of depositors. A People's Pension Plan would have
a capable, accountable, and representative governing board. It
would replace opacity with transparency, so that savers could
identify not just management fees for funds in defined contribution plans but all fees, such as the full costs of private equity funds and hedge funds. A People's Pension Plan would
behave as if long-term value mattered—for instance, by engaging with investee companies to ensure that they address climate
change and other risks. And it would provide savers easily
accessible channels to express their opinions and vote for their
representatives.

We also need to rebuild other financial institutions around their fundamental purposes. All banks worldwide can and should be better financed. We should also welcome the movement toward Community Banks and Community Development Financial Institutions (CDFIs). These are local banks strictly focused primarily on community development, aligning their mission with providing service to local savers. Not every bank has to be a CDFI, of course; global businesses often need global banks. But these local banks fill a need and can be good business.

A "Magna Carta" for Citizen Investors

This owners' manual is geared toward making the finance industry work better. The benefits, as we have seen, can be substantial. But that raises a question: the remedies we have suggested are hardly radical. Why have they not taken root? One often-overlooked reason, we believe, is that we are too willing to leave these problems to the experts. And the experts are often intermediaries who have every reason to defend current practices. If remedies for the financial system's failures have one thing in common, it is that they nearly always address the interests of the first two estates of the market, corporations and institutional investors, but neglect those of the third estate, the citizen investors.

Reformers of corporations, for instance, have sought over the last twenty-five years to define the structures and behaviors that they expect of company boards. One landmark was the multistakeholder committee led by the late Sir Adrian Cadbury, which developed voluntary standards of governance for the United Kingdom in 1991. Today, virtually every major market in the world has an authoritative, national corporate governance code in place for publicly traded companies—the United States is the principal exception.[3] Studies show that these codes have succeeded in making corporate executives answerable to boards, and that executives behave better when they know directors are watching them.[4]

The story is similar for institutional investors, which are in the midst of their own accountability evolution, to become better owners of the companies whose shares they hold on our behalf. Proliferating stewardship codes spell out how financial agents should behave as owners of public companies, in particular, how they should monitor corporate boards. As these guidelines take root, financial agents are ramping up oversight of corporate boards in their investment portfolios. Codes of corporate governance and institutional oversight are designed to mesh; just as executives change their behavior when they know they are being watched by directors, directors behave differently when they are watched by institutions that are themselves more transparent.

But if there is now a line of accountability from corporate executives through to board directors and on to institutional shareholders, who is watching the institutional investors on behalf of the ultimate providers of capital? How can we as citizen investors gain confidence that our financial agents are truly acting to best advance our interests? The six rebooting steps outlined earlier in this chapter are designed to reset the financial system, but that system won't fully function without pressure and encouragement provided by grassroots involvement. To extend the lexicon of owners' manuals, troubleshooting is up to us.

It is time for us, the citizen investors, to have a code or charter that speaks to our rights and makes our agents accountable for their responsibilities. Forces of short termism, the growing chain of agents, and the use of derivatives have created a divorce of ownership between us and the companies we own. Animating our citizens' role as watchers of the store is needed to ensure that the reforms applying to the first two estates produce a real alignment of agents with beneficiaries.

What would a Magna Carta for citizen investors demand of financial institutions?

That our financial institutions act in good faith in accordance with their essential purpose. All financial institutions should be clear about their purposes. They should be faithful to it, and not act in a way that could put the system as a whole in jeopardy. Directors or trustees should have to affirm annually that the products and services their institutions offer are consistent with the efficient achievement of that purpose. Moreover, the promise of good faith should apply not just to institutions but to the individuals within them. The authorities who oversee markets should monitor and audit these promises, ensuring minimum standards and challenging financial institutions to improve.

That our financial institutions are open and transparent. Citizen investors should be able to see in clear language, and the simplest possible math, the nature of any product or service. For asset managers, for example, citizen investors should be able to know where their money is invested, the performance of those investments, and all the costs that have been generated in achieving that performance. They should know of any potential conflict of interest, and the ethics, investment, and time horizon policies of their financial agents.

Citizen investors should have the right to engage with agents, especially where practices fall short of expectations. Agents should have the responsibility of establishing and maintaining productive avenues for engagement.

Financial markets should be aware of, and financial institutions should declare, any holding or agreement they may have that might influence their behavior, for example, in company shares or derivatives, or in a personal loan to a corporate officer. The assets of, and rights associated with, a company should never be used in a way that is not in the company's best interest.

That our financial institutions act as good owners on our behalf. Where financial agents manage assets that give them ownership or contractual rights in their portfolio companies, citizen investors should have the right to know how those agents exercise their ownership and contractual rights to improve long-term value, including how portfolio companies address environmental, social, and governance opportunities and risks. Citizen investors should have the right to a say in these decisions.

That our fiduciaries are accountable to us. No investment without representation: we citizen savers should have the right to identify, assess, and help select or approve the fiduciaries responsible for managing our money. There are many different models to accomplish this, with the main objective being to have in place skilled and prudent fiduciaries working in alignment with the long-term interests of beneficiaries.

These principles represent a starting point. If others want to debate, add to, or subtract from our civil investor charter, that would be a healthy process. The specifics of how accountability is achieved might differ in different countries, just as political representation is fashioned differently among democratic nations. The dialogue over what such standards should look like could be started by different players: civil society, regulators, participants. In our experience, many within the finance industry will support the direction we are suggesting, since most want to do the right thing. But today's incentives mean the finance industry is going to need pushing, and the reformers within the industry will need support.

We have outlined practical fixes to stem the financial industry's slow burn through our wealth. But citizen investors cannot rely on the good will of the entrenched to install such remedies. At the end of the day, it cannot just be about what "they" do with our money. It is about what we do with it.

Notes

Introduction

1. David Pitt-Watson, *Tomorrow's Investor: Building the Consensus for a People's Pension in Britain*, Royal Society for the Arts (2010), www.thersa.org /__data/assets/pdf_file/0009/366948/RSA-TI-report-Pensions.pdf.

2. These fees will include not just the "headline fees," often called the annual management charge, or total expense ratio, but also the hidden charges which she may never learn were taken from her savings.

3. Because Beth has not bought an annuity, the savings remain hers, and so if she dies before she reaches the age of ninety-five, she will be able to leave her residual pension in her will.

4. This calculation assumes that Cathy has purchased an annuity that will rise with inflation. The "money's worth" of that annuity (in other words the income generated relative to the bond investment required to defray the income payment) is 80 percent, which represents the lifetime charge. Because it is invested in bonds, returns have fallen to 2 percent. Unlike Beth, Cathy will not have any residual savings to leave in her will. For more on annuity costs in the United Kingdom see Edmund Cannon and Ian Tonks, *Money's Worth of Pension Annuities*, Department of Work and Pensions Research Report no. 563 (2009).

5. The numbers we have chosen to illustrate pension charges are indicative since charges vary from one plan to another. Further, there are no reliable data on hidden charges that we have included as a cost. Nevertheless the estimate we have given for the triplets is a fair assessment, we believe, of the median full charge for pensions taken out in that last decade. For a fuller discussion of the literature on this topic, see David Pitt-Watson, Christopher Sier, Shyam Moorjani, and Hari Mann, *Investment Costs—An Unknown*

Quantity, Financial Services Consumer Panel (November 2014), https://www.fscp.org.uk/sites/default/files/investment_david_pitt_watson_et_al_final_paper.pdf.

6. Private study obtained by the authors prepared for Her Majesty's Treasury, November 2011.

7. Thomas Philippon, "Has the US Finance Industry Become Less Efficient? On the Theory and Measurement of Financial Intermediation," National Bureau of Economic Research Working Paper no. 18077 (May 2012), http://www.nber.org/papers/w18077.

8. Ronald Gilson and Jeffrey Gordon, "Capital Markets, Efficient Risk Bearing and Corporate Governance: The Agency Costs of Agency Capitalism," Columbia Law School Coursewebs (2012), https://coursewebs.law.columbia.edu/coursewebs/cw_12S_L9519_001.nsf/0f66a77852c3921f852571c100169cb9/C52A6786C57B3B52852579830053479F/$FILE/GilGor+Oxford+Prelim+Draft.Conf+Final.011012.pdf?OpenElement.

9. For instance, see Martijn Cremers and Antti Ptajisto, "How Active Is Your Fund Manager? A New Measure That Predicts Performance" (2009), http://papers.ssrn.com/sol3/papers.cfm?abstract_id=891719.

10. Serdar Çelik and Mats Isaksson, "Institutional Investors as Owners: Who Are They and What Do They Do?" OECD Corporate Governance Working Papers no. 11 (OECD Publishing, 2013), 8.

11. Jeremy Cooper, *Super System Review* (November 12, 2009).

12. Jennifer Taub, "Able but Not Willing: The Failure of Mutual Fund Advisors to Advocate for Shareholders' Rights," SSRN (March 31, 2009), http://papers.ssrn.com/sol3/papers.cfm?abstract_id=1066831##.

13. Lauren Cohen and Breno Schmidt, "Attracting Flows by Attracting Big Clients: Conflicts of Interest and Mutual Fund Portfolio Choice" (2007), http://www.chicagobooth.edu/research/workshops/finance/docs/cohen_attractingflows.pdf.

14. John C. Bogle, *Enough: True Measures of Money, Business, and Life* (John Wiley and Sons, 2009), 82.

15. The Aspen Institute Business and Society Program, *Overcoming Short-Termism: A Call for a More Responsible Approach to Investment and Business Management* (September 9, 2009), www.aspeninstitute.org/sites/default/files/content/docs/bsp/overcome_short_state0909.pdf.

16. Scott Evans, "The Impact of Management Fees on Pension Fund Value," New York City Comptroller's Office, April 9, 2015.

17. Danyelle Jann Guyatt and Jon Lukomnik, "Does Portfolio Turnover Exceed Expectations?," *Rotman International Journal of Pension Manage-*

ment 3, no. 2 (October 2010), http://papers.ssrn.com/sol3/papers.cfm ?abstract_id=1687783.

18. "The Kay Review of UK Equity Markets and Long-Term Decision Making—Interim Report" (February 2011), http://www.bis.gov.uk/assets/bis core/business-law/docs/k/12-631-kay-review-of-equity-markets-interim -report.

19. Andrew Keay, "The Global Financial Crisis: Risk, Shareholder Pressure and Short-Termism in Financial Institutions" (2011), http://papers .ssrn.com/sol3/papers.cfm?abstract_id=1839305.

20. John Graham, Campbell Harvey, and Shiva Rajgopal, "The Economic Implications of Corporate Financial Reporting" (2005), http://faculty.fuqua .duke.edu/~charvey/Research/Working_Papers/W73_The_economic _implications.pdf.

21. One study found that executives who failed to meet two quarterly analyst consensus forecasts in a year get 24 percent less in stock and 14 percent less in cash bonuses than those who match analysts' short-term expectations. Rick Mergenthaler, Shiva Rajgopal, and Suraj Srinivasan, "CEO and CFO Career Penalties to Missing Quarterly Analysts Forecasts" (September 2008), http://hbswk.hbs.edu/item/6019.html.

22. "Breaking the Short-Term Cycle," CFA Centre for Financial Market Integrity and Business Roundtable Institute for Corporate Ethics (July 2006), www.cfapubs.org/toc/ccb/2006/2006/1.

23. Paul MacAvoy and Ira Millstein, *The Recurrent Crisis in Corporate Governance* (Stanford University Press, 2004).

24. John Bogle, who founded Vanguard as a low-fee mutual fund alternative in the United States, and the late Alastair Ross Goobey, who built the UK-based Hermes into a global force for improved corporate governance, are just two examples.

25. This book uses the term "owner" to describe the relationship an investor has with a public company when that investor holds one or more shares in the firm. However, it should be noted that some scholars assert that investors are not technically "owners" of public companies but only of the stock. Lynn A. Stout, *The Shareholder Value Myth: How Putting Shareholders First Harms Investors, Corporations and the Public* (Berrett-Koehler, 2012). In practice, market participants, and many courts, commonly treat investors effectively as owners.

26. Deputy Prime Minister Nick Clegg, Mansion House Speech, January 16, 2012, www.gov.uk/government/speeches/deputy-prime-ministers -speech-at-mansion-house.

27. *Board Practices 2012*, Institutional Shareholder Services (ISS).

28. *Spencer Stuart Board Index 2014*, www.spencerstuart.com/~/media/PDF%20Files/Research%20and%20Insight%20PDFs/SSBI2014web14Nov2014.pdf.

29. *Poison Pills in 2011*, The Conference Board (March 2011), http://www.conference-board.org/publications/publicationdetail.cfm?publicationid=1913.

30. *CEO Succession Practices 2012*, The Conference Board (April 2012), http://www.conference-board.org/publications/publicationdetail.cfm?publicationid=2168; "The Election of Corporate Directors: What Happens When Shareowners Withhold a Majority of Votes from Director Nominees," IRRC Institute and GMI Ratings (August 2012), http://irrcinstitute.org/reports/the-election-of-corporate-directors-what-happens-when-shareowners-withhold-a-majority-of-votes-from-director-nominees/; "Multiple Say-on-Pay Failures Reveal Some Common Themes," Towers Watson (May 22, 2014), www.towerswatson.com/en-US/Insights/Newsletters/Global/executive-pay-matters/2014/Multiple-Say-on-Pay-Failures-Reveal-Some-Common-Themes.

31. An example of this approach may be found in Martin Lipton, Theodore Mirvis, and Jay Lorsch, "The Proposed 'Shareholder Bill of Rights Act of 2009'" (May 12, 2009), ttp://corpgov.law.harvard.edu/2009/05/12/the-proposed-shareholder-bill-of-rights-act-of-2009/.

32. The board's significance was outlined early in Winthrop Knowlton and Ira M. Millstein, "Can the Board of Directors Help the American Corporation Earn the Immortality It Holds So Dear?," in *The US Business Corporation: An Institution in Transition* (Ballinger, 1988). See also MacAvoy and Millstein, *Recurrent Crisis*.

33. University of Chicago professor Frank Knight, of "Knightian uncertainty" fame, was an influential teacher. His students included three Nobel Prize–winning economists: Milton Friedman, George Stigler, and James M. Buchanan.

34. For example, Canadian economist Richard Lipsey wrote of perfect competition that "it is a pity it corresponds in so few aspects to reality as we know it." Richard Lipsey, *Positive Economics* (Weidenfeld and Nicholson, 1973), 299.

1

What's the Financial System For?

1. See discussion in Thomas Philippon, "Has the US Finance Industry Become Less Efficient?" On the Theory and Measurement of Financial Intermediation," National Bureau of Economic Research, Working Paper 18077 (May 2012), 6–9, http://www.nber.org/papers/w18077.

2. See World Bank data at data.worldbank.org/indicator/NV.ARG.TOTL.ZS.

3. For current figures see New York Stock Exchange data at www.nyse.com/about/listed/nya_characterstics.shtml (August 21, 2013).

4. Note that it is not just our deposits at the bank, or safe deposit boxes, that involve safe keeping. Custodians of securities also provide this service and, as a result, become involved in processing securities, foreign exchange, and other transactions.

5. Victor Rothschild, *Meditations of a Broomstick* (HarperCollins, 1977), 17, cited in Niall Ferguson, *The Ascent of Money: A Financial History of the World* (Penguin Press, 2008), 65.

6. Banks may sometimes choose to invest a portion of their deposits in cash or other securities rather than loan all of them.

7. Throughout this book we use the term "limited liability company" to mean any company which can assemble capital from multiple individuals or entities and which wholly or partially shields those providers of capital from liabilities which may be incurred by the company.

8. The abusive sale of indulgences was such a problem in the thirteenth century, the era of our time traveler, that reform of the system was a subject of the fourth Lateran council of 1215. See text of fourth Lateran council (1215), 63–66, https://www.ewtn.com/library/COUNCILS/LATERAN4.HTM.

2

Incentives Gone Wild

1. Thomas Philippon, "Has the US Finance Industry Become Less Efficient? On the Theory and Measurement of Financial Intermediation," National Bureau of Economic Research Working Paper no. 18077 (May 2012), http://www.nber.org/papers/w18077http://www.nber.org/papers/w18077.

2. During the same period, GDP per capita, which is an approximate measure of productivity, increased about tenfold. See http://www

.worldeconomics.com/Data/MadisonHistoricalGDP/Madison%20Historical%20GDP%20Data.efp. Of course, different industries have made different contributions to that increase. However, we can find no major industry where the measured increase on productivity is zero. Indeed, if one considers industries that might perform a similar "intermediation" function, such as retailing, which brings together buyers and sellers of goods, recent productivity increases have been very large. In the 1990s, retailing was responsible for a full one third of all US productivity growth. See McKinsey Global Institute, "US Productivity Growth 1995–2000" (McKinsey Global Institute, 2001).

3. Philippon, "Has the US Finance Industry Become Less Efficient?"

4. Between fund management fees, trading costs, and administrative fees, many people pay at least that much.

5. David Pitt-Watson, "Tomorrow's Investor: Building the Consensus for a People's Pension in Britain" (RSA Projects, December 2010), https://www.thersa.org/discover/publications-and-articles/reports/building-the-consensus-for-a-peoples-pension-in-britain/.

6. These calculations assume that savings are accumulated for forty years and that the pension pays out over the following twenty years. Inflation is assumed at 3 percent, and nominal returns at 6 percent. Annual payments into and out of the fund rise with inflation. Other assumptions may lead to slightly different results, but all underline the significance of what may seem like quite modest annual fees.

7. Arthur Levitt, comments on Bloomberg Radio, November 8, 2013.

8. Khaldoun Khashanah, Ionut Florescu, and Steve Yang, "On the Impact and Future of High Frequency Trading—White Paper" (Stevens Institute of Technology and IRRC Institute, May 10, 2014).

9. Bradley Hope and Julie Steinberg, "Payments to Big Brokers under Fresh Scrutiny," *Wall Street Journal*, June 13, 2014, http://blogs.wsj.com/moneybeat/2014/06/13/payments-to-big-brokers-under-fresh-scrutiny/.

10. Ibid.

11. Adam Smith, *The Wealth of Nations* (1776; repr. Alfred A. Knopf, 1991).

12. Amanda White, "Serving Itself: Why the Financial Services Industry Needs Reform," top1000funds.com, November 6, 2013.

13. Fiduciary Duties of Investment Intermediaries—Consultation Paper 215 (Law Commission, October 2013), 55–56, http://lawcommission.justice.gov.uk/docs/cp215_fiduciary_duties.pdf.

14. Jeremy Cooper, "Super in the New Age: Scale, Focus and Alignment," presentation to the Australian Superannuation Funds Association Conference, November 12, 2009, Melbourne, Australia.

15. John A. Turner and Nari Rhee, "Issue Brief: Lessons for Private Sector Retirement Security from Australia, Canada and the Netherlands" (National Institute on Retirement Security, August 2013).

16. A few funds, primarily alternative funds such as hedge and private equity funds, charge performance fees based on how well the fund does. However, in virtually all cases, those performance fees are in addition to asset-based fees.

17. Note that these are only the declared charges to the fund and do not include the cost of trading securities and other charges that are billed directly to the savers' accounts. *2013 Investment Company Fact Book* (Investment Company Institute, 2013), www.icifactbook.org/fb_ch5.html, accessed July 28, 2013.

18. "2012: Annual Global Flows Report" (Morningstar Fund Research, March 7, 2013).

19. "U.S. plan sponsors managing over $13 trillion rely on investment consultants for advice about which funds to invest in. . . . We find no evidence that these recommendations add value." Tim Jenkinson, Howard Jones, and Jose Vincente Martinez, "Picking Winners? Investment Consultants' Recommendations of Fund Managers" (Social Science Research Network, September 17, 2013), http://papers.ssrn.com/sol3/papers.cfm?abstract_id=2327042.

20. "2012: Annual Global Flows Report."

21. Keith C. Brown and W. Van Harlow, "How Good Are the Investment Options Provided by Defined Contribution Plan Sponsors?," *International Journal of Portfolio Analysis and Management* 1, no. 1 (2012): 3–31.

22. Ibid.

23. Andrew B. Weisman, "Informationless Investing and Hedge Fund Performance Measurement Bias," *Journal of Portfolio Management* 28, no. 4 (Summer 2002): 80–91.

24. See, generally, Nicholas Dunbar, *Inventing Money* (John Wiley and Sons, 2000).

25. Investors call these strategies "short volatility" because if the relationship of the prices remains stable, then it's a winning strategy. If it is volatile and if it moves in the opposite direction of what is expected, you can lose everything.

26. Paul De Grauwe, Centre for European Policy Studies Policy Brief, November 2008.

27. Technically, the most common risk models call for predictions of the future, specifically for how the price of one financial asset will move, both generally and in relation to other financial assets, in the future. These expected returns, expected volatility, and expected correlations are really just educated guesses of specific parts of future scenarios. But what that means is that for the models to predict the future, they need to know what parts of the future will look like. There are various ways to overcome that practical impossibility. By far the most common is to use some aspects of the present and the past to create the assumptions that feed the models.

28. Note that we include the leap days that would have occurred over the decade. One major problem with the mad mathematics on Wall Street is that precision implies trustworthiness, and 3,652 days sounds very exact. But using data from 3,652 days rather than 3,650 days does nothing to improve the model's ability to predict crises if the two extra days are also routine.

29. In fact the example given (De Grauwe, Centre for European Studies Policy Brief) uses thirty-seven years of data, but ten years is not an atypical period to use.

30. Kate Burgess and Robert Budden, "FSA Ends Split Capital Probe," *Financial Times*, May 21, 2007.

31. The assumption of a "one-way" market for financial assets seems a repetitive theme. One major contributor to the 2007–2008 global financial crisis was the assumption that the US residential property market would only appreciate.

32. Rupert Jones, "Split Capital Scandal Is FSA's Biggest Ever Case," *The Guardian*, July 18, 2003.

33. Bob Herz, "Lesson Learned, Relearned and Relearned Again from the Credit Crisis—Accounting and Beyond" (Financial Accounting Standards Board, September 18, 2008), http://www.fasb.org/news/09-18-08 _herz_speech.pdf.

34. Stilpon Nestor, "Evidence to the Parliamentary Commission on Banking Standards," January 4, 2013. http://www.publications.parliament .uk/pa/jt201314/jtselect/jtpcbs/27/27viii_we_c13.htm.

35. John Y. Campbell, "Diversification: A Bigger Free Lunch" (July 7, 2000), down.cenet.org.cn/upfile/36/2005417221658163.pdf. "Economists are famous for pronouncing gloomily that 'there's no such thing as a free lunch.' Yet finance theory *does* offer a free lunch: the reduction in risk that is obtainable through diversification. An investor who spreads her wealth among many investments can reduce the volatility of her portfolio, pro-

vided only that the underlying investments are imperfectly correlated. There need be no reduction in average return and thus no bill for the lunch."

36. More recently, there has been a movement to "smart" beta, or to using different factors other than market weight to determine the weight of the stocks in the index. While some of the factors, such as company revenues, may be independent of the need for active investors, others, such as the volatility of the individual stocks or low valuation stocks (as judged by common ratios such as price to earnings, price to sales, or price to book) may still be reliant upon how others in the market act and invest. Rob Arnott, the guru of smart beta, notes that it works best when the factors that determine the weighting are not linked to stock price (Bloomberg Radio interview, November 15, 2013).

37. A number of large, diversified investors, such as the California Public Employees Retirement System (CalPERS), have active engagement programs. As universal owners, they have an interest in the overall market functioning efficiently, and in the interest of the investors. See, generally, James P. Hawley and Andrew T. Williams, *The Rise of Fiduciary Capitalism: How Institutional Investors Can Make Corporate America More Democratic* (University of Pennsylvania Press, 2000). However, they tend to be concerned with systemic issues such as governance structures and risk disclosures. By contrast, activist investment managers, who deeply research and then engage with individual companies, tend to have concentrated portfolios of just a few companies, so as to reduce the diversification effect.

38. See, for example, William K. Black, "When 'Liar Loans' Flourish," *New York Times*, January 30, 2011.

39. Saving and investing for retirement is by far the dominant reason for people to invest at all. Some 92 percent of US retail investors surveyed listed savings for retirement as one of their key rationales for investing, with nearly three quarters saying it was the single most important reason. "Institute Publishes Results from the 2013 Mutual Fund Shareholder Tracking Survey," Memorandum to Pension Members No. 52-13 (Investment Company Institute, November 7, 2013).

40. Peter Brady, Kimberly Burham, and Sarah Holden, "The Success of the US Retirement System" (Investment Company Institute, 2012).

41. Technically, alpha is an intercept line on a regression of a portfolio's return against a market return and measures idiosyncratic returns of a portfolio, but it is more commonly used to be a measurement of excess return due to skill. "Excess" return can be either positive or negative.

42. Gary P. Brinson, Brian D. Singer, and Gilbert L. Beebower, "Determinants of Portfolio Performance II: An Update," *Financial Analysts Journal* 47, no. 3 (May–June 1991): 40–48.

43. Lu Wang, Whitney Kisling, and Eric Lam, "Fake Post Erasing $136 Billion Shows Market Needs Humans" (Bloomberg News Service, April 24, 2013).

44. Ibid.

45. Ibid.

46. "Findings Regarding the Market Events of May 6, 2010: Report of the Staffs of the CFTC and SEC to the Joint Advisory Committee on Emerging Regulatory Issues" (US Commodity Futures Trading Commission and US Securities and Exchange Commission, September 30, 2010).

47. Tom Lauricella, Kara Scannell, and Jenny Strasburg, "How a Trading Algorithm Went Awry: Flash-Crash Report Finds a 'Hot Potato' Volume Effect from Same Positions Passed Back and Forth," *Wall Street Journal*, October 2, 2010.

48. Ibid.

49. Wang, Kisling, and Lam, "Fake Post Erasing $136 Billion."

50. Larry Tabb, Tabb Group, "High Frequency Trading: What Is It and Should I Be Worried?," presentation to the World Federation of Exchanges, Cambridge, MA, November 2009.

51. Chris Sier, interview for this book, April 25, 2015.

52. Andrea Dang, David Dupont, and Mark Heale, "The Time Has Come for Standardized Total Cost Disclosure for Private Equity" (CEM Benchmarking, April 2015), www.cembenchmarking.com.

53. In fact, one of the authors of the present work recommended its use, first in 2002, to one of the largest bond managers in the world and, five years later, to reduce risk in a large Canadian company's pension fund, in time to save millions when the global financial crisis hit.

54. Rick Baert, "LDI Bandwagon Rolling On," *Pensions and Investments*, March 4, 2013.

55. www.tradingeconomics.com/united-states/government-bond-yield, accessed May 5, 2013.

56. "Investor Trust Study: 2013" (CFA Institute and Edelman, 2013), www.cfainstitute.org/investortrust.

57. There are issues created by the widespread adoption of cheap beta strategies. As we've seen, mass adoption of diversification can allow risks to build up in the system, even while decreasing the risk to an investor of something going wrong with any one investment. Thankfully, thought

leaders like the Royal Society of the Arts are trying to mitigate those risks and accentuate the positives. We discuss how in chapter 5.

58. "Passive Investing Has Room to Grow," *Financial Times*, September 23, 2012.

59. "Investors Shift to Low-Cost 'Tracker' Funds," *The Telegraph*, February 12, 2013.

60. www.unpri.org, accessed September 21, 2014.

61. "Public Funds Take Control of Assets, Dodging Wall Street," *New York Times*, August 19, 2013.

62. Ibid.

63. US Department of Labor, "Fact Sheet: Final Rule to Improve Transparency of Fees and Expenses to Workers in 401(k)-Type Retirement Plans" (US Department of Labor, February 2012).

64. Ibid.

3

The Return of Ownership

1. Robert Monks and Allen Sykes, "Capitalism without Owners Will Fail: A Policymaker's Guide to Reform" (Center for the Study of Financial Innovation, 2002).

2. Merriam-Webster.com defines capitalism as "an economic system characterized by private or corporate ownership of capital goods, by investments that are determined by private decision, and by prices, production, and the distribution of goods that are determined mainly by competition in a free market." Other dictionaries similarly cite private ownership as central to the definition of capitalism. www.merriam-webster .com/dictionary/capitalism, accessed September 27, 2013. Indeed, for economists such as Ronald Coase and Friedrich Hayek, the marriage of ownership and control rights is essential to the effective working of the system.

3. Warren Buffett, letter in 2002 Annual Report of Berkshire Hathaway.

4. James Saft, "The Wisdom of Exercising Patience in Investing" (Reuters, March 2, 2012). This is not a new phenomenon. The average duration of mutual fund holdings has not changed much in a quarter of a century, averaging about 1.2 to 1.5 years, according to University of Notre Dame research professor Martijn Cremers. Martin Cremers, Ankur Pareek, and Zacharias Sautner, "Stock Duration and Misvaluation" (2013), www .geneva-summit-on-sustainable-finance.ch/wp-content/ . . . /sautner.pdf.

5. Warren Buffett, letter in 1988 Annual Report of Berkshire Hathaway.

6. "Understanding High Frequency Trading," World Federation of Exchanges (May 20, 2013), www.worldexchanges.org/files/statistics/pdf/WFE_Undeerstanding%20HFT_May%202013.pdf.

7. Comments of Aaron Cowen at "The Shape of Things to Come," October 1, 2013.

8. One of the best-known exponents of this strategy was Philip Fisher, author of *Common Stocks and Uncommon Profits*, a classic textbook of practical investment. Philip A. Fisher, *Common Stocks and Uncommon Profits, and Other Writings*, 2nd ed. (Chichester, NY: Wiley, 2003).

9. Google search, July 28, 2015.

10. Danyelle Guyatt and Jon Lukomnik, "Does Portfolio Turnover Exceed Expectations?," *Rotman International Journal of Pension Management* 3, no. 2 (Fall 2010): 40. These were managers who oversee money for pension funds, endowments, insurance companies, and others, and so do not have the variable daily cash flows that can cause turnover at mutual funds.

11. Andrew Haldane, "The Short Long," speech delivered at 29th Société Universitaire Européene de Recherches Financières Colloquium: New Paradigms in Money and Finance?, May 2011, www.bankofengland.co.uk/archive/Documents/historicpubs/speeches/2011/speech495.pdf.

12. Ibid.

13. John R. Graham, Campbell R. Harvey, and Shiva Rajgopal, "The Economic Implications of Corporate Financial Reporting," *Journal of Accounting and Economics* 40, nos. 1–3 (December 2005): 3–73.

14. Ibid.

15. "The Alignment Gap between Creating Value, Performance Measurement and Long-Term Incentive Design" (IRRC Institute and Organizational Capital Partners, 2014).

16. Steve Denning, "Good News! Executives Realize They Are 'In over Their Heads'" (Forbes.com, June 11, 2013), www.forbes.com/sites/steve denning/2013/06/11/good-news-execs-see-they-are-in-over-their-heads/. There is an ongoing academic argument about the exact level of decline in return on assets and return on invested capital, but most experts agree that the decline exists and is material.

17. "Alignment Gap."

18. Ibid.

19. Steven Balsam, "Taxes and Executive Compensation," Economic Policy Institute Briefing Paper no. 344 (August 14, 2012).

20. David Hizenrath, "Clinton Proposes Limit on Executive Pay Deduction," *Washington Post*, April 9, 1993.

21. Lawrence Mishell and Natalie Sabadish, "CEO Pay and the Top 1%: How Executive Compensation and Financial Sector Pay Have Fueled Income Inequality," Economic Policy Institute Briefing Paper no. 331 (May 2, 2011).

22. Christopher Cox, "Testimony Concerning Backdating" (US Senate Committee on Banking, Housing and Urban Affairs, September 6, 2006).

23. Internal Revenue Service code, Section 162(m).

24. Elliot Blair Smith, "Companies Use IRS to Raise Bonuses with Earnings Goals" (Bloomberg, September 13, 2013).

25. See, generally, Lucian Bebchuk and Jesse Fried, *Pay without Performance: The Unfilled Promise of Executive Compensation* (Harvard University Press, 2006).

26. Raymond Gilmartin, comments to 2013 Board Leadership Conference of the National Association of Corporate Directors, Washington, DC.

27. Steve Tatton, "Executive Remuneration in the FTSE 350—A Focus on Performance-Related Pay" (Income Data Services for the High Pay Centre, October 2014). A US study found the same general result. Economic profitability accounted for only 12 percent of the variation in CEO pay. "Alignment Gap."

28. "The Financial Crisis Inquiry Report—Final Report of the National Commission on the Causes of the Financial and Economic Crisis in the United States" (Financial Crisis Inquiry Commission, January 2011).

29. Carola Frydman and Dirk Jenter, "CEO Compensation," Rock Center for Corporate Governance at Stanford University Working Paper no. 77 (March 19, 2010): "The literature provides ample evidence that CEO compensation and portfolio incentives are correlated with a wide variety of corporate behaviors, from investment and financial policies to risk taking and manipulation"; Lucian Bebchuk and Yaniv Grinstein, "Firm Expansion and CEO Pay," National Bureau of Economic Research Working Paper no. 11886 (November 2005).

30. Bebchuk and Grinstein, "Firm Expansion and CEO Pay."

31. In the United Kingdom, for example, it was RBS, which had embarked on rapid acquisition, and HBOS and Northern Rock, which had been aggressive in the market place, who found themselves in greatest trouble.

32. "Governing Banks" (Global Governance Forum/International Finance Corporation, 2010).

33. Upton Sinclair, "I, Candidate for Governor: And How I Got Licked" (University of California Press, 1994). (Originally printed 1936.)

34. Ronald J. Gilson and Jeffrey N. Gordon, "The Agency Costs of Agency Capitalism: Activist Investors and the Revaluation of Governance Rights," March 11, 2013, *Columbia Law Review*, 2013, ECGI—Law Working Paper no. 197, Columbia Law and Economics Working Paper no. 438, Rock Center for Corporate Governance at Stanford University Working Paper no. 130, http://papers.ssrn.com/sol3/papers.cfm?abstract_id=2206391.

35. "Tom Jones to Keep Citigroup Fund Unit on Song," *Financial Times*, June 16, 2003.

36. Increasingly, ownership responsibilities are being integrated into portfolio management functions. What this means practically is that portfolio analysts and portfolio managers are participating in ownership activities, such as voting. However, most firms still use separate ownership groups, which often report to compliance or legal rather than to portfolio management.

37. Authors' survey, 2014.

38. Kate Iannelli, "Going Private," National Association of Corporate Directors Leadership Blog, January 3, 2013, http://blog.nacdonline.org/category/corporate-board-composition/page/2/.

39. Blackrock, "About Us: Responsible Investment," www.blackrock.com/corporate/en-us/about-us/responsible-investment, accessed August 16, 2013.

40. Hermes Investment Management, www.hermes.co.uk/corporateinformation/Overview/Whoweare/tabid/2842/language/en-US/Default.aspx., accessed August 16, 2013; Trillium Asset Management, www.trilliuminvest.com, accessed August 16, 2013; Pax World Investments, www.paxworld.com, accessed August 16, 2013.

41. Susanne Craig, "The Giant of Shareholders, Quietly Stirring," *New York Times*, May 18, 2013.

42. Perversely, some of the industry's most regressive forces criticize efforts to be long-term owners as violations of the fund's fiduciary duties, claiming that because others also benefit, such actions run contrary to the idea of a fund's acting for the exclusive benefit of its investors or beneficiaries, even though those investors or beneficiaries would also prosper. Such arguments are increasingly being rebutted through thoughtful legal opinions, including two that won the prestigious IRRC Institute Paper Prize for 2012 and 2013. Inapt standards of fiduciary duty, as we discuss in chapter 5, are important drivers of misalignment between agents and citizen investors.

43. Gilson and Gordon, "Agency Costs of Agency Capitalism."

44. Kimberly Gladman, Agnes Grunfeld, and Michelle Lamb, "The Election of Corporate Directors: What Happens When Shareowners Withhold a Majority of Votes from Director Nominees?" (IRRC Institute and GMI Ratings, August 2012). Even in situations with a soft form of majority voting, escape hatches that allow directors to stay on in certain situations are employed so frequently they have become the norm rather than the exception: only 8 percent of directors in such companies step down soon after the election.

45. We use the pronoun "he" deliberately. In the United States in 2013, only 16.6 percent of American corporate directors were women, according to GMI Ratings. In the United Kingdom, the number was roughly 19 percent, according to Cranfield University. The highest percentage in the world is believed to be Norway, at just over 36 percent, according to GMI Ratings.

46. Warren Buffett, letter in 2002 annual report of Berkshire Hathaway.

47. Henry T. C. Hu and Bernard Black, "The New Vote Buying: Empty Voting and Hidden (Morphable) Ownership," *Southern California Law Review* 79 (2006), 811–908.

48. Ibid. That merger was also a prime example of the problems with agency capitalism. HP's management was very worried about losing the vote. It heard that Deutsche Bank, a major owner of HP's stock through its asset management arm, was likely to vote against the merger. HP's then CEO Carly Fiorina convened a conference call with high Deutsche Bank officials, not with the asset management analysts responsible for judging the proposed deal, and told them that how asset management people voted on the issue would affect Deutsche Bank's overall banking relationships with HP. The bank's senior management summoned the analysts to an emergency meeting and reportedly pressured them to reverse their vote. Deutsche wound up voting for the merger. Deutsche, of course, managed that money for thousands, if not millions, of individuals and had a fiduciary obligation to them to vote the way it saw best for them, not necessarily what was best for Deutsche Bank.

49. Henry T. C. Hu and Bernard Black, "Equity and Debt Decoupling and Empty Voting II: Importance and Extensions," *University of Pennsylvania Law Review* 156 (2008): 625–739.

50. The authors of this book have served on a number of creditor committees. On at least one occasion, we have thought that other "creditors" have hedged their positions using credit default swaps, a type of derivative. Our opinion is that their participation in the reorganization process was not helpful, as their economic interests were not in reorganizing

the company. This sounds technical and like a matter only of interest to "vulture investors" (banks and hedge funds), but the company involved was Adelphia Communications, which was the fifth largest cable television company in the United States, employing thousands of people. Destroying value in it could have cost hundreds or thousands of people their jobs.

51. Rock Center for Corporate Governance at Stanford and IRRC Institute, "Identifying the Legal Contours of the Separation of Economic Rights of Economic Rights and Voting Rights in Publicly Held Corporations" (IRRC Institute, October 2010).

52. Jon Lukomnik and Nicole Sandford, "Executive Compensation: The Alignment Myth," *Directorship*, January 24, 2013.

53. Ibid.

54. Gilmartin, comments to 2013 Board Leadership Conference of the National Association of Corporate Directors.

55. Conversation with Jon Lukomnik, September 2011.

56. Jon Lukomnik, "U-Turn for Executive Comp?" (September 13, 2011), www.sinclaircapital.com/blog/.

57. Charles M. Elson and Craig K. Ferrere, "Executive Superstars, Peer Groups and Overcompensation: Cause, Effect and Solution," *Journal of Corporation Law* 38, no. 3 (Spring 2013): 487–531.

58. "New Executive Compensation Research: Peer Group Benchmarking Inherently Flawed and Inflationary," press release (IRRC Institute, September 22, 2012).

59. "Alignment Gap."

60. Ibid.

61. Capital Institute, "Evergreen Direct Investing: Co-creating the Regenerative Economy," September 2013.

62. Ben Protess, "New York Stock Exchange Settles Case over Early Data Access," *New York Times*, September 14, 2012.

63. Securities and Exchange Commission, "Order Approving a Proposed Rule Change Amending the NYSE Amex Options Fee Schedule to Provide for Additional Co-location Services and Establish Related Fees" (August 15, 2012), www.sec.gov/rules/sro/nysemkt/2012/34-67665.pdf.

64. Elisse Walter, comments at PricewaterhouseCoopers Investors' Exchange, Chicago, IL, September 24, 2013.

65. Jacob Goldstein, "Putting a Speed Limit on the Stock Market," *New York Times*, October 8, 2013.

66. Khaldoun Khashanah, Ionut Florescu, and Steve Yang, "On the Impact and Future of High Frequency Trading" (Stevens Institute of Technology, May 10, 2014).

67. www.shareaction.org.uk, accessed August 16, 2013; www.cdproject .net, accessed August 16, 2013; www.fandc.com. Author David Pitt-Watson is a founder of Hermes EOS; author Stephen Davis is a non-executive director of the firm.

68. Ceres, www.ceres.org, accessed August 16, 2013.

69. ICGN Global Governance Principles, www.icgn.org.

70. www.sharegate.com, accessed November 11, 2013.

71. Ibid.

72. John Endean, "The Untapped Power of Individual Investors," *Wall Street Journal*, October 5, 2014.

73. Ibid.

74. Aspen Institute, "Overcoming Short-Termism: A Call for a More Responsible Approach to Investment and Business Management" (Aspen Institute, September 9, 2009).

75. Hu and Black, "New Vote Buying."

4
Not with My Money

1. Funston Advisory Services, "Fiduciary Audit Report of the South Carolina Retirement System Investment Commission" (Funston Advisory Services, April 18, 2014). Author Jon Lukomnik participated in the review.

2. Ben W. Heineman Jr., and Stephen Davis, *Are Institutional Investors Part of the Problem or Part of the Solution?* (Committee for Economic Development and Yale School of Management-Millstein Center for Corporate Governance and Performance, October 2011), 13.

3. Some scholars assert that institutional investors are not technical owners of public companies even though they own company stock. Lynn A. Stout, *The Shareholder Value Myth: How Putting Shareholders First Harms Investors, Corporations and the Public* (Berrett-Koehler Publishers, 2012). Others such as Yale Law School's Jon Macey counter that shareowner value is the default objective of public corporations regardless of the legal distinction. See a May 1, 2013, debate at the American Enterprise Institute at www.aei.org/events/2013/05/01/shareholder-value-theory-myth-or -motivator/.

4. Keith Ambachtsheer, Ronald Capelle, and Hubert Lum, "The Pension Governance Deficit: Still with Us" (Social Science Research Network, 2008), http://papers.ssrn.com/sol3/papers.cfm?abstract_id=1280907. Critics

rightly caution that while the study finds correlation between fund governance and performance, causation is elusive. In other words, outperformance could help produce good governance rather than the other way around. Also, the period of four years examined by the authors is relatively short given retirement timeframes.

5. To illustrate, apply the academic projection to the real world. Let's plug in numbers for an employee at age thirty who starts with a $50,000 a year salary and typical contributions to a 401(k). She would wind up with a $318,000 nest egg at a poorly run fund; the same level of pay and savings would produce some $404,000 at a well-governed fund. For a worker earning $100,000 at the start, the twenty-year outcome would be $590,000 as compared with an optimum $753,000. The price tag for subpar accountability would seem to be substantial if the Ambachtsheer gap holds up under further investigation.

6. *Super System Review Final Report—Part One Overview and Recommendations* (Super System Review, June 30, 2010), www.afr.com/rw/2009-2014/AFR/2010/07/05/Photos/0d280174-87d8-11df-bbd0-8f855dd2fda9_SSR%20Final%20Report%20Part%201.pdf, section 6.1.

7. Kathryn L. Dewenter, Xi Han, and Paul H. Malatesta, "Firm Values and Sovereign Wealth Fund Investments," *Journal of Financial Economics* 98, no. 2 (November 2010): 256–78.

8. Lauren Pavlenko Lutton, Katie Rushkewicz, Kailin Liu, and Xin Ling, *Morningstar 2011 Mutual Fund Stewardship Grade Research Paper* (Morningstar Fund Research, March 2011), http://corporate.morningstar.com/us/documents/methodologydocuments/MethodologyPapers/StewardshipGradeMethodology.pdf.

9. Gordon L. Clark, "Pension Fund Governance 1: Expertise and Organisational Form" (Pennsylvania State University, College of Information Sciences and Technology), February 16, 2004, http://citeseerx.ist.psu.edu/viewdoc/download?doi=10.1.1.198.5727&rep=rep1&type=pdf.

10. Jennifer Taub, "Able but Not Willing: The Failure of Mutual Fund Advisers to Advocate for Shareholders' Rights," *Journal of Corporation Law* 34, no. 3 (2009): 844–93.

11. Lauren Cohen and Breno Schmidt, "Attracting Flows by Attracting Big Clients: Conflicts of Interest and Mutual Fund Portfolio Choice," www.chicagobooth.edu/research/workshops/finance/docs/Cohen_Attracting Flows.pdf.

12. Martijn Cremers, Joost Driessen, Pascal Maenhout, and David Weinbaum, "Does Skin in the Game Matter? Director Incentives and Gov-

ernance in the Mutual Fund Industry," *Journal of Financial and Quantitative Analysis* 44 (2009): 1345–73.

13. Fiona Stewart and Juan Yermo, "Pension Fund Governance: Challenges and Potential Solutions," OECD Working Papers on Insurance and Private Pensions no. 18 (OECD Publishing, 2008), doi:10.1787/241402256531.

14. Josh Lerner, Ann Leamon, and Vladimir Bosiljevac, "Measurement, Governance and Long-Term Investing" (World Economic Forum, March 2012), www3.weforum.org/docs/WEF_IV_MeasurementGovernanceLongtermInvesting_Report_2012.pdf.

15. Simon C. Y. Wong, "Why Stewardship Is Proving Elusive for Institutional Investors," *Butterworths Journal of International Banking and Financial Law* (July–August 2010), http://papers.ssrn.com/sol3/papers.cfm?abstract_id=1635662.

16. Jonathan Stempel, "NY Mets Owner Wilpon Sued over Madoff Losses" (Reuters, July 30, 2010).

17. A. Wood, D. Wintersgill, and N. Baker, "Pensions Landscape and Charging: Quantitative and Qualitative Research with Employers and Pension Providers" (Department of Work and Pensions, 2012).

18. Co-authors Stephen Davis and Jon Lukomnik are associated with Funston Advisory.

19. "Local UK Pension Schemes Waste Millions on High Fees," *Financial Times*, March 29, 2015.

20. Clark, "Pension Fund Governance."

21. *Pension Plans: Additional Transparency and Other Actions Needed in Connection with Proxy Voting*, Government Accountability Office GAO 04-749 (August 2004), www.gao.gov/assets/250/243646.pdf.

22. In the United Kingdom, there is a similar split between the pension regulator and the FCA. The former is criticized for lacking the powers to intervene before problems arise, and is instead restricted to "closing the barn door after the horse has bolted."

23. www.apra.gov.au/Super/PrudentialFramework/Documents/Final-SPS-510-Governance-November-2012.pdf and *FSC Superannuation Corporate Governance Policy—Raising the Bar*, http://fsc.org.au/downloads/file/submissionsfile/fscsupercorporategovernancefinal.pdf.

24. See www.rijksoverheid.nl/nieuws/2013/07/09/wetsvoorstel-versterking-bestuur-pensioenfondsen-aanvaard.html.

25. *OECD Guidelines for Pension Fund Governance* (Organisation for Economic Co-operation and Development, June 2009), www.oecd.org/daf/fin/private-pensions/34799965.pdf.

26. *Review into the Governance Efficiency, Structure, and Operation of Australia's Superannuation System: Final Report* (2010), www.afr.com/rw /2009-2014/AFR/2010/07/05/Photos/0d280174-87d8-11df-bbd0-8f855dd2fda9 _SSR%20Final%20Report%20Part%201.pdf, p. 11.

27. *Achieving the Right Balance: CalPERS Board Governance Study-Final Report* (Funston Advisory Services, September 2011), www.calpers .ca.gov/eip-docs/about/board-cal-agenda/agendas/boardgov/201110/item3 attachb.pdf. Two of this book's coauthors, Lukomnik and Davis, were associated with the study.

28. Reports provided to Davis in April 2012 courtesy of PFZW and PGGM.

29. One 2008 academic study found that Dutch beneficiaries would also accept a higher premium or lower retirement benefit if that is necessary to invest more responsibly. Derk Erbé, "StilleKapitalisten: Eensociologischonderzoek over de invloed en controle van deelnemers op het beleggingsbeleid van hunpensioenfonds" (University of Amsterdam, 2008).

30. See Triodos Bank, www.triodos.co.uk.

31. www.top1000funds.com/analysis/2013/08/16/calpers-a-new-framework -of-economy/.

32. *CalPERS Beliefs: Thought Leadership for Generations to Come* (June 2014), p. 5, www.calpers.ca.gov/docs/board-agendas/201501/full/day1/itemo1 -04-01.pdf.

33. Towers Watson, *We Need a Bigger Boat* (August 2012).

34. United Nations Global Compact, UNEP Finance Initiative, Principles for Responsible Investment, *Fiduciary Duty in the 21st Century* (September 2015).

35. Generation Investment Management, "Sustainable Capitalism" (February 15, 2012), www.generationim.com/media/pdf-generation-sustainable -capitalism-v1.pdf.

36. See the UK code at www.frc.org.uk/Our-Work/Codes-Standards /Corporate-governance/UK-Stewardship-Code.aspx; the Dutch at www .eumedion.nl/en/public/knowledgenetwork/best-practices/best_practices -engaged-share-ownership.pdf; and South Africa's at http://c.ymcdn.com /sites/www.iodsa.co.za/resource/resmgr/crisa/crisa_19_july_2011.pdf?hh SearchTerms=%22responsible%22.

37. The authors are founders (Stephen Davis, Jon Lukomnik) and a director (David Pitt-Watson) of the ICGN.

38. Institutional Investor Responsibilities (2013), https://www.icgn.org /policy/guidance.

39. www.youtube.com/watch?v=5YGc4zOqozo.

40. David Benoit, "Carl Icahn Wants to Create Twitter Movement," *Wall Street Journal*, September 9, 2013, http://blogs.wsj.com/moneybeat/2013/09/09/carl-icahn-wants-to-create-twitter-movement/.

41. http://navalny.livejournal.com/.

42. "Access Blocked to Major Opposition Sites and Navalny's Blog," *Moscow Times*, March 14, 2014, www.themoscowtimes.com/news/article/access-blocked-to-major-opposition-sites-and-navalnys-blog/496148.html.

43. See http://blogs.law.harvard.edu/corpgov/.

44. www.dealbreaker.com.

45. Speech by Secretary of State Hillary Rodham Clinton to the Community of Democracies (Krakow, July 3, 2010), http://iipdigital.usembassy.gov/st/english/texttrans/2010/07/20100703224911ptellivremoso.4888836.html#axzz3nyrKbWVZ.

46. *Fact Sheet on Non-Governmental Organizations in the US*, January 12, 2012, http://iipdigital.usembassy.gov/st/english/texttrans/2012/01/20120130171036romao.1718823.html#axzz2eKQtP9A8.

47. "You're Making a Killing in Darfur" (Save Darfur Coalition, October 1, 2007), www.youtube.com/watch?v=y31TNgu-Nf4. See also Investors Against Genocide at www.investorsagainstgenocide.org.

48. See www.aodproject.net.

49. Megan Darby, "No Greenwash: Investors Urged to Disclose Climate Strategy" (Responding to Climate Change, September 9, 2014), www.rtcc.org/2014/09/30/no-greenwash-investors-urged-to-disclose-climate-strategy/.

50. For instance, see "New Study: More U.S. Mutual Fund Companies Supporting Climate Change Resolutions, but Big Firms Still Lagging," Ceres media release (June 5, 2013), www.ceres.org/press/press-releases/new-study-more-u.s.-mutual-fund-companies-supporting-climate-change-resolutions-but-big-firms-still-lagging.

51. www.350.org.

52. See "Mutual Funds and CEO Pay" (AFL-CIO Executive Paywatch), www.aflcio.org/Corporate-Watch/CEO-Pay-and-You/Mutual-Funds-CEO-Pay.

53. See www.shareaction.org. Coauthor Stephen Davis is a non-executive trustee of ShareAction.

54. See www.proxydemocracy.org/fund_owners.

55. Shareholder Association for Research and Education, www.share.ca.

56. Trade Union Congress: Member Trustees, https://www.tuc.org.uk/economic-issues/pensions-and-retirement/member-trustees.

57. CFA Institute, "Pension Trustee Code of Conduct," www.cfainstitute
.org/ethics/codes/pension/Pages/index.aspx.
58. Responsible Endowments Coalition, www.endowmentethics.org.
59. www.pushyourparents.org.
60. *Murninghan Post*, August 29, 2013, http://murninghanpost.com
/2013/08/29/lets-bend-the-arc-of-money-and-power-toward-justice/.
61. For example, Paul Woolley at the Centre for the Study of Market
Dysfunctionality, London School of Economics. See www.lse.ac.uk/fmg
/researchProgrammes/paulWoolleyCentre/home.aspx.

5

The New Geometry of Regulation

1. P. Harle, E. Luders, T. Pepanides, S. Pfetsch, T. Poppensiekr, and U.
Stegemann, "Basel III and European Banking," McKinsey Working Papers
on Risk no. 26 (McKinsey, 2010). Economist Andy Haldane notes that the
Glass-Steagall Act, which was the response to the 1929 Depression, had
thirty-seven pages. Other comparators include Basel I with thirty pages
in 1988 and Basel III in 2010 with 616. Basel I had five different risk
weights and could be calculated using pad and pen. It was there "to support, not supplant" management decisions. Basle III involves several million calculations. In the United Kingdom, there was one regulator for every
eleven thousand staff in 1980. Today there is one for every three hundred. In 1930, reports to the Office of the Comptroller of the Currency
contained about eighty entries. By 1986, there were 547 Excel columns;
by 2011, there were 2,271 such columns. Andy Haldane, "The Dog and the
Frisbee," speech to Economic Policy Symposium, Jackson Hole, WY, August 31, 2012.
2. Rather more enlightening on the factors associated with banking
collapse is a paper by R. A. Brealey, I. Cooper, and E. Kaplanis. They find
that the key factors were association with US banks, the simple leverage
ratio of the bank, and the fragility of its financing—that is, the likelihood
that lenders will withdraw funds. They point out that the fundamental
problem with Basel III is that it aims to control the wrong thing. It focuses
on risk, that is, the "known unknowns" for each bank, rather than uncertainty, that is, "unknown unknowns" for the system as a whole. R. A
Brealey, I. Cooper and E. Kaplanis, "International Propagation of the
Credit Crisis: Implications for Bank Regulation," *Journal of Applied Corporate Finance* 24, no. 4 (2012): 36–45.

3. Haldane, "The Dog and the Frisbee."

4. Similarly, the problem of "externalities" could be solved, albeit at great cost, if we were all given rights to clean air, which the polluter could buy from us. However, the transaction costs associated with doing so would be very high. For further discussion, see R. H. Coase, *The Firm, the Market, and the Law* (University of Chicago Press, 1988).

5. See "Reducing the Impact of Regulation on Business," updated December 19, 2012, which includes the commitment to operate a " 'one on two out' rule for business regulation"; www.gov.uk/governmentgovernment/policy/reducing-the-impact-of-business-on-regulation.

6. Indeed, one can observe that regulatory bodies are often established when companies or industries are privatized.

7. See interview at www.pbs.org/now/shows/501/credit-traps.html.

8. Ibid.

9. Michael Daniel, comments before the National Association of Corporate Directors, Washington, DC, October 13, 2014.

10. This would be the assumption of equilibrium economics, which may underpin some atomized approaches to regulation. We would caution that positive self-correcting behavior should not be taken for granted, and that the job of the regulator is to help construct a system where such an assumption can, by and large, be made. Incidentally, that is exactly the approach the world's best cybersecurity regulators have taken. They have created frameworks and architecture, rather than attempt to create a rigid set of rules. They recognize that rigidity becomes fragility when imposed on a fast-moving environment.

11. In making this suggestion, we are not trying to define outcomes but, rather, to encourage a system where competition will result in structures that better meet the goals of the financial system.

12. In a series of citizen juries undertaken for Britain's Royal Society of Arts, jurors generally wanted to create a system where you "could give your money away to someone who would look after it properly on your behalf until you retire." Such a description comes quite close to the notion of fiduciary management.

13. This is an edited version of the definition of fiduciary duty used by John Kay, in his report for the UK government. For those wishing to explore this topic further within the investment industry, we would recommend the report of the UNEP Finance Initiative; see www.unepfi.org/fileadmin/documents/fiduciaryII.pdf; and the work of ShareAction (formerly FairPensions) in the United Kingdom, at www.fairpensions.org.uk/redisovering-fiduciary-duty.

14. See Francis Fukuyama, *Trust: The Social Virtues and the Creation of Prosperity* (Penguin, 1996): "One of the most important lessons we can learn from an examination of a nation's economic life, is conditioned by a single pervasive characteristic: the level of trust inherent in society."

15. See, for example, Keith L. Johnson and Frank Jan de Graaf, *Modernizing Pension Fund Legal Standards for the 21st Century* (February 2009), www.oecd.org/corporate/corporateaffairs/corporategovernanceprinciples/42670725.pdf.

16. David Pitt-Watson is co-chair of the UNEP FI initiative.

17. See http://www.unepfi.org/fileadmin/documents/fiduciaryII.pdf.

18. *The Kay Review of UK Equity Markets and Long-Term Decision Making: Final Report* (The National Archives, July 2012), http://webarchive.nationalarchives.gov.uk/20121204121011/http://www.bis.gov.uk/assets/biscore/business-law/docs/k/12-917-kay-review-of-equity-markets-final-report.pdf.

19. http://lawcommission.justice.gov.uk/areas/fiduciary_duties.htm.

20. *Code of Conduct for Members of a Pension Scheme Governing Body* (CFA Institute Centre for Financial Market Integrity, May 2008), www.cfainstitute.org/learning/products/publications/ccb/Pages/ccb.v2008.n3.1.aspx.

21. See James Hawley, Keith Johnson, and Ed Waitzer, "Reclaiming Fiduciary Balance," *Rotman International Journal of Pension Management* 4, no. 2 (Fall 2011), www.reinhartlaw.com/Publications/Documents/art111020%20RIIS.pdf.

22. Stephen Davis, Jon Lukomnik, and David Pitt-Watson, "Active Shareowner Stewardship: A New Paradigm for Capitalism," *Rotman International Journal of Pension Management* 2, no. 2 (Fall 2009), http://papers.ssrn.com/sol3/papers.cfm?abstract_id=1493279.

23. The industry's argument against applying fiduciary standards to brokers are two-fold. The first argument is that they are just selling financial products. But that ignores the information asymmetry between brokers and their clients. The second is that the added cost of complying with a fiduciary standard in a litigious society such as the United States will mean that some brokers will refuse to provide advice. That may well be true, but the question is, what type of advice is now being provided, and what will be provided in the future? An overall reduction in advice, but where none of the advice is conflicted and all benefits the client, may be a preferred outcome.

24. "ESG Rethink Can Add 40 Basis Points per Month: Hermes" (Top 1000 Funds, May 18, 2014), http://www.top1000funds.com/news/2014/05/16/esg-rethink-can-add-40-basis-points-per-month-hermes/.

25. FSC Standard No. 20, *Superannuation Governance Policy* (Financial Services Council, March 2013).

26. The service was renamed the PRI Academy. See www.priacademy.org.

27. See, for example, Alfred Marshall, *Principles of Economics*, bk. 4, chap. 7 (Macmillan, 1920).

28. Such a model is associated with Gary Becker, the Nobel Prize–winning economist. However, similar calculations would have been familiar to Jeremy Bentham.

29. The configuration of this approach can be made more complex by introducing personal preferences for altruistic behavior or for risk avoidance. However, the basic logic remains similar.

30. Dan Ariely, *The Honest Truth about Dishonesty* (HarperCollins, 2012).

31. See ibid.

32. Consider, for example, the list of major regulatory challenges faced by JP Morgan Chase that were announced in just one month, August 2013. The Federal Housing Finance Agency sued the bank, alleging it fraudulently claimed that the loans behind some $33 billion in mortgage derivatives met underwriting guidelines. The Securities and Exchange Commission and the US Attorney's Office were prosecuting the bank for its public statements about a $6 billion trading loss fancifully nicknamed "the London whale" after the market heft of the trader who caused the blowup. The SEC also was investigating how the bank came to hire the children of well-connected Chinese in a potential bribery scheme. The US Attorney continued to explore the bank's potential manipulation of the energy markets, even after the bank paid a $410 million settlement to the US energy regulator, but did not admit or deny criminality in that situation. Meanwhile, the New York State and Connecticut attorneys general sent JP Morgan Chase subpoenas relating to an investigation about the criminal manipulation of Libor, the benchmark interest rate that affects who owes how much for trillions of dollars of contracts (Barclays, Deutsche Bank, UBS, Citigroup, Royal Bank of Scotland, and HSBC Holdings also reportedly received subpoenas).

33. Ariely undertook an experiment with those filling in insurance declarations, and discovered that those who signed at the top that they would provide accurate information did so to a greater degree than those who declared at the end of the form that they had provided such information.

34. The first statutory audit was introduced for joint stock banks following the collapse of the City Bank of Glasgow in 1878. The bank did not enjoy limited liability, so its shareholders became liable for its debts.

35. We note that the role of prudence as an audit principle remains controversial. The statements we have made about its abandonment relate primarily to international accounting standards. We note that following the 2008 crisis, some moves have been made to reintroduce the concept, albeit with a lower priority than it had historically.

36. See "UK and Irish Banks' Capital Losses—Post Mortem" (LAPFF Forum, 2011), www.lapfforum.org/Publications/latest-research/files/LAPFF _Post_Mortem_report.pdf/view.

37. James R. Doty, speech to Weinberg Center at the University of Delaware, October 8, 2014.

38. It need not apply to routine contracts, such as airlines hedging their fuel costs. A minimum value threshold could form part of any such disclosure rule.

39. Stephen Davis, Jon Lukomnik, and David Pitt-Watson, "Towards an Accountable Capitalism," Private Sector Opinion, Issue 13 (2009), Global Corporate Governance Forum, International Finance Corporation.

40. See www.financialstabilityboard.org/cos/key_standards.htm.

41. James Saft, "The Wisdom of Exercising Patience in Investing," (Reuters, March 2, 2012), http://www.reuters.com/article/2012/03/02/us -patience-saft-idUSTRE8210O620120302. This is not a new phenomenon. The average duration of mutual fund holdings has not changed much in a quarter of a century, averaging about 1.2 to 1.5 years. "The Mutual Fund Industry in 2003: Back to the Future," remarks by John C. Bogle, founder and former chairman, The Vanguard Group, January 14, 2003, Boston, MA.

42. "Investment Horizons: Do Managers Do What They Say?" (IRRC Institute and Mercer, February 2010).

43. See "Colocation: NYSE Euronext's US Liquidity Center" (NYSE Technologies, 2010), www.nyse.com/pdfs/Colocation-NYSE-Euronext-US -Liquidity-Center.pdf.

44. Khaldoun Kashanah, Ionut Florescu, and Steve Yang, "On the Impact and Future of HFT" (IRRC Institute, May 10, 2104), http://irrcinstitute .org/projects.php?project=73.

45. J. Franks, C. Mayer, and S. Rossi, "Ownership: Evolution and Regulation," LSE seminar paper, January 2003.

46. The way market discipline has been interpreted is a focus on financial disclosures. That is understandable, since Basel II basically focuses on the financial institutions and not the entire financial system in which they operate. See "International Conversion of Capital Measurement and Capital Standards" (Basel Committee on Banking Supervision, June 2006).

47. For example, during the passage of the Dodd-Frank Act (the keystone regulation passed in the United States to regulate banks following the 2008 crisis), it was reported that six thousand lobbyists were employed to make sure it did not cut off lucrative revenue streams to the finance industry. See http//:thenation.com/article/174113/how-wall-street-defanged-dodd-frank.

48. See Nassim Nicholas Taleb, *The Black Swan: The Impact of the Highly Improbable*, 2nd ed. (Random House, 2010), 284.

6

The Queen's Question

1. "The Queen Asks Why No One Saw the Credit Crunch Coming," *The Telegraph*, November 5, 2008.

2. Sky News, December 14, 2012, www.youtube.com/watch?v=wADO zwSTJGQ.

3. See Higher Education Statistics Agency, www.hesa.ac.uk/content /view/1897/239.

4. See Economic Departments, Institutes and Research Centres in the World, Edirc.repec.org.

5. There are some honorable exceptions to this rule. William White of the OECD and John Plender of the *Financial Times* would count among them.

6. Adam Smith was professor of moral philosophy at Glasgow University and is supposed to have fallen into a tanning pit while focusing on a conversation with a friend about economics. Author Isaac Asimov claimed, almost certainly apocryphally, that Gauss was interrupted in the middle of solving a mathematics problem to be told his wife was dying. "Tell her to wait a moment 'til I am done" was his reply. See http://en.wikipedia.org/wiki /Adam_Smith and http://en.wikipedia.org/wiki/Carl_Friedrich_Gauss.

7. Babylonian Talmud, Shabbos 31a.

8. En.Wikipedia.org/wiki/Adam_Smith.

9. Pitt speech on introducing his budget, February 17, 1792, quoted in John Kenneth Galbraith, *A History of Economics* (Hamish Hamilton, 1987), 61.

10. Adam Smith, *The Wealth of Nations* (Oxford University Press, 2008), bk 1, chap 2.

11. Smith claimed that 240 times the number of pins could be created in this way than by an artisan working alone.

12. See Adam Smith, *The Wealth of Nations*, bk. 1, chap. 7.

260   Notes to Pages 159–167

13. Other economists of the same era also sought to turn economics into a science like physics. Stanley Jevons, for example, is described as "wanting to make human behavior as predictable as gravity." Eric Beinhocker, *The Origin of Wealth: Evolution, Complexity, and the Radical Remaking of Economics* (Random House, 2005), 34.

14. Leon Walras, *Elements of Pure Economics*, trans. W. Jaffe (Richard Irwin, 1954), 71.

15. Ibid., 428.

16. Both measured in terms of other goods whose consumption and production are forgone.

17. Gauss's biography is available at the University of Goettingen website, www.uni-goettingen.de/en/62596.html.

18. By the time of the crisis, most economists and financial analysts were no longer using a normal curve but had adjusted it in various ways. Previous work had shown that financial markets tend to have "fat tails"; or, to put it another way, extreme events happen more often than a traditional Gaussian distribution would predict. The adjustments to the shape of the curve were many, but the fundamental assumption, that the variability of the outcomes was predictable, was largely unchallenged.

19. International Monetary Fund, "IMF Performance in the Run-up to the Financial and Economic Crisis: IMF Surveillance in 2004–07" (International Monetary Fund, Independent Evaluation Office, January 10, 2011), http://www.ieo-imf.org/ieo/pages/NewsLinks107.aspx.

20. Myron Scholes and Robert Merton were both directors of Long-Term Capital Management. Wikipedia.org/wiki/Long_Term_Capital_Management.

21. John Maynard Keynes, *General Theory of Employment Interest and Money* (Snowball Publishing, 2012), bk. 5, chap. 21.

22. Friedrich von Hayek, "The Pretense of Knowledge," Nobel Prize acceptance speech, 1974, http://www.nobelprize.org/nobel_prizes/economic-sciences/laureates/1974/hayek-lecture.html.

23. John Kenneth Galbraith, *A History of Economics* (Hamish Hamilton, 1987), 125. Galbraith goes on to note, "One of the costs . . . [of mathematical economics] . . . was the removal of the subject several steps further from reality" (259).

24. Andrew Scott, professor of economics at London Business School, in his private review and critique of this chapter, October 2014.

25. Smith, *Wealth of Nations*, bk. 4, Introduction.

26. Quoted in Niall Ferguson, *Civilization: The West and the Rest* (Penguin 2011), 287.

27. David Brooks, "The Legacy of Fear," *New York Times*, November 10, 2014.

28. Andrew Scott, professor of economics at London Business School, in his private review and critique of this chapter, October 2014.

29. He went on, incorrectly, as it would later prove, to say that this propensity is to be "in no other race of animals." Smith, *Wealth of Nations*, bk. 1, chap. 2.

30. R. H. Coase, "The Lighthouse in Economics," in *The Firm, the Market, and the Law*, chap. 6 (University of Chicago Press, 1988).

31. Coase might also have noted that in making this bimodal distinction, economists were separating away those parts of the economy (what they called public goods) where economic models do not predict at all well, thus leaving economic models to cover "private goods." They chose this route rather than noting that transaction costs in all goods complicated the economic models they were using.

32. Coase, *The Firm, the Market, and the Law*, 15.

33. Andrew Scott, private interview for this book, October 2014.

34. En.wikipedia.org/wiki/There_are_known_knowns.

35. Some economists, notably Frank Knight at the University of Chicago, have written extensively about the dichotomy between predictable risk and uncertainty, which cannot be calculated. But many continue to focus only on risk.

36. Nassim Nicholas Taleb, *The Black Swan: The Impact of the Highly Improbable* (Random House, 2010), xxxix.

37. Andrew G. Haldane, "Tails of the Unexpected," speech given at University of Edinburgh, June 8–9, 2012, p. 20, http://www.bankofengland.co.uk/publications/Documents/speeches/2012/speech582.pdf.

38. From Haldane, "Tails of the Unexpected." The ratios are calculated on Table 2. Haldane compares an event four standard deviations from the mean, which under the predictions of a normal curve would have a probability of 0.003, with actual outcomes of events in the natural, social, and economic world. The economic events he looks at are more than one hundred times more likely to occur than the normal curve would predict. Haldane calls for "a fairly fundamental rethink of the core risk management tools currently used by many financial firms."

39. Citation can be found at www.theinvisiblegorilla.com/biographies.html.

40. The video can be accessed at www.youtube.com/watch?v=IGQmdoK_ZfY.

41. As leading participants in the corporate governance movement that encouraged some of these actions, the authors themselves must accept some of the blame for encouraging this form of contracting.

42. Smith, *Wealth of Nations*, bk. 5, chap 1.

43. Alfred Marshall, *Principles of Economics* (Macmillan, 1946), 303.

44. Kenneth Arrow, *Information and Economic Behaviour* (Federation of Swedish Industries, 1973), 24. For discussion, see O. Williamson, *The Economic Institutions of Capitalism* (Free Press, 1985), 405.

45. John R. Hicks, "'Revolutions' in Economics," in Spiro J. Latsis, ed., *Method and Appraisal in Economics* (Cambridge University Press, 1976), 207–18. Quoted in Williamson, 386.

46. In his words, "Organisations, markets and economies are not just like evolutionary systems, they truly, literally are evolutionary systems." Beinhocker, *Origin of Wealth*, 187.

47. The navigational skills and commercial incentives that took European sailors around the Cape of Good Hope were the same ones that led Columbus to sail west across the Atlantic to America.

48. The voyages of Chinese admiral Zheng He took place between 1405 and 1433. Philip Snow, *The Star Raft: China's Encounters with Africa* (Cornell University Press, 1989).

49. Perhaps the seventeenth-century Dutch playwright Joost van der Vondel caught the spirit of the age with this ditty: "We Amsterdammers journey . . . , Where ever profit leads us, to every sea and shore, For love of gain, the wide world's harbors we explore." Quoted in David Landes, *The Wealth and Poverty of Nations* (Little, Brown, 1998).

50. Landes, *Wealth and Poverty of Nations*, 217.

51. As Geoffrey Hodgson put it, institutions are "the systems of established and prevalent social rules that structure social interaction." See Geoffrey M. Hodgson, "What are Institutions?," *Journal of Economic Issues* 40, no. 1 (March 2006), http://www.geoffrey-hodgson.info/user/image/whatare institutions.pdf.

52. Oliver Williamson makes this point well. Quoting Karl Llewellyn, he notes that in studying contracts, we would do well to focus less on the letter of the law than on the purpose served by it. Llewellyn notes that contracts create a "framework which almost never accurately indicates real working relations, but affords a rough indication around which such relations vary, an occasional guide in cases of doubt, and a norm of ultimate appeal when the relations cease in fact to work." Williamson, *Economic Institutions of Capitalism*, 4–5.

53. This is the law in the UK. For further discussion see http://www
.icaew.com/en/archive/library/subject-gateways/law/insolvency/legal
-alert/when-directors-can-be-personally-liable-on-company-insol-
vency.

54. Thomas Philippon, "Has the US Finance Industry Become Less Efficient? On the Theory and Measurement of Financial Intermediation,"
Stern School of Business, New York University, September 2014.

55. Williamson, *Economic Institutions of Capitalism*, 22.

56. Ineteconomics.org.

57. Interview with George Soros: "Why We Need to Rethink Economics" (June 2013), ineteconomics.org.

58. April 2015.

59. www.aspeninstitute.org/policy-work/business-society/purpose-of
-corporation, accessed October 10, 2014.

60. Robert H. Frank, Thomas Gilovich, and Dennis T. Regan, "Does
Studying Economics Inhibit Cooperation?," *Journal of Economic Perspectives* 7, no. 2 (Spring 1993): 159–71.

61. Sumantra Ghoshal, "Bad Management Theories Are Destroying
Good Management Practices," *Academy of Management Learning and Education* 4, no. 1 (2005): 75–91.

62. Menachem Wecher, "Business Schools Increasingly Require Students to Study Ethics," *US News and World Report*, September 20, 2011.

7

People's Pensions, Commonsense Banks

1. Studies demonstrate that in practice, collective pensions offer higher
and more predictable retirement incomes than individual saving. For example, David Pitt-Watson and Harinder Mann, *Collective Pensions in the UK*
(RSA, 2012) cite six separate studies comparing individual and collective
pension provision. The two look at the cost of pensions where there is no annuity market, and savers need to know they have a 97.5 percent chance of
having adequate savings. These studies suggest individual savings would cost
83 to 145 percent more than collective savings. Other studies that allow for
annuity purchase on retirement suggest an upside of 25 to 45 percent. *Collective Pensions in the UK II* (RSA, 2014), by the same authors, cites a study by
AON Hewitt modeling both systems. It suggests an upside of over 30 percent
for a collective system of pension provision, and a more predictable outcome.

2. See, for example, David Pitt-Watson, *Pensions for the People: Addressing the Savings and Investment Crisis in Britain* (RSA, 2009). In recent years, in Europe, there has been a move away from investment in simple asset structures (which may be imperfect in matching the promise but are more robust in the event of inflation) toward "liability-driven investing."

3. The average duration of the liabilities of such a collective pension savings fund will depend on the nature of the workforce being provided for. But in any continuing plan, there will always be long-lived liabilities, and the average duration is usually many years.

4. These figures are based on a pension lasting sixty years, forty in accumulation and twenty in decumulation. The example is explained in more detail in David Pitt-Watson, *Tomorrow's Investor: Building the Consensus for a People's Pension in Britain* (RSA, 2010).

5. As we have seen in chapter 2, you need to beware of the investment manager who tries to persuade you that they are better than the next and can make more money by buying and selling shares. There is little evidence to suggest that many can do this. Indeed, given that investment managers compete against one another, for every winner, there will also be a loser. See William Sharpe, "The Arithmetic of Active Fund Management," *Financial Analysts Journal* 47 (January–February 1991): 7–9.

6. In Britain and the United States they were generally established as company plans, and in the Netherlands as industry plans.

7. There are variants on annuities which do not have promised payouts, but this is the basic structure.

8. See en.m.wikisource.org, *Dictionary of National Biography 1885–1900*, vol. 59, "Robert Wallace 1697–1771."

9. Throughout this book, we have been critical of the misuse of predictive models. That doesn't mean models and probability distributions are useless. They need to be revisited periodically so as to be calibrated for new information, and their limitations understood. "Set it and forget it" is rarely, if ever, a good idea. In this case, calculating the actuarial events for a pension fund should be revisited periodically, and the contribution rates, investment program, and benefit levels adjusted accordingly.

10. Unfortunately, this trust among a particular employment or cultural or religious group is sometimes abused. Criminal justice calls these types of frauds affiliation scams.

11. Survey data on expectations may be found in David Pitt-Watson, *Tomorrow's Investor-Pensions for the People: Addressing the Savings and In-*

vestment Crisis in Britain (RSA, 2009), www.thersa.org/__data/assets/pdf
_file/0010/220141/Tomorrows_Investor_Pensions-for-the-people.

pdf; and
Aziz Boghani and Elizabeth Evans, *Survey Findings: Urgent Need for Accountable, Trustworthy and Transparent Investments* (RSA, 2009), www
.thersa.org/__data/assets/pdf_file/0018/215145/TI-Final-Pension-Survey
-Results-2009.pdf.

12. Mark Maremont and Mike Spector, "Buyout Firms Push to Keep
Information under Wraps," *Wall Street Journal*, November 4, 2014, http://
online.wsj.com/articles/buyout-firms-push-pension-funds-to-keep
-information-under-wraps-1415142588.

13. In 2011, the Millstein Center for Corporate Governance and Performance, then at the Yale School of Management, launched a multistakeholder
research inquiry into the idea of an authoritative national governance
code for the United States. Nearly every other significant market has a corporate governance code of some kind.

14. In the United States, for example, the SEC had proposed that mutual
fund boards be composed of 75 percent independent directors and that the
chair be independent of the fund company. Though the rule was overturned on procedural grounds, many mutual fund groups effectively follow the proposal as a way of aligning interest.

15. See *ICGN Statement of Principles for Institutional Investor Responsibilities* (International Corporate Governance Network, 2013) and *ICGN
Global Governance Principles* (International Corporate Governance Network, 2014), www.icgn.org.

16. See CalPERS's discussion of the review and subsequent changes in
the system's own governance at www.calpers.ca.gov/index.jsp?bc=/about
/organization/board/governance-policies.xml.

17. *Issue Brief: RSIC Makes Progress on Key Fiduciary Audit Recommendations* (Retirement System Investment Commission, October 2014),
http://www.rsic.sc.gov/PDFs/IssueBrief1Oct2014.pdf.

18. "All aboard the Change Express as Railpen Leaves the Station"
(Top1000Funds.com, October 29, 2014), http://www.top1000funds.com
/profile/2014/10/29/all-aboard-the-change-express-as-railpen-leaves-the
-station/.

19. Reports provided to the authors in April 2012 courtesy of PFZW
and PGGM.

20. One 2008 academic study found that Dutch beneficiaries would
also accept a higher premium or lower retirement benefit if that is necessary to invest more responsibly. Derk Erbé, "Stille Kapitalisten: Een sociologisch onderzoek over de invloed en controle van deelnemers op het

beleggingsbeleid van hun pensioenfonds" (University of Amsterdam, 2008).

21. See, for instance, the 2014 survey at www.nestpensions.org.uk /schemeweb/NestWeb/includes/public/docs/NEST-insight-2014.PDF.pdf.

22. Nell Minow, testimony before the US House Committee on Oversight and Government Reform, October 6, 2008.

23. CalPERS is the California Public Employees Retirement System, and CalSTRS the California State Teachers Retirement System.

24. www.gmi3d.com/home.

25. "The Morningstar Stewardship Grade for Funds" (Morningstar, 2010).

26. www.nestpensions.org.uk/schemeweb/NestWeb/includes/public/docs /NEST-phrasebook,PDF.pdf.

27. An SEC example shows what *not* to do; the commission rightly required mutual funds to disclose how they vote at the companies in their portfolios, but then gave no guidance about how funds should report. Today the information is arduous for investors to dig up and costly for analysts to put side by side.

28. The model we have used for the People's Pension is borrowed from best practice around the world. In particular, the underlying structure is of Collective Defined Contribution (CDC), which gives a balance of high and predictable outcomes with limited need for an external party to guarantee the pension payment. These are found in Holland and Denmark. To be successful, such structures have to have good governance and regulation. CDC funds could readily be used by individual employers or by groups of employers instead of the 401(k) and similar individual savings structures found in the United States, United Kingdom, and Australia. They can be established on an individual company basis or for entire industries; since they do not involve an employer covenant, they do not need to be established separately for every employer. They are particularly relevant for the decumulation period of a pension (i.e., the time when the pension is in payment), since they allow the effective sharing of longevity risk. For further discussion of collective pensions, see Pitt-Watson and Mann, *Collective Pensions in the UK*, and Pitt-Watson and Mann, *Collective Pensions in the UK II*. Both publications contain references to the many studies that compare collective pensions to individual savings.

29. John Kenneth Galbraith, *A History of Economics* (Hamish Hamilton, 1987), 141.

30. Brian Pitman in evidence to the Future of Banking Commission (Which Publications, 2010), 19.

31. There is a certain irony here. From a bank's point of view, ignoring taxes, it can fund its lending from whatever mix of equity, deposits, and other borrowing it chooses. Similarly, an investor who was equally invested in each of those asset classes would achieve the same return from whatever funding mix the bank chose, since its lending book would not have changed. Of course, as citizen investors, we do indeed have an interest in all these forms of bank borrowing, through our deposits and through our pension and other assets. But our money is not invested in a way which considers our requirements holistically. Instead, different agents invest different elements of it. Equity managers encouraged banks to borrow more, in order to make a higher return on equity indifferent to the fact that this might be putting depositors and bondholders in jeopardy. For further discussion, see A. Admati, P. DeMarzo, M. Hellwig, and Pl. Pfleiderer, "Fallacies, Irrelevant Facts and Myths in the Discussion of Capital Regulation: Why Bank Equity Is Not Expensive," Stanford University Rock Center for Corporate Governance Paper no. 86 (Stanford University, 2010).

32. Anat Admati, and Martin Hellwig, *The Bankers' New Clothes: What Is Wrong with Banking and What to Do about It* (Princeton University Press, 2013).

33. John Sutherland, discussion at ICGN Annual Conference, Amsterdam, 2014.

8

Capitalism

1. One area where banks can claim to have made substantial productivity improvements is in transferring money. Indeed, Paul Volcker, former chairman of the US Federal Reserve, declared that in the past generation, "the ATM is the only financial innovation he [Volcker] can think of which has improved society." Alan Murray, "Paul Volcker: Think More Boldly," *Wall Street Journal*, December 14, 2009.

2. For example, a US federal court found that an electrical engineering company and the record keeper of its 401(k) plan had violated fiduciary duty. The result: $37 million less in savings than there should have been. John F. Wasik, "Finding, and Battling, Hidden Costs of 401(k) Plans," *New York Times*, November 7, 2014.

3. The United States is an exception, as it has no national authoritative corporate governance code.

4. Nolan Haskovec, *Working Paper: Codes of Corporate Governance: A Review* (Yale School of Management-Millstein Center for Corporate Governance and Performance, June 2012), http://web.law.columbia.edu/sites /default/files/microsites/millstein-center/Codes%20of%20Corporate%20 Governance_Yale_053112.pdf.

Index

Sarbanes-Oxley Act (US), 10
Save Darfur Coalition, 120
Savers. *See* Citizen investors/savers
Schmidt, Breno, 102
Scholes, Myron, 260*n*20
Schwartz, Barry, 52
Scott, Andrew, 171
SEC (Securities and Exchange Commission), 52, 88, 91, 107, 204, 257*n*32, 265*n*14, 266*n*27
SHARE. *See* Shareholder Association for Research and Education (SHARE)
Share price, 66, 71, 148
ShareAction, 89, 111, 121, 225
Sharegate, 90–91
Shareholder activism, agency capitalism and, 76
Shareholder Association for Research and Education (SHARE), 121
Shareholder resolutions, mutual fund votes on, 102
Shareowners: board of directors and, 18; rollback of powers, 11
Short volatility strategies, 239*n*25
"The Short Long" (Haldane), 66
Short-term buying and selling, 150–51
Short-termism, 8, 10, 63–66, 68, 71, 148, 228. *See also* Economic attention deficit hyperactivity disorder
Sier, Chris, 53–54
Silicon Valley, 70, 182
Simons, Dan, 174
Sinclair, Upton, 74
Smart beta, 241*n*36
Smith, Adam, 13, 161, 184, 259*n*6, 259*n*11; classical economics and,

157–59; on purpose of economics, 166, 192; on trading, 169; ownership and, 62; self-interest and, 180; specialization and, 30; trust and money management and, 33, 176
Social capital, 181
Social forces, economic forces and, 179–80
Social institutions, globalization and, 186–87
Social media: fostering accountability and, 114–19; scrutiny of funds and, 224–25
Social mobility, finance industry and, 4–5, 24
Socially responsible investors, 77
Soros, George, 189
Specialization: in finance industry, 30–33; productivity and, 158–59; reducing number of agents, 58–59
Stanford University, Rock Center for Corporate Governance, 82–83
State of Wisconsin Investment Board (SWIB), 59
Statement on Institutional Investor Responsibilities, 113–14
Stausboll, Anne, 110, 111–12
Stewart, Fiona, 103
Stichting Pensioenfonds Zorg en Welzijn (PFZW), 111, 206
Stock market crash (2013), 51
Stock options, executive compensation and, 69–71, 83–84
Stock price, 8, 50, 64, 67, 70–71, 72, 84–85, 146, 223
Stock, holding period of traded, 4, 63–65